ENERGIZE
YOUR TEAMS

POWERFUL TOOLS FOR COACHING COLLABORATIVE TEAMS IN PLCs AT WORK®

foreword by **JOELLEN KILLION**

THOMAS W.
MANY

MICHAEL J.
MAFFONI

SUSAN K.
SPARKS

TESHA FERRIBY
THOMAS

with **BRIAN GREENEY**

Solution Tree | Press
a division of
Solution Tree

555 North Morton Street
Bloomington, IN 47404
800.733.6786 (toll free) / 812.336.7700
FAX: 812.336.7790

email: info@SolutionTree.com
SolutionTree.com

Printed in the United States of America

Library of Congress Cataloging-in-Publication Data

Names: Many, Thomas W., author. | Maffoni, Michael J., author. | Sparks,
   Susan K., author. | Thomas, Tesha Ferriby, author. | Greeney, Brian,
   other.
Title: Energize your teams : powerful tools for coaching collaborative
   teams in PLCs at work / Thomas W. Many, Michael J. Maffoni, Susan K.
   Sparks, Tesha Ferriby Thomas with Brian Greeney.
Description: Bloomington, IN : Solution Tree Press, [2021] | Includes
   bibliographical references and index.
Identifiers: LCCN 2021025335 (print) | LCCN 2021025336 (ebook) | ISBN
   9781952812279 (paperback) | ISBN 9781952812286 (ebook)
Subjects: LCSH: Teaching teams. | Professional learning communities.
Classification: LCC LB1029.T4 M36 2021 (print) | LCC LB1029.T4 (ebook) |
   DDC 371.14/8--dc23
LC record available at https://lccn.loc.gov/2021025335
LC ebook record available at https://lccn.loc.gov/2021025336

Solution Tree
Jeffrey C. Jones, CEO
Edmund M. Ackerman, President

Solution Tree Press
President and Publisher: Douglas M. Rife
Associate Publisher: Sarah Payne-Mills
Art Director: Rian Anderson
Managing Production Editor: Kendra Slayton
Copy Chief: Jessi Finn
Senior Production Editor: Suzanne Kraszewski
Content Development Specialist: Amy Rubenstein
Copy Editor: Evie Madsen
Proofreader: Elisabeth Abrams
Text and Cover Designer: Abigail Bowen
Editorial Assistants: Sarah Ludwig and Elijah Oates

To all who persevered through the trials and tribulations of educating students during the pandemonium that was the 2020–2021 school year: As educators, you never wavered in what you valued because of the pandemic and remained true to the mission of ensuring high levels of learning for all. You are my heroes.

—Tom Many

To Sophia and Michael: Life is full of intricate, breathtaking moments. You both offered me the perspective to love and persevere through it all. The journey to you continues.

—Michael Maffoni

This book is dedicated to Chris Bryan, Heather Clifton, Cindy Harrison, Brenda Kaylor, and Joellen Killion who were all part of the original "Kitchen Cadre" and with whom we first began to explore the idea of coaching collaborative teams. Thanks for sharing your experience, expertise, insights, and ideas; you helped to inspire this work.

—Susan Sparks

To Tony: Without you, none of this would have been possible. Thank you for your unconditional love and constant support. I love you with all of my heart.

—Tesha Ferriby Thomas

ACKNOWLEDGEMENTS

Turning our vision into reality took a tremendous effort by a host of people. We would like to thank the team at Solution Tree Press for their belief in us and in the idea of coaching collaborative teams. None of this would have been possible without the support and encouragement of Douglas Rife, Sarah Payne-Mills, and everyone else at Solution Tree Press. We would especially like to recognize the wonderful work of Suzanne Kraszewski, a gifted and accomplished editor who has guided us through the writing of three books with patience, passion, and persistence. We feel Suzanne is an integral and indispensable part of our team.

We would also like to thank Cecilia Cortez de Magallanes, Anita Jiles, and everyone else at the Texas Elementary Principals and Supervisors Association (TEPSA) for providing the authors with opportunities to share our thinking with their members. It has been our privilege to write and partner with TEPSA for more than a decade.

We truly believe that if we are to achieve the goal of high levels of learning for all, it is not enough to participate in conferences, attend workshops, or engage in book studies. It is imperative that schools "learn by doing" and embrace the idea of coaching teams around improving their PLC practice. With the publication of *Amplify Your Impact* (PLC structures), *How Schools Thrive* (PLC culture), and this latest book *Energize Your Teams* (developing highly effective PLCs), we offer colleagues across the country a trilogy of resources to assist with our collective efforts to improve the professional practice of collaborative teams.

Solution Tree Press would like to thank the following reviewers:

Kim Ballestro
Assistant Principal
Carterville Junior High School
Carterville, Illinois

Breez Longwell Daniels
Thermopolis, Wyoming

Michael Harris
Principal
John Marshall Middle Enterprise School
Oklahoma City, Oklahoma

Jed Kees
Principal
Onalaska Middle School
Onalaska, Wisconsin

Benjamin Kitslaar
Principal
West Side Elementary
Elkhorn, Wisconsin

JoAnna McIlroy
Educational Consultant

Brad Mitchell
Principal
Timothy Christian High School
Elmhurst, Illinois

Kim Timmerman
Principal
Adel DeSoto Minburn Middle School
Adel, Iowa

David Pillar
Assistant Director
Hoosier Hills Career Center
Bloomington, Indiana

Visit **go.SolutionTree.com/PLCbooks** to download
the free reproducibles in this book.

TABLE OF CONTENTS

Reproducible pages are in italics.

PART I

INTRODUCTION TO COACHING COLLABORATIVE TEAMS IN A PLC AT WORK

CHAPTER 1

CHAPTER 2

PART II

MODULES FOR COACHING COLLABORATIVE TEAMS

CHAPTER 5

Guaranteed and Viable Curriculum. **77**

CHAPTER 6

A Balanced and Coherent System of Assessment **115**

CHAPTER 7

Productive Data Conversations. **151**

CHAPTER 8

PART III

ONE TEAM'S TRANSFORMATION

CHAPTER 9

ABOUT THE AUTHORS

Thomas W. Many is an educational consultant in Denver, Colorado. Tom retired as the superintendent of schools in Kildeer Countryside CCSD 96 in Buffalo Grove, Illinois. Tom's career included twenty years of experience as superintendent, in addition to serving as a classroom teacher, learning center director, curriculum supervisor, principal, and assistant superintendent. District 96 earned the reputation as a place where the faculty and administration worked together to become one of the premier elementary school districts in the United States during his tenure as superintendent.

Tom has worked with developing professional learning communities (PLCs) in school districts around the world. He has proven to be a valuable resource to those schools beginning their journey, offering special insights into developing the kind of coaching cultures that support the creation of high-performing collaborative teams.

In addition to more than fifty articles, Tom is the coauthor of *Amplify Your Impact: Coaching Collaborative Teams in PLCs at Work®* and *How Schools Thrive: Building a Coaching Culture for Collaborative Teams in PLCs at Work* with Michael J. Maffoni, Susan K. Sparks, and Tesha Ferriby Thomas; *Learning by Doing: A Handbook for Professional Learning Communities at Work* with Richard DuFour, Rebecca DuFour, Robert Eaker, and Mike Mattos; *Concise Answers to Frequently Asked Questions About Professional Learning Communities at Work* with Mike Mattos, Richard DuFour, Rebecca DuFour, and Robert Eaker; *Aligning School Districts as PLCs* with Mark Van Clay and Perry Soldwedel; and *How to Cultivate Collaboration in a PLC* and *Leverage: Using PLCs to Promote Lasting Improvement in Schools* with Susan K. Sparks. He is a contributing author for *The Collaborative Teacher: Working Together as a Professional Learning Community*.

To learn more about Tom's work, follow @tmany96 on Twitter.

Michael J. Maffoni, an educator since 1987, has a diverse background that includes experience as a teacher, principal, and central administrator in a variety of districts in Colorado. He also teaches courses in educational leadership as an affiliate faculty member at Regis University.

Michael is the former director of professional learning communities (PLCs) for Jeffco Public Schools in Golden, Colorado. During his tenure, Michael led PLC implementation in over one hundred schools throughout the district. His collaborative leadership was instrumental in developing integrated PLC support systems, monitoring processes, and aligning professional learning. Three schools in Jeffco are nationally recognized model PLC schools.

Michael specializes in increasing educator and student learning by developing agency to coach and support collaborative teams. Additionally, he coaches leadership teams to scale PLC implementation in any size school system, both large and small.

He has presented at state and national events on topics related to continuous improvement for schools, teams, and individual educators. Michael has coauthored articles on increasing the effectiveness of collaborative teams and is a coauthor of *Amplify Your Impact: Coaching Collaborative Teams in PLCs at Work* and *How Schools Thrive: Building a Coaching Culture for Collaborative Teams in PLCs at Work*.

To learn more about Michael's work, follow @mjmaffoni64 on Twitter.

Susan K. Sparks is an educational consultant in Denver, Colorado. Susan retired in 2008 as the executive director of the Front Range Board of Cooperative Educational Services (BOCES) for Teacher Leadership, a partnership with the University of Colorado Denver. Susan spent her career in St. Vrain Valley School District as a teacher and with four different BOCES as staff developer, assistant director, and executive director. She consults internationally in collaborative cultures, conflict resolution, contract negotiations, and community engagement.

She provides professional development and training in facilitating professional learning communities, impacting results through interpersonal effectiveness, managing challenging conversations, and creating collaborative teams.

Susan contributed to *The Collaborative Teacher: Working Together as a Professional Learning Community* and coauthored *Amplify Your Impact: Coaching Collaborative Teams in PLCs at Work*; *How Schools Thrive: Building a Coaching Culture for Collaborative Teams in PLCs at Work*; and *How to Cultivate Collaboration in a PLC* and *Leverage: Using PLCs to Promote Lasting Improvement in Schools*.

To learn more about Susan's work, follow @sparks12_susan on Twitter.

Tesha Ferriby Thomas, EdD, is a school improvement facilitator and language arts consultant at the Macomb Intermediate School District in Macomb County, Michigan where she supports struggling districts and school leaders by helping them embed systemic practices that result in improved student achievement. Her passion for the power of professional learning communities (PLCs) has grown over the twenty-five years she has worked to support PLC implementation as a teacher, department chairperson, assistant principal, and assistant superintendent for curriculum and instruction.

She is a coauthor of *Amplify Your Impact: Coaching Collaborative Teams in PLCs at Work* and *How Schools Thrive: Building a Coaching Culture for Collaborative Teams in PLCs at Work*. She presents regularly at local, state, and national conferences on topics ranging from writing across the curriculum to implementing an instructional learning cycle in a PLC. She has been a member of the Michigan Learning Forward board and the Michigan Department of Education Surveys of Enacted Curriculum Steering Committee, and is a National Writing Project fellow. She earned a doctoral degree from the University of Michigan–Flint, where she researched the impact of coaching on PLCs.

To learn more about Tesha's work, follow @tferribythomas on Twitter.

Brian Greeney, EdD, is the assistant superintendent of innovation, teaching, and learning for Willis Independent School District in Texas. His district has achieved multiple Model PLC school recognitions since 2015. He is also a Solution Tree educational consultant who works with teams, campuses, and districts throughout the United States on empowering collaborative teams through the PLC process to guarantee that all students learn at high levels.

Previously, Brian was the principal of Klein Oak High School in Spring, Texas. He and his staff implemented PLC at Work strategies resulting in increased graduation rates and growth in all major accountability areas. At the time, Klein Oak was one of only four high schools in the United States with over 4,000 students to be recognized as a Model PLC campus by Solution Tree. Before serving as principal at Klein Oak, Brian was a middle school principal, associate principal, assistant principal, AP government teacher, and swim coach.

Brian has received multiple honors including N2Learning Transforming School Leader, C.A.S.E. Equity Champion, Secondary Principal of the Year, Klein Superintendents Initiative Award Winner, and Stars of Tomorrow Outstanding Teacher on two occasions, and was named a USA National Open Water Swim Coach.

He earned his bachelor of arts degree from the University of Texas at Austin, his master of education degree from Prairie View A&M University, and doctor of education in educational leadership with a superintendent certification from Sam Houston State University. He also has a business fellowship degree from the Rice Executive Education program.

To learn more about Brian's work, follow @DrGreeney on Twitter.

To book Thomas W. Many, Michael J. Maffoni, Susan K. Sparks, or Tesha Ferriby Thomas for professional development, contact pd@SolutionTree.com.

FOREWORD

By Joellen Killion

Coaching matters—not only is this the title of the book I coauthored with Chris Bryan and Heather Clifton (Killion, Bryan, & Clifton, 2020), but it is also a succinct summary of research about the impact of coaching in multiple fields, including education. Coaching builds capacity, accelerates transfer of learning to practice, and refines and sustains practice over time.

Coaching is frequently considered a practice that occurs between a coach and a client. In schools, this view means change will likely be slow, accomplished one teacher at a time. A common challenge with coaching, particularly in schools, is the ratio of coaches to staff members. Coaching teams, working one-with-some rather than one-on-one, as we describe it in *Coaching Matters*, exponentially increases the likelihood that more teachers access coaching and reap its benefits.

Often team coaching equates to team facilitation. Facilitation differs from coaching, and that distinction is particularly important in team settings. As facilitator, the coach sets the agenda, guides the team's work, advises on process and content, handles conflict and dysfunctional team members, assesses the team's work, and repeats the cycle. When teams are coached rather than facilitated, they learn how to accomplish their work and to become both efficient and effective on their own. They build capacity to be a productive team rather than a group of individuals. The coach engages the team leader and members to understand what is working, what's getting in the way, how to select the best ways to accomplish their work, and how to measure their success. In other words, the coach builds the team's expertise to become highly functioning.

For coaches who work with teams, the balance between direct facilitation and coaching is important to move the team from dependence to independence through intentional gradual release of responsibility and control. When facilitating, the coach assumes more responsibility and control for the team's work. This might be necessary when a team is dysfunctional, new to one another or to the work, or just learning collaborative skills to work together. Maintaining tight reins on the team's work over time as a facilitator, however, limits a team's movement toward becoming a fully functioning, independent team, in which members demonstrate shared responsibility for team success.

Coaches, when coaching rather than facilitating, cultivate a team's capacity for collaborative expertise, reducing the variability in student learning experiences that occurs across classrooms. Collaborative expertise is the ability of team members to be equally expert in their work and to have shared agency and efficacy for the results of their work. Collaborative expertise means that all members of a team are equally equipped with the knowledge, skills, attitudes, and practices for high-quality instruction. Team members work together to understand students, content, and pedagogy; assess the current state; plan instruction to meet the needs of students; implement instructional decisions with consistency; assess and evaluate their effectiveness; and learn from their experience.

Energize Your Teams: Powerful Tools for Coaching Collaborative Teams in PLCs at Work provides what coaches and teams need to succeed in building collaborative expertise. It offers the resources coaches need to build the capacity of team members and leaders to work together efficiently and effectively. It unpacks the five essential PLC conditions and what is required to meet each. It pairs the conditions with background text, tools, and processes to meet each condition. The resources address the *why, what, how,* and *now what* of the PLC process. The addition of the *now what* integrates coaching to follow up with individuals and teams to support implementation of their learning within practice and reflection in, on, and for practice. Coaching moves team and individual learning from the meeting room to the classroom and from knowing about to applying learning to achieve results for students.

As I think about the definition of *energize* and the message in this book, I visualize how transformed a school becomes when individuals work within a community to move from individual expertise to collaborative expertise. Thomas W. Many, Michael J. Maffoni, Susan K. Sparks, Tesha Ferriby Thomas, and Brian Greeney have assembled, created, and shared the tools necessary for teams to collaborate on what matters most to them, to learn with and from each other, and to generate the force that moves them all toward the greater good—results for students and each other.

Those who coach, supervise, facilitate, or participate in learning communities will use the resources included in *Energize Your Teams* to create the movement toward collaborative expertise for student success. The resources guide principals to coach and support team leaders and teams to clarify goals and processes, to be purposeful and intentional with their time, and to assess their progress. The book offers team leaders navigation tools and processes to clarify and complete essential learning tasks, including unpacking the curriculum, generating assessments, holding data conversations, examining student and teacher work, monitoring team effectiveness, and moving from facilitator to coach. The resources make the processes transparent for all team members so they can be energized, empowered, and engaged to gain fluency and flexibility in collaborative work. And, most important, the resources provide the tools to keep learning for educators at the forefront of the work as a catalyst for action. After all, it is only through learning that deep, sustained change is possible. Learning becomes the heartbeat of the collaborative process and energizes any community.

When faced with questions or challenges about redirecting teams that are PLC lite, getting teams started, or moving functional teams to the next level of mastery, leaders, coaches, and facilitators will find within *Energize Your Teams* the energy that lights up the work, that catalyzes action, and brings joy, verve, and passion into the core work of every PLC.

Reference

Killion, J., Bryan, C., & Clifton, H. (2020). *Coaching matters* (2nd ed.). Oxford, OH: Learning Forward.

A Call to Action

Never before, researchers say, have so many experts in so many countries focused simultaneously on a single topic and with such urgency.

—MATT APUZZO AND DAVID D. KILPATRICK

When the world was struck with the COVID-19 pandemic, epidemiologists and infectious disease experts from around the globe immediately sprang into action, collaboratively searching for a vaccine. Never before has the scientific community worked so closely together to develop multiple vaccines for a deadly virus in such a short amount of time. These scientists didn't have the luxury of time to conduct years and years of research; the world urgently needed a vaccine, so scientists immediately got to work. They answered the call to action and, by doing so, they saved people's lives.

Educators, too, have the power to save people's lives, although not from a deadly pandemic. When schools deeply implement the PLC process, they can increase achievement and change students' lives for the better. This book is a call to action for all schools that call themselves PLCs (and those that want to become PLCs) to stop settling for *PLC lite*—to move from an interest in learning more about the PLC process to engaging in the work with enough depth to become proficient (DuFour, DuFour, Eaker, Many, & Mattos, 2016). It's time to reject superficial implementation efforts that result in pseudo PLCs. It's time to fight for deep implementation of the PLC process. Mediocre implementation is not good enough to achieve the results students need and deserve. It's time *all students can learn* becomes words we, as educators, live by. We must insist all our policies, practices, and procedures support the belief that learning is the fundamental purpose of our school.

It's time to stop procrastinating and putting off the hard work of becoming a PLC. As DuFour and Reeves (2016) point out: "Too many schools have adopted the [PLC] label without committing to the substance of the professional learning community process" (p. 71). The PLC process requires that educators work together in collaborative teams; establish a guaranteed and viable curriculum; use formative assessments; and use the results of those assessments to impact instruction and interventions (DuFour & Reeves, 2016).

We must act. We must do. We must commit to shifting the way we think about improving our schools from attending workshops and *learning, learning, learning* to engaging in job-embedded professional development and *doing, doing, doing*.

Finally, we believe it is time to commit to coaching collaborative teams as the primary way of delivering professional development. If we accept that collaborative teams are the fundamental building block and the engine that drives PLCs (DuFour et al., 2016), we must commit to deepening our collective understanding of the PLC process by coaching teams around improving their PLC practice.

The goal of working as highly effective teams that thrive in collaborative cultures and produce unprecedented levels of student learning is an aspiration worth fighting for. It is our hope that this text will support you and your school as you answer this call to action.

INTRODUCTION

I have been impressed with the urgency of doing. Knowing is not enough; we must apply. Being willing is not enough; we must do.

—LEONARDO DA VINCI

In our work with schools all over the world, we meet with principals, school leaders, and staff committed to the Professional Learning Communities at Work (PLC at Work) process and to working collaboratively in teams—a foundational element of the PLC process (DuFour et al., 2016). They have committed resources and time to training to build their collective knowledge of the process. They often wonder, however, why training has not translated into changes in their practice. They wonder what is preventing them from moving from theory to practice, from learning to doing. The answer to these questions has been the focus of our work with schools: the very best way to move a school from *PLC lite* to *PLC right* is by coaching collaborative teams.

One of the most rewarding professional activities we (the authors) engage in is working directly with administrators, coaches, and teacher teams across the United States. During this work we often find that, although schools are employing basic concepts of PLCs, they are doing so at superficial levels. While teachers may meet in teams, review assessment data, and even speak the "PLC language," many schools seeking our help are struggling to use the model to improve teacher practice and increase student achievement. Team members seem willing to do the work, but they have difficulty operationalizing PLC concepts at deep levels. In these cases, it is our job to use coaching techniques that will help move schools from *knowing* to *doing*. These experiences, along with extensive research on coaching and collaboration, are what have shaped the content of this book.

Our previous books, *Amplify Your Impact: Coaching Collaborative Teams in PLCs at Work* and *How Schools Thrive: Building a Coaching Culture for Collaborative Teams in PLCs at Work*, provide the foundation for this companion book. In *Amplify Your Impact* (Many, Maffoni, Sparks, & Thomas, 2018), we provide the rationale for why school leaders should embrace the practice of coaching collaborative teams; we present a framework for this coaching based on three concepts—clarity, feedback, and support; we describe a tool schools and districts can use to coach collaborative teams—the strategy implementation guide (SIG)—and a practical process school leaders can use to help teams develop this tool; and we present the Pathways for Coaching Collaborative Teams tool (Thomas, 2015) to assist coaches in guiding team conversations.

In *How Schools Thrive* (Many, Maffoni, Sparks, & Thomas, 2020), we share more concrete ideas and strategies for coaching collaborative teams around the successful implementation of the essential elements of a PLC. While *Amplify Your Impact* offers strategies that help teams with the implementation of the more explicit tasks of PLCs—things like prioritizing and unwrapping standards, identifying learning targets, developing common assessments, holding productive data conversations, and using protocols to ensure that results drive decisions—*How Schools Thrive* shifts attention to coaching teams around the essential elements of the PLC process—continuous improvement, collective inquiry, action orientation, and a focus on results—drilling deeper into the more complex aspects of the PLC process.

Amplify Your Impact and *How Schools Thrive* introduce a framework and processes proven through our work in schools as successful with coaching collaborative teams to higher levels of effectiveness in dozens of schools across the United States. We know coaching provides teams with more clarity, ongoing feedback, and continuous support of their efforts to improve, which substantially increases the likelihood of implementing the PLC process successfully. Simply stated, coached teams go further faster than un-coached teams (Joyce & Showers, 2002; Killion & Harrison, 2007; Neufeld & Roper, 2003; Thomas, 2019).

In this book, we provide school leaders with concrete methods and materials to help build shared knowledge and strengthen collaborative teams' PLC practice. We include key coaching points, important vocabulary, protocols that foster a deeper understanding of PLCs, and links to resources leaders can use to extend professional development activities. While this book can be used independently, readers of the trilogy will appreciate that concepts from *Amplify* and *Thrive* culminate into applicable professional development here in *Energize*. The beauty of this book is that schools at any level of PLC implementation can use it, from those just beginning the journey to those who have been practicing PLCs for a number of years and are ready to re-energize their teams!

A Flexible Format

We intentionally structured *Energize Your Teams* so those who are coaching teams (principals, department heads, instructional coaches, teacher leaders, or others) can identify an area of need, locate that topic in the book, and deliver a meaningful professional development experience in an hour or less. This flexible format allows coaches to differentiate professional development by content and format. Coaches can deliver modules to grade-level or departmental teams or to the faculty as a whole.

This book is organized into three parts.

- Part I presents a practical overview of coaching collaborative teams in a PLC.

- Part II includes professional development activities that support the five essential prerequisites of a PLC: (1) educators work in collaborative teams, rather than in isolation, and take collective responsibility for student learning; (2) collaborative teams implement a guaranteed and viable curriculum, unit by unit; (3) collaborative teams monitor student learning through an ongoing assessment process that includes frequent, team-developed common formative assessments; (4) educators use the results of common assessments to improve individual practice, build the team's capacity to achieve its goals, and intervene and enrich on behalf of students; and (5) the school provides a systematic process for intervention and teaching (DuFour & Reeves, 2016).

- Part III offers a glimpse into how one organization transformed the PLC process in their schools by coaching collaborative teams.

Part I: Introduction to Coaching Collaborative Teams in a PLC

Chapter 1 provides an overview of the five prerequisite conditions of a PLC (DuFour & Reeves, 2016) and describes how school leaders can use this book to facilitate coaching collaborative teams.

Chapter 2 introduces a continuum of PLC practice and describes a way practitioners can use it to reflect on how deeply their collaborative teams are implementing the PLC process.

Chapter 3 identifies the characteristics of effective coaching and presents a coaching cycle built on research, experience, and evidence from the field. The coaching cycle is designed to support collaborative teams and describe how coaching impacts teams' PLC practice.

Part II: Modules for Coaching Collaborative Teams

The purpose of this middle section of the book is to provide those responsible for coaching collaborative teams with a single source of targeted professional development activities they can use as a springboard to deeper learning or differentiated coaching based on the level of each team's PLC practice.

In each of chapters 4 through 8, we focus on a single prerequisite condition of PLCs as the main topic of professional development modules coaches can grab to help teams grow.

- Chapter 4 presents tools to support educators' work in collaborative teams as they take collective responsibility for student learning.

- Chapter 5 supports coaches as they coach collaborative teams to implement a guaranteed and viable curriculum, unit by unit.

- Chapter 6 helps coaches support collaborative teams as they monitor student learning through an ongoing assessment process that includes frequent, team-developed common formative assessments.

- Chapter 7 focuses on supporting teams as educators use the results of common assessments to improve individual practice, build the team's capacity to achieve its goals, and intervene and enrich on behalf of students.

- Chapter 8 helps coaches support teams in the systematic process for implementing intervention and teaching.

Each individual module is organized using a consistent three-section format.

1. **Before the learning:** These sections include an overview and provide the rationale, purpose, desired outcome, key coaching points, and important vocabulary associated with the module.

2. **During the learning:** These sections contain directions (similar to a lesson plan) for using each module, a step-by-step process around an article or activity to engage

teams in the experience, and an opportunity for reflection. These sections identify the *why*, *what*, and *how* for each prerequisite condition of a PLC.

3. **After the learning:** These sections provide coaches with strategies for helping teams identify the next steps they should take to operationalize each specific aspect of the PLC process.

Part III: Practical Implications for Coaching Collaborative Teams in a PLC

Finally, we conclude with a case study from a practitioner's point of view describing how one district successfully shifted the focus of coaching from individual teachers to collaborative teams using the SIG and pathways tools to delve more deeply into the PLC practice of collaborative teams.

Know Better to Do Better

As school leaders, we sometimes assume because we know something, our staff know it too; but what leaders know and expect is often different than what teams know and are able to do. By coaching collaborative teams on specific PLC practice, leaders and coaches help them improve the quality of collaboration, which leads to improved teaching and learning. Like Maya Angelou is credited as saying, *when we know better, we do better*. We believe *Energize Your Teams* will be a constant companion to those coaching teams so they can help teams know better and do better.

PART I

INTRODUCTION TO COACHING COLLABORATIVE TEAMS IN A PLC AT WORK

CHAPTER 1

Energize Your Collaborative Teams

Coaching creates positive energy and professional renewal that revitalizes and benefits the school culture in a lasting way.

—SANDRA A. TRACH

Think about a time when the teachers in your school were excited about a new initiative. You probably felt a buzz throughout the building—an air of excitement and anticipation that something great was about to happen. You might have noticed teachers getting along with one another and committed to working together to accomplish a goal. Wasn't that a wonderful feeling?

This kind of climate does not have to be an apparition. By coaching collaborative teams, schools can create this feeling of renewal and excitement on a regular basis, developing a culture that embraces a growth mindset and supports teachers improving their practice. Schools that have developed this kind of climate and culture encourage educators to explore ideas and try out new instructional strategies without fear of retribution if those strategies don't work. These schools have created an atmosphere where educators expect collaboration and growth instead of one where educators work in isolation and accept the status quo. However, these expectations for growth do not stand alone; these schools have committed to coaching teams—and so can yours!

To help teachers improve their teaching and implement new policies, practices, and procedures, many schools employ instructional coaches. The number of instructional coaches in the United States doubled between 2000 and 2015, with most instructional coaching conducted one-to-one (Domina, Lewis, Agarwal, & Hanselman, 2015). In many cases, school leaders assign instructional coaches to work with struggling or new teachers to improve individual practices. Typically, the coach and teacher meet to discuss a goal for improvement, and then the instructional coach co-plans with the teacher or even models an instructional practice, so the teacher can see a strategy in real time. Finally, the teacher implements the new strategy while the coach observes and offers feedback.

There is no question that coaching individual teachers is an effective strategy. "With coaching, the quality of teachers' instruction improves by as much as—or more than—the difference between a novice and a teacher with five to 10 years of experience" (Kraft & Blazar, 2018, p. 69). Knowing this, why do school leaders limit the scope of their coaching initiatives to one individual at a time? Wouldn't it be more efficient to coach multiple teachers at the same time—especially if those teachers share a common goal?

Financial constraints often limit the number of coaches schools employ. When a school only has one or two instructional coaches who serve teachers individually, only a small number of teachers will have the opportunity to work with a coach. Utilizing those same two coaches to work with class, course, or grade-level teacher teams increases efficiency exponentially. Instead of working with one teacher at a time, coaches simultaneously support multiple teachers in improving their collective practice. After all, "Quality teaching is not an individual accomplishment, it is the result of a collaborative culture that empowers teachers to team up to improve student learning beyond what any one of them can achieve alone" (Carroll, 2009, p. 13). Coaching collaborative teams increases the capacity of teachers across the school in far greater numbers than coaching individual teachers one-to-one.

In addition to improving efficiency, coaching teams also improves the effectiveness of the implementation of the PLC process. Coaches provide teams with guidance and support on specific PLC practices, nudging teams toward deeper and deeper levels of implementation. When teams improve the effectiveness of their PLC practice, the effectiveness of team members' classroom instruction also improves. While there are times when one-to-one coaching is needed, coaching collaborative teams moves the development of PLCs further and faster than coaching individual teachers ever will (see figure 1.1).

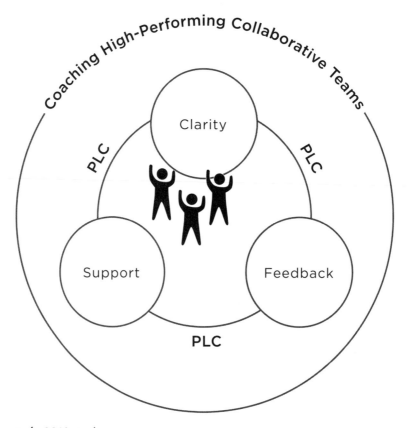

Source: Many et al., 2018, p. 4.

Figure 1.1: A framework for coaching in a PLC.

The Three Cornerstones

In *Amplify Your Impact* (Many et al., 2018), we present a framework for coaching collaborative teams based on the three cornerstones of clarity, feedback, and support. When schools combine coaching with collaboration by coaching teams, they promote the growth of many—not just one.

Clarity

The process begins with clarity because teams need a clear understanding of their goals to attain them. When beginning to implement the PLC process, team members often ask the question, "What should this look like?" Together, the coach and team can paint a vivid picture of what it looks like to be a high-performing team. To help visualize this picture, we recommend schools and districts work together to create a strategy implementation guide (SIG) that describes various levels of PLC implementation. The SIG created at the school or district level can be an excellent opportunity for professional development. The SIG consists of a series of anchor statements and a matching progression of indicators describing different levels of implementation (beyond proficient, proficient, and below proficient) for each PLC element the SIG highlights. We recommend the school or district SIG be based on the following five prerequisite conditions of a PLC (DuFour & Reeves, 2016).

1. Educators work in collaborative teams, rather than in isolation, and take collective responsibility for student learning.

2. Collaborative teams implement a guaranteed and viable curriculum, unit by unit.

3. Collaborative teams monitor student learning through an ongoing assessment process that includes frequent, team-developed common formative assessments.

4. Educators use the results of common assessments to improve individual practice, build the team's capacity to achieve its goals, and intervene and enrich on behalf of students.

5. The school provides a systematic process for intervention and teaching.

These conditions lay the foundation for a successful PLC. When any one of these conditions is missing, it becomes far more difficult for teams to function at high levels. We recommend the SIG at a minimum include these conditions. See figure 1.2 (page 12) for a sample SIG.

Collaborative Teams

The first prerequisite is to strategically organize teachers into meaningful teams that share common goals for improving student learning. As teams work together to achieve these goals, they develop a sense of collective responsibility for the success of all students—not just those individual teachers see in their classrooms every day. A true sense of *team* grows over time, which leads to a cohesive faculty, reduced teacher turnover, and a positive atmosphere (Barber, Chijioke, & Mourshed, 2010; DuFour, 2010; Eaker & Dillard, 2017; Fulton & Britton, 2011; McLaughlin & Talbert, 2006).

Anchor Statements	Beyond Proficient	Proficient	Below Proficient
Educators work in collaborative teams, rather than in isolation, and take collective responsibility for student learning.	Teachers meet weekly in collaborative teams for a minimum of sixty minutes during the regular school day. They utilize norms, goals, and protocols and work interdependently to improve their practice and enhance student learning.	Teachers meet weekly in collaborative teams for a minimum of forty-five minutes during the regular school day. They write norms and goals, and participate in common planning to improve student learning.	Teachers meet weekly in collaborative teams for a minimum of forty-five minutes per week outside the regular school day. They work together on topics of mutual interest and share ideas, materials, and resources.
Collaborative teams implement a guaranteed and viable curriculum, unit by unit.	Teams prioritize and unwrap standards, identify learning targets, write *I can* statements, create common pacing guides, and commit to teach—rather than cover—the curriculum.	Teacher teams prioritize and unwrap standards, identify learning targets, and follow pacing guides created by the district or the publisher.	Teachers deliver lessons based on what they know the best, like the most, have materials for, or what is included in the textbooks.
Collaborative teams monitor student learning through an ongoing assessment process that includes frequent, team-developed, common formative assessments.	Teacher teams work collaboratively to create valid and reliable common formative and summative assessments they administer every few weeks throughout the school year.	Teacher teams share the responsibility for creating common formative and summative assessments they administer on a regular basis throughout the school year.	Teacher teams rotate the responsibility for creating common summative assessments they administer periodically throughout the school year.
Educators use the results of common assessments to improve individual practice, build the team's capacity to achieve its goals, and intervene and enrich on behalf of students.	Teacher teams analyze common formative and summative assessment results to identify which students need more time and support and which instructional strategies they should retain, refine, or replace.	Teacher teams analyze the results of common formative and summative assessments to identify which students need more time and support.	Teacher teams review summative assessment results to monitor student progress or generate grades.
The school provides a systematic process for intervention and extension.	Teacher teams provide students with extension and remedial support as well as targeted and timely interventions that are systematic, practical, effective, essential, and directive, without missing direct instruction in another core subject.	Teacher teams provide students with remedial support as well as targeted interventions that are systematic, practical, effective, essential, and directive.	Teacher teams provide students with opportunities to receive additional remedial support.

Source: Many et al., 2018, pp. 59–60.

Figure 1.2: Sample SIG.

Guaranteed and Viable Curriculum

One of the most important tasks of a highly effective team is to develop a guaranteed and viable curriculum, which is the second prerequisite condition. In this process, team members work together to prioritize the essential standards, identify the highest leverage learning targets, and craft *I can* statements in student-friendly language. Teams also develop a common scope and sequence to ensure students have the ability to learn what teachers deem the essentials in the time allotted. This work leads to an aligned curriculum teacher teams deliver consistently to all students (DuFour & Marzano, 2011; Marzano, 2003; Marzano, Warrick, & Simms, 2014).

Common Assessment Process

When teams practice the third prerequisite, they develop common formative and common summative assessments to measure student proficiency. During this process, team members agree on the targets they will measure and the depth of knowledge levels necessary for proficiency, and they intentionally design assessment items that align with those expectations. They also develop agreements on the logistics of how and when they will deliver common assessments so they can easily compare results across all classrooms in a timely manner.

Focus on Results

One of the most important responsibilities of a team is to analyze common assessment results, which is the fourth prerequisite. Team members come together to review students' performance on specific knowledge, skills, and dispositions by comparing results across the class, course, or grade level. While these data provide teachers with information about individual students and subgroups, highly effective teams also use these data to reflect on the effectiveness of their own instructional practice.

Intervention and Extension

Finally, highly effective teams utilize samples of student work and the results of common assessments to identify which students are having difficulty demonstrating proficiency on which essential standards. These teams create systematic ways to provide opportunities for intervention and remediation by ensuring struggling students have access to more time and support in specific skill areas. In addition, highly effective teams use the same data to identify students who excel in specific areas and provide them with opportunities for extension and acceleration.

When teachers understand these prerequisite conditions of PLCs, it is more likely they will put them into practice. Consider that best practice dictates teachers provide students with a rubric for success before they begin working on an assignment. The same is true here; the SIG defines the success criteria for a high-performing collaborative team. A SIG describes levels of PLC practice coaches and teams can use to pinpoint members' current level of practice in relation to one or all of the five prerequisite conditions of a PLC.

While we recommend team members use the SIG to identify their current reality, we realize they are sometimes so immersed in their work it can be difficult to accurately ascertain their progress. Sometimes the practices you *think* you are using are only that—*what you think*. When coaches become involved in the process, however, they bring a new perspective that a team's perceptions have not influenced. To shed new light on the subject, we encourage coaches to use the SIG to prompt inquiries into the level of a team's PLC practice and implementation, and to seek evidence that confirms the accuracy of the team's perceptions of progress. In addition, coaches use the SIG to help teams set small, attainable goals for moving toward *next practice* (the next level of best practice).

The SIG is analogous to a team's "flight plan." It clearly identifies the team's starting point and final destination, gives them direction, and helps them measure progress along the way. In fact, the professional development chapters in this book align with the five prerequisite conditions to help leaders maintain their focus on these important factors. If you have not yet worked with your staff to create a SIG, we refer you to chapter 3 of *Amplify Your Impact* (Many et al., 2018, p. 47) for more information about how to engage in this important, foundational work.

Feedback

An outcome of successfully implementing the PLC process is transformative change. Teams use data to reflect on their practice and make changes that lead to increased student learning. However, "without feedback, there can be no transformative change" (Brown, 2012, p. 197). By providing teams with ongoing, differentiated feedback, the coaching process helps teams deepen their reflection and initiate transformative change. To help coaches deliver effective feedback to teams, we provide the SIG (see Clarity, page 11) and the Pathways for Coaching Collaborative Teams (pathways) tool (Many et al., 2018; Thomas, 2015). The pathways tool assists coaches in guiding team conversations. The tool is composed of matrices with a series of questions that focus on a different aspect of each of the four critical questions of a PLC (DuFour et al., 2016):

1. What knowledge, skills, and dispositions should every student acquire as a result of this unit, this course, or this grade level?

2. How will we know when each student has acquired the essential knowledge and skills?

3. How will we respond when students do not learn?

4. How will we extend the learning for students who are already proficient? (p. 36)

By collaboratively discussing the answers to the four critical questions with a coach's guidance, teams receive the support they need to deepen their understanding of the PLC process and move forward in the instructional learning cycle (Many et al., 2018). A sample pathways tool appears in figure 1.3. To learn more about the pathways tool, see chapter 5 in *Amplify Your Impact* (Many et al., 2018, p. 85).

The SIG and the pathways tool guide coaches toward objective feedback based on concrete evidence rather than subjective feedback based on opinion. The purpose of coaches' feedback is to help teams improve their PLC practice, which leads to transformed instruction and higher levels of student learning.

When coaches provide teams with differentiated feedback that brings clarity to the team's goals, ongoing support becomes vital for the team to achieve those goals. Anthony Muhammad points out, "Leadership is a balance between support and accountability; support has to precede accountability. Accountability is unethical if it's not preceded by support" (Crow, 2012, p. 20).

Prioritizing Standards	Identifying Targets	Determining Proficiency	Planning Units	Analyzing Strategies
Which standards provide endurance?	What targets did the unwrapping process reveal?	How would you rewrite this target in student-friendly terms?	What targets will you be instructing on next?	What instructional strategies will you use?
Which standards provide readiness for the next level of learning?	Where does the current curriculum address these targets?	What are the prerequisite skills and vocabulary necessary to master this target?	What instructional strategies will you all agree to use during this unit?	Which strategies worked well when this unit was taught in the past? How do you know?
Which standards provide leverage?	Which targets are not adequately addressed in your current curriculum?	To what DOK level should students show mastery?	Approximately how much time will you spend teaching each target?	Which strategies did not work well last time this unit was taught? Why did they not work?
Which standards are most often assessed by standardized tests?	To what DOK level will you teach each target?	What will students create, produce, or be able to do when they master this target?	To what DOK level will you teach each target?	How can you alter these strategies to make them more successful?
If you could only teach ten standards in this course, which would they be? Why?	How will you pace your course curriculum to include these targets?	How will you grade or score this target?	What data, evidence, or student work should your team bring to the next meeting?	What strategies should you delete from this unit?
		What models of proficiency do you have or can you create?		What additional best-practice strategies should you try?

Source: Many et al., 2018, p. 91.

Figure 1.3: Pathways tool for PLC critical question one.

Support

Just like students, teacher teams need differentiated support. The pathways tool we present in *Amplify Your Impact* functions as a means of providing this differentiated support (Many et al., 2018). As we mention in the Feedback section, the original pathways tool is based on the four critical questions of a PLC (DuFour et al., 2016) and the tasks that teams engage in as they respond to each question. For example, in the first critical question, "What knowledge, skills, and dispositions should every student acquire as a result of this unit, this course, or this grade level?" (DuFour et al., 2016, p. 36), one of the pathway tasks is to prioritize standards. In addition, we have developed a new set of pathways for the five prerequisite conditions of highly effective teams (see the reproducibles on pages 242–248).

Once the coach and team identify a team's current reality on the SIG and develop a SMART (strategic and specific, measurable, attainable, results oriented, and time bound; Conzemius &

O'Neill, 2014) goal for next steps, coaches guide the team to the pathway that will best support the team in attaining its goal. If the team's goal is to do a better job of creating valid and reliable common assessments (prerequisite three, *Collaborative teams monitor student learning through an ongoing assessment process that includes frequent, team-developed, common formative assessments*), the coach directs the team to the Pathway for critical question two: "How will we know when each student has acquired the essential knowledge and skills?" (DuFour et al., 2016, p. 36). Alternatively, coaches can guide teams using the new pathways for prerequisite conditions of highly effective teams introduced in this book (see the reproducibles on pages 242–248). Either way, coaches use the pathways to lead teams through a series of important questions about the work they have (or have not) engaged in related to PLC critical question two.

If the SIG represents the "flight plan," the Pathways are the "preflight checklist." While the SIG provides the destination, the Pathways provide a checklist of actions and procedures that must be functioning to get "the plane off the ground." It is important to reiterate that the SIG and the Pathways work best when educators use them together. When teams are clear on where they are going *and* receive guidance on the specific tasks that will help them get there, PLCs will go further faster.

Table 1.1: Prerequisite Conditions and the Four Critical Questions of a PLC

Five Prerequisite Conditions of PLCs (foundation of the SIG)	Educators work in collaborative teams, rather than in isolation, and take collective responsibility for student learning.	Collaborative teams implement a guaranteed and viable curriculum, unit by unit.	Collaborative teams monitor student learning through an ongoing common assessment process that includes frequent, team-developed common formative assessments.	Educators use the results of common assessments to improve individual practice, build the team's capacity to achieve its goals, and intervene and enrich on behalf of students.	The school provides a systematic process for intervention and teaching.
The Four Critical Questions of Learning in a PLC (foundation of the pathways tool)		Question one: What knowledge, skills, and dispositions should every student acquire as a result of this unit, this course, or this grade level?	Question two: How will we know when each student has acquired the essential knowledge and skills?	Question three: How will we respond when students do not learn? Question four: How will we extend the learning for students who are already proficient?	Question three: How will we respond when students do not learn? Question four: How will we extend the learning for students who are already proficient?

Sources: Adapted from DuFour et al., 2016; DuFour & Reeves, 2016.

The design of the coaching framework (clarity, feedback, and support) guides coaches as they help teams improve their PLC practices. It is a blueprint of coaching that leads teams to do their very best work. To continue in this vein, we created additional Pathways for the five prerequisite conditions of highly effective teams (see the reproducibles, pages 242–248). When coaches utilize these Pathways, they encourage teams to engage in cycles of continuous improvement and collective inquiry that lead to increased student learning.

The next chapter provides a continuum of PLC practice—the context for PLC lite, PLC right, and PLC tight. Both teams and their coaches can use this continuum to measure and manage the growth and development of highly effective collaborative teams.

CHAPTER 2

A Continuum of Practice for PLCs

A Professional Learning Community is an ethos that infuses every single aspect of a school's operation. When a school becomes a professional learning community, everything in the school looks different than it did before.

—ANDY HARGREAVES

During a team coaching session in a small district in Iowa, the principal asked one of the authors, Michael Maffoni, the question, "What constitutes a highly effective professional learning community, and how do I recognize one when I see it?" Unfortunately, many leaders ask the very same question, which is why we developed a framework for coaching collaborative teams. The *Amplify Your Impact* framework (Many et al., 2018) is built on the cornerstones of clarity, feedback, and support and includes SIGs and Pathways tools to support those who coach teams. When schools utilize the SIG and Pathways tools to coach teams, they obtain a much clearer understanding of what constitutes a highly effective PLC and how to recognize one when they see it. It is difficult to calculate exactly how many schools are functioning as high-performing PLCs because the term has become so commonplace. In fact, some educators use the term PLC:

> To describe every imaginable combination of individuals with an interest in education—a grade-level teaching team, a school committee, a high school department, an entire school district, a state department of education, a national professional organization, and so on. In fact, the term has been used so ubiquitously that it is in danger of losing all meaning. (DuFour, 2004, p. 6)

Becoming a PLC is not an event or something that happens all at once. Principals and teacher leaders might be able to identify turning points or breakthrough moments, but they don't wake up one morning and find their school or district a fully functioning and highly effective PLC. To paraphrase DuFour (2018), becoming a PLC requires passion and persistence.

PLC is also not something you *do*; a PLC is something you *are*. The most effective leaders recognize that becoming a PLC is a journey or pilgrimage—an ongoing and never-ending process of discovery and professional growth. As coauthors Cathy Riggins and Debbie Knowles (2020) state, "There are no shortcuts to operating as a true PLC" (p. 53).

While there are no advanced levels of PLC training, there are advanced levels of PLC practice. The challenge for principals and teacher leaders is to recognize the current level of practice at their school, identify next logical steps, and commit to implementing the PLC process deeply enough to attain the results they seek.

Any principal or group of teacher leaders committed to coaching collaborative teams wants to know two things: (1) what constitutes a highly effective PLC and (2) the current level of PLC practice in their school. The mantra of those coaching teams in a PLC is, "It's not about what's wrong; it's about what's next," so knowing current levels of PLC practice for a school or team helps identify the next steps in implementing the PLC process.

School leaders also want to know what a highly effective PLC looks like, sounds like, and feels like; it's important to coach teams toward an agreed-on standard of best practice. In *Amplify Your Impact* and *Thrive*, we describe a coaching framework built on clarity, feedback, and support that introduces specific SIG and pathways tools (Many et al., 2018, 2020). While the design of SIG and Pathways facilitates coaching collaborative teams, school leaders can also use them to identify and articulate the policies, practices, and procedures of a highly effective PLC.

The terms *PLC lite* and *PLC right* (DuFour & Reeves, 2016) describe different stages of PLC development. In addition, Robert Eaker and Janel Keating have coined the term "PLC tight," which identifies teams that have gone beyond PLC right as they embed PLC practices in the culture of their school (R. Eaker, personal communication, September 2020). These descriptions have proven useful ways of looking at levels of implementation. However, the duality of the *lite* versus *right* description has also proven to be limiting as a way for principals and teacher leaders to ascertain their schools' progress; those who coach teams realize that becoming a PLC is just not that simple.

For example, both lite and right schools engage in similar work. Schools do not operate exclusively in one category or the other. Becoming a PLC is not an either/or proposition, and using terms such as *lite* and *right* to describe where a school is in the process of becoming a PLC suggests a dichotomy that does not exist.

> "When the PLC process is implemented deeply and sustained over time, schools can experience dramatic improvement in learning by both students and adults. PLC lite is an exercise in futility that helps neither students nor the educational systems that serve them."
>
> **—Richard DuFour and Douglas Reeves**

A Continuum of Competence

In reality, implementing the PLC process is best thought of as on a continuum. By adapting the work of Thomas Gordon and Noel Burch (1974) and the four stages of competence, we created a continuum of PLC practice to help principals and teacher leaders identify how their schools are progressing through the various stages of becoming a PLC.

Gordon and Burch (1974) describe the four stages of competence as follows.

1. Unconscious incompetence

2. Conscious incompetence

3. Conscious competence

4. Unconscious competence

The stages (see figure 2.1) describe how individuals and organizations learn new skills or gain mastery of new information.

One level is not better or worse than another, and the levels do not reflect value or relative worth. The labels Gordon and Burch attach to each stage describe a natural progression all learners transition through as they master a new skill.

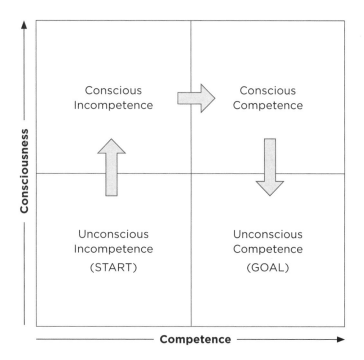

Source: Adapted from Gordon and Burch, 1974.

Figure 2.1: The four stages of competence.

Four Stages

The four stages of competence (see figure 2.1) are applicable to any organization. The value is that the stages always move in the same direction following the same sequence, thus making this framework a reliable tool to determine the level of individual or group learning associated with any initiative.

Stage 1: Unconscious Incompetence

Unconsciously incompetent individuals or groups simply don't know what they don't know. They are blissfully unaware of how ineffective they are or even what they need to do to become effective. In fact, this group may honestly believe their current practice is just fine and often resists a coach's efforts to help them improve.

Stage 2: Conscious Incompetence

Consciously incompetent individuals or groups know what they don't know, but not how to do it. People in this stage recognize the need to improve and often seek out information about better ways of working. Mistakes are common in the early stages of any initiative, so coaching and feedback are particularly helpful in this stage.

Stage 3: Conscious Competence

Consciously competent individuals or groups know what they know and can put new skills or knowledge into practice, but it takes concerted and persistent effort to be successful. In this stage, coaching focuses on creating systems and patterns of behavior that promote success.

Stage 4: Unconscious Competence

Unconsciously competent individuals or groups know what is effective and have become so competent that executing the new skill or aptitude has become second nature. Groups and individuals create routines that become habits of practice, and coaches help them innovate and move from best practice to *next practice* (the next level of best practice).

The four stages of competence also describe levels of PLC practice. To be compatible with the PLC process, those coaching teams would likely rename the stages but, even with new verbiage, the underlying concepts remain the same.

> "There are powerful ways to leverage the four stages if you are a leader. The first is in the area of coaching and teaching."
>
> **—Wally Schmader**

By shifting Gordon and Burch's (1974) language to align with the vernacular of PLCs, it is possible to explore more specific dimensions of a school's PLC practice. A continuum of PLC practice would begin with schools where a PLC is nowhere in sight (stage 1); then PLC lite schools in the early stages of development (stage 2); to PLC right schools that are "farther down the road" (stage 3); and finally, to PLC tight schools where the PLC process is part of the school's culture (stage 4). If you are exploring the idea of coaching teams, your school probably falls somewhere within the middle two categories of PLC lite and right. Teams functioning in the middle two stages possess a foundational knowledge of PLCs and operate in a "sweet spot" for coaching. However, *Energize Your Teams* is designed as a resource to support teams operating in all four stages of development. We hold firm to the belief that teams just beginning their PLC journey will benefit from coaching. We also believe that even the best collaborative teams can improve.

> An essential characteristic of a true professional learning community is continuous improvement—a "persistent disquiet with the status quo" and a constant search for a better way to achieve goals and accomplish the purpose of the organization are inherent in the PLC culture.
>
> **—Richard DuFour, Rebecca DuFour, and Robert Eaker**

Four Stages of Competence in a PLC

In the following section, we apply this four-stage model to the PLC journey.

Stage 1: PLC Is Nowhere in Sight

This is the unconscious incompetence stage. A surprising number of schools have not yet begun to explore the PLC process. When visiting schools in this stage, you would likely experience a palpable sense of complacency along with an extraordinary level of comfort and satisfaction with the status quo. For these schools, a PLC is nowhere in sight.

Few, if any, of the faculty have attended training, and professional development is reserved for principals. Efforts to coach teams that are unconsciously incompetent about PLCs should focus on building readiness for the idea of implementing the PLC process. By challenging past practice, building shared knowledge, and "tilling the soil" to prepare for a shift in school culture, the coaching of collaborative teams can be an important step in the right direction. Coaching helps facilitate difficult conversations concerning teachers' beliefs about students and the idea of working together as collaborative teams.

> "Although many schools around the world have claimed to embrace the professional learning community (PLC) process, it would be more accurate to describe the current state of affairs in many schools as PLC lite."
>
> **—Richard DuFour and Douglas Reeves**

Stage 2: PLC Lite

This is the conscious incompetence stage. The faculty in PLC lite schools buys in to the idea of PLCs, and those individuals coaching teams focus on building shared knowledge, developing common language, and creating the necessary structures to support collaborative teams.

Teachers in these schools are comfortable meeting to share ideas, materials, and suggestions about delivering the curriculum. They review standards documents the district makes available, administer assessments publishers develop, use data to identify students who are not proficient, and offer students *opportunities* for additional time and support.

The signature characteristic of teams in this stage is *learning*. Coaches must be mindful that while teachers in PLC lite schools are interested in learning more about the PLC process, they have not been engaged in the work long enough or with enough depth to become proficient. These teams benefit most from specific and nonjudgmental feedback.

Schools described as *PLC lite* are moving in the right direction and if the faculty and staff remain committed, stay focused on doing the right work, and continue their efforts to drive the PLC process deeper into the school's culture, they will begin to generate more consistent results. As Riggins and Knowles (2020) advise, "Change doesn't happen overnight and it is only sustainable when teams stay focused on the right work" (p. 53). For this reason, it's important for coaches to celebrate when teacher teams recognize these *lite* practices and are determined not to accept past practice as the norm.

"An excellent test for distinguishing between a genuine PLC [PLC right] and a school engaged in PLC lite is the school's attention to the four questions that drive the work of collaborative teams in a PLC."

—Richard DuFour and Douglas Reeves

Stage 3: PLC Right

This is the conscious competence stage. Teams in this stage are all about *doing*. The biggest difference between PLC lite and PLC right is that teams operating as *PLC right* demonstrate a commitment to the right work and have developed habits of professional practice around best PLC practices. In schools that have successfully operationalized the PLC process, collaboration between and among teachers results in action. This is where the shift from *learning* to *doing* takes place.

In schools referred to as *PLC right*, many teachers have attended training along with their principal and together create systems and routines to support the PLC process. Teachers and students feel empowered as evidence of higher levels of learning becomes more prevalent. The faculty moves beyond buy-in to ownership as a result of seeing the way the PLC process promotes higher levels of collective efficacy and student achievement.

In PLC right schools, teams routinely identify and unwrap essential standards and regularly administer common formative and summative assessments. They use assessment data and samples of student work to monitor student progress *and* reflect on the effectiveness of their own instructional practice. These teams create a schoolwide and systematic pyramid of interventions (DuFour et al., 2016) to provide more time and support when students have not learned and opportunities to extend their learning when they have.

Schools operating in the PLC right stage have effectively operationalized the PLC process and developed behaviors and routines that promote high levels of learning for their students. These schools have also built structures that support productive collaborative teams.

"A professional learning community is an ethos that infuses every single aspect of a school's operation. When a school becomes a professional learning community, everything in the school looks different than it did before."

—Andy Hargreaves

Stage 4: PLC Tight

This is the unconscious competence stage. Eaker and Keating describe teams who have implemented the PLC process with the most depth and expertise as *PLC tight* (R. Eaker, personal communication, September 2020).

Teachers in these schools are deeply committed to the PLC process. For teams in this stage, collective inquiry, continuous improvement, and an action orientation focused on results have become habits of professional practice.

In PLC tight schools, the school culture anchors the PLC process. In fact, the PLC process is so deeply engrained that it routinely survives the loss of key administrators or teacher leaders. The recruitment and selection process for teachers and administrators reflects a commitment to PLCs; even new teacher orientation is built around developing an understanding of the three big ideas of a PLC—(1) a focus on learning, (2) a collaborative culture, and (3) a results orientation (DuFour et al., 2016). Resources such as *Learning by Doing* (DuFour et al., 2016) and *Taking Action* (Buffum, Mattos, & Malone, 2018) are excellent guides for empowering schools and teams to move toward PLC tight.

> "A comprehensive study of the world's best-performing school systems finds that these systems function as professional learning communities."
>
> **—Michael Barber, Chinezi Chijioke, and Mona Mourshed**

From PLC Lite to PLC Tight

It takes a real commitment for educators to fully engage in the PLC process, but when it happens, it is *PLC right*; and when PLC right becomes a habit of professional practice, it evolves into *PLC tight*. We have also seen honest attempts to implement PLCs that have little impact on teaching and learning. These well-intended efforts result in trivial and temporary changes and when that happens, it is *PLC lite*.

There is no doubt that implementing PLCs well is hard work. In fact, coauthors Richard DuFour and Michael Fullan (2013) state, "even those individual schools that have implemented the PLC process successfully will find it difficult to sustain the process unless the larger system provides a more positive and supportive context" (p. 3). One way to provide this kind of positive, supportive context is by coaching collaborative teams. Just as students perform at higher levels when their teachers coach them, collaborative teams will perform at higher levels when their leaders coach them. When principals and teacher leaders provide coaching on specific skills and strategies to improve teams' PLC practices, they inevitably move toward PLC tight.

Just as there are degrees of effectiveness associated with implementation of the PLC process, there are differences in the effectiveness coaching has on collaborative teams. In chapter 3, we will focus on the difference between *coaching lite* and *coaching right*.

CHAPTER 3

The Team Coaching Cycle

I believe that wherever there is mastery, coaching is occurring, and whenever coaching is done, mastery will be the outcome.

—ANDREA J. LEE

Collaborative teams thrive when there is predictability to their processes and routines. Knowing what to expect provides clarity, direction, and a sense of comfort. These attributes were evident during one observation of a coaching session with a collaborative team at a mid-sized middle school in Missouri. During the visit, the coach used the *Amplify Your Impact* coaching cycle to anchor the team's conversation and shared a graphic of the cycle with the team members. Seeing the graphic and knowing the stage they were in helped the team understand their next best steps for moving forward. One member of the team commented, "You know, providing us a visual of the cycle gave us something to relate to. I think seeing it was foundational. We know there is a road map for our work ahead. I'm excited!" This conversation brought about a sense of optimism that the coach would be a guide, helping them navigate their collective work.

In chapter 2, we presented the continuum of PLC practice to illustrate the task school leaders face as they work to implement PLCs deeply enough to impact teaching and learning in their schools. Regardless of the level of implementation, teams of teachers in schools operating as PLCs lite, PLCs right, and PLCs tight engage in similar work. These teachers work together to identify essential standards, design assessments, analyze data, and create and implement interventions and extensions; but the trajectory of improvement is not at the same rate or of the same magnitude for schools in different places on the continuum. The most effective school leaders understand this, and they also understand the difference between knowing about PLCs and actually implementing the PLC process successfully. They realize that while teachers and administrators can attend workshops, seminars, and institutes, no amount of training by itself will ever be enough. The *only* way they can hope to change teachers' day-to-day practice and create a lasting impact on their schools is by driving the PLC process deeply into the school's culture over an extended period of time.

School leaders often ask, "What is the most efficient and effective way to move a school from PLC lite to PLC right to PLC tight?" We believe the answer to that question is clearer now than ever before; the best way to move schools toward deeper levels of implementation is to coach collaborative teams around improving their PLC practice.

> "What most people consider coaching, we consider support."
>
> **—Michael Cary Sonbert**

There are countless resources describing the characteristics of coaching, and while there are general agreements on effective and ineffective practices, there is no definitive list of what does and does not constitute good coaching. It would be a mistake to suggest there is an explicit list of the precise actions coaches must take, or to point to a specific situation and say, "These are the things good coaches do." *Effective coaching* is complex; it blends elements of structure, process, experience, and expertise with more specialized skills like building trust, paraphrasing, providing feedback, and facilitating decision making.

Learning Forward senior advisor Joellen Killion (2008) writes extensively about coaching *and identifies two categories of coaching she calls coaching light* and *coaching heavy*. Killion (2008) writes, "Coaching light occurs when coaches want to build and maintain relationships more than they want to improve teaching and learning" (p. 1). She continues, "Coaching heavy occurs when coaches ask thought-provoking questions, uncover assumptions, and engage teachers in dialogue about their beliefs and goals rather than focusing only on teacher knowledge and skills" (Killion, 2008, p. 3). Killion (2008, 2010) makes it clear: if coaching is to impact student learning, it must move beyond congenial relationships and offer more than support to individual teachers. Having a weekly conversation or monthly check-in with a coach to talk about how things are going will not improve a teacher's practice.

Coaching Versus Supporting

Educators tend to conflate the terms *coaching* and *supporting*. School leader and teacher trainer Michael Cary Sonbert (2020) explains that support includes things like discussing a lesson, sharing materials, or talking about students and instructional practice. In his mind, *support* is a conversation that is "not terribly structured, no skill is modeled, no practice occurs, and there aren't any deadlines or deliverables at the end of it" (Sonbert, 2020, p. 5). Sonbert (2020) sees coaching as being opposite in nearly every way, arguing that *coaching* is "structured and focused. It is heavy on modeling, practice, design, and feedback. It is directive and grounded in data" (p. 5). Leaders would be wise to remember that support helps us *feel* better, while coaching helps us *do* better.

Killion's (2008) and Sonbert's (2020) distinctions between the different categories of coaching individual teachers apply equally well to the coaching of collaborative teams. Comparing PLC lite, PLC right, and PLC tight schools provides a way to explore how different dimensions of the PLC process impact student learning. Likewise, contrasting Killion's and Sonbert's descriptions of coaching approaches provides a way to study the effect coaching collaborative teams can have on improving teaching and learning in schools. Because most schools are functioning somewhere on the continuum between PLC lite and PLC right, for the sake of clarity and consistency, we will use the terms *coaching lite* and *coaching right* when referring to the process of coaching collaborative teams.

"Changing teaching and student learning takes time yet the speed of change can be accelerated when coaches work at least part of their day with teams of teachers."

—Joellen Killion, Cindy Harrison, Chris Bryan, and Heather Clifton

Coaching Lite Versus Coaching Right

Most teachers and administrators are familiar with the kind of coaching when a teacher who is new to the profession or experiencing difficulty works one-on-one with a coach to hone, shift, and sharpen his or her classroom management or instructional strategies. More often than not, this kind of coaching focuses on improving an individual teacher's curricular knowledge and instructional strategies in core subject areas like reading, mathematics, and science. This kind of coaching can also support implementation of new initiatives, achievement of schoolwide goals, or the use of recently purchased online tools.

These teacher-centric approaches begin with a deficit orientation (the teacher has a problem the coach must fix), have limited access to resources (no one coach has enough time, energy, and expertise to help all teachers), and rely heavily on the perception of teachers and coaches to measure progress.

Interactions between teachers and coaches in this kind of coaching have an invitational tone, and building and maintaining positive relationships are a high priority. The coaching can be personal or professional, emotional or academic, formal or informal, and the coach's opinion, comfort level, and knowledge play a significant role in determining the goals and direction of the coaching relationship. Teachers often describe this kind of coaching as affirming, encouraging, and supportive.

In these coaching relationships, coaches encourage teachers to self-select improvement goals based on their individual interests or in response to deficits coaches identify during the formal evaluation process. It is not unusual for every teacher on the same team to have a different improvement target and, because of the one-on-one nature of the approach, teachers typically work alone, in isolation away from their colleagues, while coaches focus on individual rather than collective improvement. A meta-analysis of sixty instructional coaching evaluations by Kraft and Blazar (2018) confirms and establishes coaching as an integral part of professional development for teachers. We acknowledge this is a proven, effective strategy for improving an individual teacher's practice; it may even align with the prevailing belief systems in some schools, but it's just not enough.

"Coaching is about intentionally and strategically building skill. It's not about leaving notes and hoping."

—Michael Cary Sonbert

Shifting the emphasis of a school's coaching from individual teachers to collaborative teams substantially increases the number of teachers who benefit. Simply put, it amplifies the impact of coaching!

Educational authors like Tom Carroll (2009), Sharon Kruse, Karen Seashore Louis, and Anthony Bryk (1994), Judith Warren Little (2006), and Cynthia D. McCauley and Ellen Van Velsor (2003) believe the impact of coaching *individual* teachers will always be suboptimal because strategies that focus on improving schools one teacher at a time "[do] not develop the interdependence, collaboration, and collective effort essential to improving results" (as cited in DuFour & Marzano, 2011, p. 66).

According to DuFour and Marzano (2011), research shows, "the best way to improve the effectiveness of individual teachers is not . . . through individualistic strategies that reinforce educator isolation" (p. 67). Likewise, improvement "strategies that focus solely on improving individuals will fail to improve schools because meeting that challenge [improving schools] requires building collective capacity" (DuFour & Marzano, 2011, p. 66).

Instead of coaching individual teachers using a one-on-one approach, the most effective schools and districts place greater emphasis on coaching collaborative teams using a one-on-many approach. In this way, coaches work with more teachers in the same amount of time and, as Killion and Harrison (2017) observe, "When coaches work with teams, they substantially increase the effect of their effort" (p. 161).

The following is from instructional coaches in Olathe, Kansas, who recognized that what they already knew about effective coaching practices with individual teachers applied equally well to collaborative teams. Their testimonial is an example of how one school district shifted its coaching priorities in an effort to accelerate the improvement of teaching and learning.

The Olathe Kansas Public School District is a large system composed of over sixty schools. The district has a long history of coaching individual teachers, focusing on improving their instructional strategies in specific content areas. Each coach in Olathe supports multiple schools and, because of the large number of classrooms, teachers historically have received different levels and frequency of coaching support.

Coaches received extensive training and leaned heavily on cognitive coaching and coaching cycles. *Cognitive coaching* promotes reflective conversations with teachers, and *coaching cycles* ensure better alignment to a results orientation for teacher and student learning.

Olathe benefitted from having strong central office– and school-based leaders who worked hard to align expectations and districtwide systems of support. Their strategic plan focused on districtwide PLC implementation. Olathe recognized the importance of team practice focused on the three big ideas of a PLC (focus on learning, collaboration, and results orientation; DuFour et al., 2016). Over many years, school leaders, guiding coalition members, and coaches participated in a series of trainings around the PLC process.

As Olathe began PLC implementation, leaders noticed variability in the effectiveness of teams and quickly recognized that teams would benefit from coaching support. This, however, would require a revision to their traditional approach and a shift from individuals to teams. It also would require a shift from coaching content (mathematics, science, and writing) and instructional strategies to coaching elements of the PLC process.

To make this switch, leaders and coaches read and trained on the framework in *Amplify Your Impact* (Many et al., 2018). The coaches demonstrated a shared commitment to embed team coaching in all grade- and department-level meetings. Working together, they created a SIG and practiced providing feedback to teams. In parallel, coaches utilized the pathways tool to identify specific next steps with teams.

Initially, the coaches believed coaching teams was a new process and required a different skill set. A collective sense of frustration and disequilibrium set in despite their belief that coaching teams was essential to improved PLC practice. Overall, they seemed to set aside what they knew about coaching and began to ask questions such as, "Are we doing this—coaching teams—correctly?"

When asked, "What do you know about good coaching?" the Olathe coaches experienced a collective aha moment. They realized the actions and skills they had been utilizing when coaching individual teachers (such as setting goals, feedback, paraphrasing, and implementing coaching cycles), with a few vital adjustments around audience and content, were transferable to coaching teams. Coaches were thankful for the agreed-on standard of best practice the SIG and the pathways tool provided, which served to unite their efforts.

Olathe coaches made the connection that many of the skills and processes used to coach individual teachers were transferrable to teams. The primary difference for Olathe was their ability to make the paradigm shift from coaching individual teachers centered on content and scattered definitions of instructional practice to a focus on coaching teams in the PLC process based on their SIG, an agreed-on standard of excellence.

Coaching collaborative teams involves more than simultaneously coaching several teachers who just happen to be in the same grade level or department. If the kind of coaching teachers experience while working as a team shares and mimics what coaches would do with individual teachers, that is coaching a group, not a team, and we would characterize it as *coaching lite*.

> "The focus must shift from helping individuals become more effective in their isolated classrooms and schools, to creating a new collaborative culture based on interdependence, shared responsibility, and mutual accountability."
>
> **—Richard DuFour and Robert J. Marzano**

Coaching lite and coaching right share some common characteristics; both are affirming and encouraging. They both require coaches to build and maintain trustworthy relationships. If trust is the foundation of a healthy coaching relationship, then confidentiality, honesty, and integrity are the cornerstones of that foundation. Just as with coaching individual teachers, all of these are critical to building positive working relationships between coaches and teacher teams.

Both coaching lite and coaching right assume teachers' best intentions, and coaches resist the temptation to be judgmental, make assumptions about the capacity of teams to succeed, prematurely offer solutions to problems, or pretend to have all the answers.

Coaching lite and coaching right both require a high level of competency on a host of specific coaching strategies and skills, perhaps the most important of which is communication. The most effective coaches excel at listening, reflecting, paraphrasing, and providing nonjudgmental feedback. Communication involves verbal and nonverbal cues, and the best coaches have learned it's not enough to *hear* what teachers say; they must make a sincere effort to *understand* what teachers are trying to communicate.

Some would argue that good coaching is simply good coaching, and while there are many similarities between coaching lite and coaching right, there are significant differences including the audience for and content of the coaching collaborative teams receive.

Coaching right promotes collaboration by capitalizing on the power of collective inquiry. Having all team members involved and learning *together* through a process of collective inquiry and continuous improvement builds capacity of the entire team and develops a sense of *collective* efficacy.

Coaching right engages teams in a collaborative data-driven goal-setting process based on an agreed-on standard of best practice. Rather than coaching around discrete instructional skills and strategies, coaching collaborative teams is grounded in the essential elements of the PLC process, and each member of the team shares a common goal for which they are held mutually accountable. In coaching right, it is the coach's job to help teacher teams become more competent in and confident with collaborating about teaching and learning.

Coaching collaborative teams focuses on the team's assets in an effort to improve specific PLC practices. Those coaching collaborative teams focus on the five prerequisite conditions of a PLC we presented in chapter 1 and the actions associated with them. This type of coaching empowers teachers' expertise; because the coaching focuses on student results and how instructional strategies contribute to those results, coaching becomes a catalyst for lasting professional change.

Leaders can determine if the coaching culture in their school is trending lite or right by asking and answering the following questions. When schools are coaching right, coaches can answer these questions affirmatively.

1. Does the team clearly know and understand the current reality of their PLC practice? (The coach uses the SIG to help the team reach consensus and answer this question.)

2. Does the team know the next steps the members need to take to continue improving their PLC practice? (The coach uses the Pathways to help the team reach consensus and answer this question.)

3. Does the team have concrete evidence of improved PLC practice?

Coaching Versus Coaches

We subscribe to the belief that developing highly effective collaborative teams is about *coaching*, not *coaches*. While not all schools employ coaches, most schools have a combination of administrators and teacher leaders who, through coaching, can help teams improve their professional practice. University education assistant professors Matthew A. Kraft and David Blazar (2018) have it right when they write, "The role of coach may be performed by a range of personnel, including administrators, master teachers, curriculum designers, external experts, and other classroom teachers" (p. 70). Fundamentally, we believe everyone should be willing to coach and receive coaching in the interest of improving their professional practice.

One of the most persistent myths is that principals can't, or shouldn't coach, but others such as Knight and colleagues (2019) and Psencik (2011) challenge this view. They believe not only *can* principals coach, they *should* coach and look for opportunities to engage in effective coaching behaviors whenever possible.

The primary rationale for believing principals can't coach is based on the belief that the line between *coaching* and *evaluation* is blurry and difficult to define. Sonbert (2020) argues that an easy and effective way to eliminate confusion on which role the principal is engaged in is to use a different document for each task.

In this scenario, when evaluating teachers, building principals utilize the formal, district-, or state-approved evaluation instrument. When principals or others in administrative roles are coaching, they rely on the SIG and pathways tools. After all, coaching is not about what's wrong, it's about what's next, and the notion that principals can't or shouldn't coach reflects an outdated understanding of how best to help teachers *and* teams improve their practice.

Given the belief that action rather than role defines coaching, the critical question becomes, *What defines good coaching?* When educators ask, "What are the characteristics of a good coach?" there are two basic beliefs. First, good coaching is less about the title and more about the work. Second, good coaching utilizes a well-defined coaching cycle to ensure each team member engages in an effort to improve the team's PLC practice.

> "The work OF a team must include work ON the team. When we take time to work ON the team, the work OF the team improves."
>
> **—Walt Kozlowski**

The Coaching Cycle

According to student-centered coaching expert and author Diane Sweeney (2011), organizing coaching into cycles is a powerful way to create structure and promote sustained collaboration over an extended period of time. Sweeney and coauthor Leanna S. Harris (2017) define a coaching cycle as "job embedded professional development that is ongoing and data driven" (p. 3). Sweeney (2011) argues that coaching cycles share three characteristics: (1) they involve in-depth work with teachers over an extended period of time; (2) they are grounded in formal or informal data; and (3) they involve regular interaction for planning and feedback.

More broadly, a coaching cycle should include key elements of the continuous-improvement process and help teams (1) gather objective data; (2) determine current reality; (3) identify next steps; (4) facilitate professional development; and (5) apply new learning. (See figure 3.1, page 34.)

A coaching cycle is both circular and recursive, which allows coaches and teams to repeat any steps that will lead them to greater clarity, higher levels of precision, and lasting proficiency around the skills necessary to promote the development of highly effective collaborative teams.

It is difficult to determine exactly how long a coaching cycle should last. Based on our experience, coaching cycles can range from as short as two to four weeks (based on a unit of study) to as long as six to nine weeks (based on the academic calendar). Whatever length of time, the

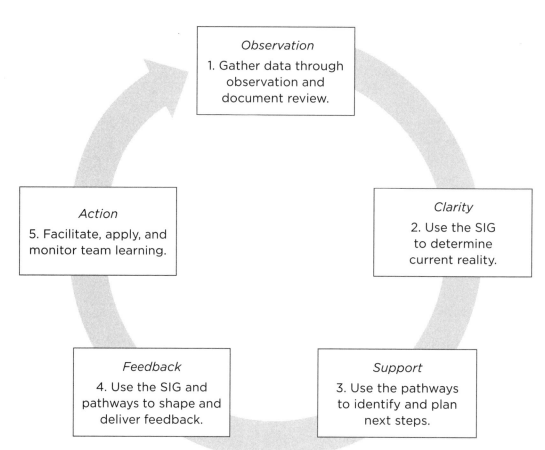

Figure 3.1: The team coaching cycle.

coaching cycle should be "short enough to feel urgent and long enough to allow for change to happen" (Sonbert, 2020, p. 102).

Step 1: Gather Data Through Observation and Document Review

> "Often I get asked about what tool or form should be used to collect data. We intentionally haven't created one because, ultimately, the tool you use is much less important than what you collect data on and how you collect it."
>
> **—Michael Cary Sonbert**

The first step of a team coaching cycle involves collecting any relevant team-generated documents, artifacts, or products, followed by an observation to document the team's professional practice. A significant difference between coaching lite and coaching right is that the former is based on perception, while the latter is grounded in data. When a coaching cycle is not grounded in data, the coaching will undoubtedly be less effective.

Step 2: Use the SIG to Determine Current Reality

"This isn't happening *to* you. It's *for* you."

—Michael Cary Sonbert

In step 2 of the coaching cycle, the coach uses the data he or she collected in step 1 along with the SIG to provide teams with an evidence-based assessment of the team's current reality. The SIG also helps define the relative strengths and vulnerabilities of the team's PLC practice. When a team reflects on its effectiveness, there is a tendency to base the assessment of the team's current reality on beliefs and perceptions, rather than on observable evidence. This practice can lead teams to have a more optimistic and, at times, unrealistic view of their PLC practice. When one makes a judgement or decision based on perception, it is often influenced by bias or emotion; however, if an assessment or decision is rooted in observation, there is tangible, visual evidence that eliminates bias and emotions.

In the second step of the coaching cycle, a coach's role is to shift the team's collective understanding from *what we think* is the level of our PLC practice to *what we know* is the level of our PLC practice. This shift requires the coach and team to use the data they collect during the first phase of the coaching cycle and an agreed-on standard of best PLC practice (the SIG) to determine where they are in terms of implementing the PLC process.

During a debriefing session, team members look at the observational data to determine where they align with the descriptors on the SIG. This process yields the following four specific benefits.

1. It helps the team clearly identify current practice.

2. It informs the team about possible next steps.

3. It promotes the development of common language.

4. It promotes the alignment of PLC practices among and between teams in a school or across a district.

Because teams work on multiple SIG anchors simultaneously, it is likely members will identify multiple descriptors that all contribute to an accurate description of their current PLC practice.

Determining the one indicator that *best* reflects the team's work is important. Accurately identifying the team's currently reality on the SIG helps teams determine next steps and goals for improvement. Consider these questions to prioritize descriptions of a team's current reality. In order to make this assessment, a coach considers both the SIG's anchor statements and the associated descriptors at the Beyond Proficient, Proficient, and Below Proficient levels.

- Which anchor statement and descriptor have the greatest potential impact to improve teaching and learning?

- Which anchor statement and descriptor provide an opportunity for a quick win?

- Which anchor statement and descriptor strike the right balance of effectiveness and efficiency?

Step 3: Use the Pathways to Identify and Plan Next Steps

> "If we assume the best of our teachers, we must assume that if they knew how to do the thing they need to do to impact students more, they would do it."
>
> **—Michael Cary Sonbert**

When individuals come together to identify next steps, the result can be a catalyst that unifies the team's direction. Determining next steps begins when coaching helps teams align the prerequisite condition identified on the SIG in step 2 with the corresponding PLC pathway in step 3. For example, if a team determines it needs to analyze the results of common formative and common summative assessments to identify which students need more time and support, members would use the Pathways for Prerequisite Four: Educators use the results of common assessments to improve individual practice, build the team's capacity to achieve its goals, and intervene and enrich on behalf of students. The team would then follow the pathway task titled "Analyze assessment data." (See the sample SIG and pathways tools on pages 239–248 in the appendix; note, teams can also use the pathways in *Amplify Your Impact*).

Once they determine the appropriate Pathway, team members review the tasks listed in the "Analyze assessment data" column and discuss each question until they identify one they don't know how to accomplish or one they can't answer. This single question becomes the *next step* the team will focus on during their coaching cycle. The work of the coach here is, in effect, to lead a gap-analysis process.

Step 4: Use the SIG and Pathways to Shape and Deliver Feedback

> "Most school leaders do not ask their teachers to practice. This is largely because they think practice will be uncomfortable, or because they're not confident in their ability to model effectively and provide precise feedback."
>
> **—Michael Cary Sonbert**

It is not unusual for a team to identify multiple pathway questions (step 3) as possible next steps. In situations where teams struggle to prioritize what to do next, a coach can be directive. If a team is more self-directed and could benefit from considering a few options, the coach may choose to provide collaborator-level feedback. Alternatively, the coach can pose a reflective question to a team when members need a simple connection to move forward.

As teams and their coach decide on next steps, members arrive at a final decision by consensus. The standard definition of *consensus in the PLC process* is, "When all points of view have been heard and the will of the group is evident—even to those who oppose it" (DuFour et al., 2016, p. 33). When there is a common goal, teams gain momentum.

Step 5: Facilitate, Apply, and Monitor Team Learning

> "You want to make sure that every team you're coaching is in a constant state of practicing and learning."
>
> **—Michael Cary Sonbert**

At this step in the cycle, those coaching teams create opportunities for teachers to practice the skill that will most improve student outcomes. Teams learn at different rates and in different ways, and, while it is true that professional development that meets the needs of one team may be ineffective with others, professional development is *necessary* for teams to sustain momentum and continue to learn. As teams learn more, they will do better.

In this step of the coaching cycle, a coach customizes professional development to match each team's learning needs. For example, a team that identifies the next step of analyzing common formative assessment (CFA) data might observe another team's process and debrief with its members afterward. A different team might opt to read a professional article about analyzing CFA data and reflect together before implementation.

Similarly, schools can facilitate and adjust professional development to scale in a variety of ways. If several teams have similar goals, such as designing assessment questions that match the appropriate levels of depth of knowledge, a school could utilize staff meeting time and learn together. If the goal is unique to one particular team, a school might schedule professional development during the team's planning time. Professional development expert and author Hayes Mizell (2010) notes:

> A school that organizes team-based professional development and expects all teachers and administrators to consistently participate—though for different purposes, at different times, in different ways—demonstrates that it is serious about all educators performing at higher levels. As a result, the entire school is more focused and effective. (p. 18)

Differentiating professional learning that meets the needs of each team will help teams meet their specific goals and continue their movement through the coaching cycle.

While professional development helps teams build shared knowledge, the true test is whether teachers can apply that knowledge in the context of their classrooms. The value of testing new ideas and rehearsing what educators learn cannot be overstated, which is why it is so important to provide teams with adequate time and space to practice their new learning.

As teams attempt to implement their new learning, some will transition smoothly. These teams will need coaching check-ins, feedback, and additional learning less frequently. Other teams will struggle to make the shift. These teams may need more frequent and consistent contact with their coach to stay on track. Teams thrive on feedback that provides objective evidence of how they are progressing. No matter how the implementation process is going for a team, finding opportunities to celebrate even the smallest of victories can help members continue the journey forward.

The Intersection of Coaching and Professional Development

Let's be real—without job-embedded professional development, any plan will likely fall short. Professional development is best when it accentuates team strengths and aims to alleviate the gaps in PLC practice. When teams engage in coaching cycles, identification of systemwide patterns and trends may begin to emerge. Over time, this "balcony view" helps those coaching teams identify professional development needs for individual teams and the faculty as a whole.

The next five chapters in this book offer what we call *grab-and-grow* professional development activities that support a team's ongoing learning—materials any school leader or educator tasked with coaching teams can grab to grow a team or staff's PLC knowledge and skill. Each chapter corresponds to one of the five prerequisites of a PLC (DuFour & Fullan, 2013) and contains professional development modules to support teams through the coaching cycle. Through these next chapters, we hope to answer one question principals constantly ask us as we work in schools: "What is the best way to train our staff?"

PART II

MODULES FOR COACHING COLLABORATIVE TEAMS

CHAPTER 4

Highly Effective Collaborative Teams

Prerequisite one: Educators work in collaborative teams, rather than in isolation, and take collective responsibility for student learning (DuFour & Reeves, 2016).

Coaching teams to collaborate effectively can be a challenge, but it is possible. There is a common misconception that teachers know how to collaborate (many don't) and are comfortable collaborating with others (many aren't). Simply telling teachers to "go and collaborate" often results in team meetings that are as unproductive as working in isolation.

The task of creating high-performing collaborative teams begins with an examination of *why* teams should collaborate. Years of deeply held cultural norms that time-honored stereotypes reinforce (such as the heroic teacher singlehandedly saving the world), combined with past practice, current schedules, archaic belief systems, and modern-day demands on teachers' time, conspire against the idea of collaborating with colleagues. While any of these could be potential barriers, none is enough to prevent coaches from working to develop highly effective collaborative teams.

After grappling with important cultural beliefs about the value of collaboration, there are logistical questions leaders must explore before embarking on the task of creating meaningful teams. School leaders should consider *how* to approach a range of issues, including finding time to collaborate, defining the makeup and membership of collaborative teams, and creating a common language.

Five Keys to Effective Team Meetings

When teachers become anxious about collaborating, individuals coaching teams should examine what impact each of the five keys of effective team meetings—(1) focus, (2) structure, (3) roles and responsibilities, (4) relationships, and (5) process—is having on collaborative teams (Sparks, 2008, p. 33). All these keys contribute to the team's productivity in different ways. When team meetings become unproductive or burdensome, the root of the problem is likely related to the lack of implementation for one of the five keys of highly effective teams.

41

Focus

Highly effective collaborative teams require a clear focus on the right work; without it, meetings quickly become confusing. Educational consultant Susan K. Sparks (2008) believes, "The professional learning community model has helped shift the focus of teams from casual conversations about individual students and climate issues to rich dialogue about student learning" (p. 34).

Structure

Teams that ignore the importance of structure find their meetings can quickly spiral into chaos. While structure is necessary for collaboration, structure alone is not enough to make teams productive. The structures teams use to be productive are most effective and efficient when they flow naturally from the work of teams.

Roles and Responsibilities

Without clearly defined roles and responsibilities, team meetings devolve into a form of institutional anarchy. When establishing roles, it is best to define, then assign; if teams cannot define what a role is responsible for doing, that role is unnecessary.

Relationships

Negative or toxic relationships can inhibit a team's efforts to be productive. Renowned educator and best-selling author Roland Barth (2019) makes the point that the relationship among adults in the building is one of the essential elements of successful schools. He argues that positive, productive, and professional relationships have a greater impact on the school's overall effectiveness than any other factor.

Process

Process for its own sake is ineffective; it is like kryptonite to collaboration. The ineffective use of process leads to dysfunctional team meetings. Teachers will engage in process if they believe it will help them accomplish the task at hand. Likewise, teachers will disengage if they think the process is irrelevant or too complex and time consuming.

According to DuFour and Marzano (2011), "Perhaps the biggest mistake leaders make in attempting to create a collaborative culture is to assign teachers or principals into groups and encourage them to collaborate—with little other direction or support" (p. 79). Teacher, author, international speaker, and project-based learning expert Trevor Muir (2019) believes leaders should view providing training for teachers around effective teaming practices as an investment in their success. DuFour and Marzano (2011), Muir (2019), and others advocate for the conscious, purposeful, and intentional coaching of collaborative teams.

Synopsis of Chapter 4 Modules

The first prerequisite of a PLC states, *Educators work in collaborative teams, rather than in isolation, and take collective responsibility for student learning* (DuFour & Reeves, 2016). The first module in the chapter provides the rationale for *why* collaboration is essential to the success of PLCs. The second module explores *how* teacher leaders and principals create the conditions for highly effective collaborative teams. The third module helps teams understand *what* they can do to operationalize the five keys to an effective team meeting.

Module 4.1: Why Are Collaboration—and Collaborative Teams—Critical to the Success of a PLC?

This module focuses on understanding why collaboration is important. Along with an overview of the research, participants will develop common language and an appreciation for the importance of working collaboratively. By participating in the Repeat Before Response strategy and the Are We a Group or a Team? activity, teachers will have an opportunity to explore their beliefs about collaboration.

Module 4.2: What Conditions Should Schools Consider Before Establishing Collaborative Teams?

There are many things principals, coaches, and teacher leaders should consider before establishing teams, and this module delves into some of the practical questions they must answer before establishing collaborative teams. For example, "How can schools create time for teachers to collaborate?" or "How does the creation of a common language impact the effectiveness of collaboration?" or "How should the school organize the membership of collaborative teams to maximize opportunities for collaboration?"

The answers to these questions are all within the purview of principals, coaches, and teacher leaders. We have found that creating the conditions necessary for successful collaboration is collective effort that reflects what faculty and staff value. The most effective schools realize that developing a schoolwide consensus on answers to these and other questions early in the process of becoming a PLC goes a long way to ensuring collaborative teams will be successful.

Module 4.3: How Do Teams Operationalize the Five Key Elements of Effective Team Meetings?

The final module in this chapter identifies the five keys to effective team meetings. Each of the five keys—(1) focus, (2) structures, (3) roles and responsibilities, (4) relationships, and (5) process—plays a different role in helping promote positive and productive team meetings. When any of the keys are missing, team productivity suffers. This module explores these keys to effective and efficient team meetings and provides opportunities for teachers to reflect on how their team behaviors align with widely accepted best practice.

Like diamonds, each of the keys to effective team meetings is multifaceted. For example, structures encompass things like team norms, SMART goals, agendas and minutes, and protocols, each of which could be a topic for additional study. Simple things like an assessment schedule or use of asynchronous tools may offer opportunities for ongoing collective inquiry. Likewise, the use of protocols is included in the discussion of process, yet there are dozens of different protocols for analyzing assessment data or examining student work. Within each of the five keys is a variety of factors that those who coach teams may want to explore with teams in greater depth or over an extended period of time. This module is designed to provide an overview in a single professional development session or allow for a deep dive into one or all of the keys to collaboration across multiple sessions.

This last module is best thought of as an opportunity for teachers to learn together or as a starting point for further investigation. We intentionally designed the professional development activities in this module to be flexible, and they can be delivered to an individual team or the entire faculty. Present the module as one experience or divided into multiple opportunities to learn about the keys to effective and efficient team meetings.

Why Are Collaboration—and Collaborative Teams—Critical to the Success of a PLC?

Section I: Before the Learning

Rationale—Why It Matters

DuFour and his colleagues (2016) make it clear: "The very reason any organization is established is to bring people together in an organized way to achieve a collective purpose that cannot be accomplished by working alone" (p. 75). Indeed, people accomplish more by working together than working alone, but what educators do in schools doesn't always align with what they know to be best practice. If the fundamental purpose of schools is to ensure high levels of learning for all, it makes sense to bring people together, form collaborative teams, and devote collective efforts to that purpose.

Outcomes

Following are the goals of this module.

1. Build a common vocabulary.

2. Build an awareness of the importance of collaboration in a PLC; teachers will understand why by working together they will create better solutions than they could by working alone.

SIG and Pathways

SIG for prerequisite one (page 239) and the Pathways for Prerequisite One to Five (1.1–5.3; pages 243–248)

Key Coaching Points

Following are the key coaching points of this module.

1. **Introduce and define collaboration:** Explain that research shows teachers working together as collaborative teams is more effective and efficient than teachers working alone; evidence does not support teachers working in isolation as a more effective strategy.

2. **Identify collaboration as a non-negotiable (or tight aspect) and one of the five prerequisites of a PLC:** Challenge the notion by asking why leaders still *accept* the practice of working in isolation in some schools, while leaders in other schools *expect* the practice of working in collaboration.

Important Vocabulary and Terms

Collaboration: This is the systematic process in which people work together, interdependently, to analyze and impact professional practice in order to improve individual and collective results.

Cooperation: People share resources but continue to work independently.

Dependent: This is the quality or condition of relying on others to accomplish your professional goals.

Independent: This is the quality or condition of being self-sufficient and relying on yourself to accomplish your professional goals.

Interdependent: This is the quality or condition of being mutually accountable to others for the accomplishment of your professional goals.

Isolation: This is the condition of working alone, of being separate and not connected to others.

Section II: During the Learning

Preparation—Time and Materials

Complete this module in forty-five minutes. The ideal group size is four teachers per group, seated at tables, but the activity will work with between three and six participants per group. Groups will need chart paper, markers, and a sheet of standard 8 ½ × 11-inch paper. Participants will also need the following handouts.

- "Why Should We Collaborate?" (page 48)
- "Are We a Group or a Team?" (page 50)

Step 1: Getting Ready to Learn—Repeat Before Response Activity (Ten Minutes)

Ask participants to work silently and individually to review the handout "Why Should We Collaborate?" (page 48). As each person reviews the handout, he or she should choose three statements that resonate with them and highlight them (four minutes).

When the group has finished reviewing and highlighting the handout, have everyone stand, find a partner from another table group, and decide who will be *person one* and who will be *person two*. Ask person number one to share a statement that resonated with him or her and explain *why* it was important. Next, ask person two to paraphrase what person one said. Finally, person one confirms that what person two paraphrased was accurate and adds anything he or she omitted. Repeat with person two being the first to speak (six minutes).

After everyone has had an opportunity to share at least one statement with their partner, have the teachers return to their original small groups and prepare for step 2 of the module.

Step 2: Interactive Strategy, Protocol, or Activity—Are We a Group or a Team? (Thirty Minutes)

In preparation for this activity, whoever is facilitating the professional development creates a table with three columns and a row corresponding to each table group participating in the training on a piece of chart paper. Each table will need a facilitator, time keeper, recorder, and reporter. Pass out a piece of 8 ½ × 11-inch paper to each participant. Ask participants to draw a horizontal line—like drawing the equator—on their paper.

1. Follow the directions on the "Are We a Group or a Team?" activity sheet (page 50) and complete steps 1 through 7.

2. After completing the activity, write *isolation, cooperation,* and *collaboration* at the top of columns one, two, and three, respectively, on the chart paper. Ask each table group to identify (a) what happened during the simulation (that, overall, the number of correct letters in the correct sequence improved each round) and (b) which behaviors contributed to the group's improvement from one round to the next. Ask the teams to reflect on whether these behaviors are present on their teams.

3. Return to the directions and complete the remaining tasks as outlined in steps 8 through 10.

Culminate the exercise by asking participants to imagine one of their colleagues asks them, "Why should we collaborate?" As a group, reflect on what you would want the colleague to understand, and develop a succinct response. Have the reporter write the team's consensus on chart paper.

Step 3: Personal Reflection (Five Minutes)

Ask participants to reflect about why teachers should collaborate. How does the faculty feel about working with colleagues? Do they view collaboration as an opportunity or an obligation? Did anything discussed cause you to reconsider how your team operates? What questions are you still wrestling with, and what do you want to learn more about? Have participants record and retain their reflections until the next team meeting; they will be used in section III as the starting point for a debriefing of today's training.

Section III: After the Learning

Next Steps and Follow-Up for Coaching Teams

Your first task as a coach is to help teachers understand *why* collaboration is important. The goal for this section—*the debrief*—is to focus the team's attention on reaching consensus on why it is important that schools promote collaboration and collaborative teams as *the* way teachers approach their work. Possible questions or tasks for the team to consider might include the following.

1. Using a round-robin approach, give each participant a chance to share his or her biggest takeaway from the professional development activity. Each participant should identify the *one* thing he or she believes should definitely be a priority among the faculty.

2. Review the questions and comments generated by participants during step 3, the personal reflection. Are there any patterns? Is there a consensus on any of the questions? Are there particular topics the team wants or needs to learn more about?

3. Schedule a visit to another team or school with a reputation for being a highly effective collaborative team. Design some look-fors for the visit based on the questions generated during the personal reflection in step 3 of the module.

4. Establish a timeline for the team to implement its plan for moving forward at the next collaborative team meeting where members will identify the conditions that must be present to promote the development of highly effective collaborative teams.

Why Should We Collaborate?

"The single most important factor for successful school restructuring and the first order of business for those interested in increasing the capacity of their schools is building a collaborative internal environment" (Eastwood & Louis, 1992, p. 215).

When groups, rather than individuals, are seen as the main units for implementing curriculum, instruction, and assessment, they facilitate development of shared purpose for student learning and collective responsibility to achieve it (Newmann & Wehlage, 1995).

"[High-achieving schools] build a highly collaborative school environment where working together to solve problems and to learn from each other become cultural norms" (WestEd, 2000, p. 12).

"The key to ensuring that every child has a quality teacher is finding a way for school systems to organize the work of qualified teachers so they can collaborate with their colleagues in developing strong learning communities that will sustain them as they become more accomplished teachers" (National Commission on Teaching and America's Future, 2003, p. 7).

"Collaboration and the ability to engage in collaborative action are becoming increasingly important to the survival of public schools. Indeed, without the ability to collaborate with others, the prospect of truly repositioning schools . . . is not likely" (Schlechty, 2009, p. 237).

"It is time to end the practice of solo teaching in isolated classrooms" (Fulton, Yoon, & Lee, 2005, p. 4).

Teacher collaboration in strong professional learning communities improves the quality and equity of student learning, promotes discussions that are grounded in evidence and analysis rather than opinion, and fosters collective responsibility for student success (McLaughlin & Talbert, 2006).

"Quality teaching is not an individual accomplishment, it is the result of a collaborative culture that empowers teachers to team up to improve student learning beyond what any one of them can achieve alone" (Carroll, 2009, p. 13).

"High-performing, high-poverty schools build deep teacher collaboration that focuses on student learning into the culture of the school. Structures and systems are set up to ensure teachers work together rather than in isolation, and "the point of their collaboration is to improve instruction and ensure all students learn" (Chenoweth, 2009, p. 17).

Teachers should be provided with more time for collaboration and embedded professional development during the school day and year. . . . Expanding time for collaboration during the school day "facilitates the development of effective professional learning communities among teachers" (Farbman, Goldberg, & Miller, 2014, p. 25).

"When teachers work together on collaborative teams, they improve their practice in two important ways. First, they sharpen their pedagogy by sharing specific instructional strategies for teaching more effectively. Second, they deepen their content knowledge by identifying the specific standards students must master. In other words, when teachers work together they become better teachers" (Many & Sparks-Many, 2015, p. 83).

"We must stop allowing teachers to work alone, behind closed doors and in isolation in the staffrooms and instead shift to a professional ethic that emphasizes collaboration. We need communities within and across schools that work collaboratively to diagnose what teachers need to do, plan programs and teaching interventions and evaluate the success of the interventions" (Hattie, 2015, p. 23).

Source: DuFour, DuFour, Eaker, Many, & Mattos, 2016.

page 1 of 2

References

Carroll, T. (2009). The next generation of learning teams. *Phi Delta Kappan*, *91*(2), 8–13.

Chenoweth, K. (2009). It can be done, it's being done, and here's how. *Phi Delta Kappan*, *91*(1), 38–43.

DuFour, R., DuFour, R., Eaker, R., Many, T. W., & Mattos, M. (2016). *Learning by doing: A handbook for Professional Learning Communities at Work* (3rd ed.). Bloomington, IN: Solution Tree Press.

Eastwood, K. W., & Louis, K. S. (1992). Restructuring that lasts: Managing the performance dip. *Journal of School Leadership*, *2*(2), 212–224.

Farbman, D. A., Goldberg, D. J., & Miller, T. D. (2014, January). *Redesigning and expanding school time to support Common Core implementation*. Washington, DC: Center for American Progress. Accessed at https://cdn.americanprogress.org/wp-content/uploads/2014/01/CommonCore-reprint.pdf on October 20, 2015.

Fulton, K., Yoon, I., & Lee, C. (2005, August). *Induction into learning communities*. Washington, DC: National Commission on Teaching and America's Future. Accessed at www.nctaf.org/documents/NCTAF_Induction_Paper_2005.pdf on January 10, 2010.

Hattie, J. (2015, June). *What works best in education: The politics of collaborative expertise*. London: Pearson. Accessed at www.pearson.com/content/dam/corporate/global/pearson-dot-com/files/hattie/150526_ExpertiseWEB_V1.pdf on September 30, 2015.

Many, T. W., & Sparks-Many, S. K. (2015). *Leverage: Using PLCs to promote lasting improvement in schools*. Thousand Oaks, CA: Corwin Press.

McLaughlin, M. W., & Talbert, J. E. (2006). *Building school-based teacher learning communities: Professional strategies to improve student achievement*. New York: Teachers College Press.

National Commission on Teaching and America's Future. (2003, January). *No dream denied: A pledge to America's children*. Washington, DC: Author.

Newmann, F. M., & Wehlage, G. G. (1995). *Successful school restructuring: A report to the public and educators*. Madison, WI: Center on Organization and Restructuring of Schools.

Schlechty, P. C. (2009). *Leading for learning: How to transform schools into learning organizations*. San Francisco: Jossey-Bass.

WestEd. (2000). *Teachers who learn, kids who achieve: A look at schools with model professional development*. San Francisco: Author.

MODULE
4.1

Are We a Group or a Team?

Complete the following ten steps to understand the differences between cooperation and collaboration.

1. Give the following directions to teams: "I will show you a triangle graphic comprised of twenty-five randomly placed capital letters (twenty-five out of twenty-six—none repeated). You have ten seconds to study the triangle, and you may *not* write during those ten seconds. When I remove the triangle, record as much as you can remember. Score your work based on the number of correct letters in the correct location on the triangle."

2. Show the first triangle for ten seconds, and then remove it from view (see the sample triangles).

Y

Q Z J

P C F H I

R X V A M O G

T J E W U B L N K

3. When everyone is finished looking, show the triangle again. Have individuals score their recordings and find the average for their table team. Report out and chart the averages.

4. Using the same data, direct teams to determine their team score by compiling their individual results into a team total—there is still a total of twenty-five possible, so each letter only counts once, even if all team members got it correct. But every letter counts, even if only one member got it correct. Report out and record team scores. Point out the positive impact of cooperating—more heads are better than one.

5. Give the following directions to teams: "I will now show you a new triangle—same format, different letter placement. You have ten seconds to view it. The difference this time is that you only need to create one triangle as a team, and you will have one minute to figure out how you want to do it."

6. Monitor planning time (one minute). Give a cue, show the second triangle for ten seconds, and then remove it from view. Tell teams to compile their recordings for their team triangle.

F

K P D

V A G T O

E Q I L C W J

M U B R Y H N X S

7. Once everyone is finished, show the second triangle again. Have teams determine their team scores—report out and chart.

8. Ask participants to look at data and point out the significant gains between team totals and team results. Ask them to briefly talk about how and why their teams improved. Ask for individuals to share and chart their responses. Be sure to probe for ideas such as: clear, common goal; clear individual expectations; individual strengths factoring into work division; data used for reflection and improvement; trust; accountability to teammates; communication; and strategies for sharing.

9. Once you chart all responses, ask participants to reflect on a team that they currently work with and answer *yes* or *no* to each question you are about to pose. Using the charted responses, ask a question based on each response. For example, "Does your team have a clear, common goal?"

10. Finally, suggest that the responses on the chart reflect the differences between cooperative teams and collaborative teams to conclude the activity. Highlight the potential of increasing student achievement (getting results no one is able to get when working alone or in cooperative groups) when educators understand and commit to true collaboration.

Source: Buffum, A., Mattos, M., & Malone, J. (2018). Taking action: A handbook for RTI at Work. *Bloomington, IN: Solution Tree Press.*

MODULE 4.2

What Conditions Should Schools Consider Before Establishing Collaborative Teams?

Section I: Before the Learning

Rationale—Why It Matters

Even the most well-intentioned teachers struggle to function as a highly effective collaborative team if they do not have access to critical resources; time and again, we have seen the PLC process lose momentum if the right conditions are not present. Principals and teacher leaders must consider a number of factors to ensure conditions are right for teams.

Outcomes

One of the most common mistakes principals make is to assign teachers to teams and tell them to "go and collaborate." It is far more effective if school leaders recognize the chances of creating highly effective collaborative teams are much greater if certain conditions are in place early in the process of implementing PLCs.

Following are the goals of this module.

1. Teachers recognize that certain conditions are essential for developing highly effective teams.

2. Teachers understand these conditions are well within the purview of any school.

SIG and Pathways

SIG for prerequisite one (page 239) and the Pathways for Prerequisite One to Five (1.1–5.3; pages 243–248)

Key Coaching Points

1. Certain conditions promote the development of highly effective teams. Having those conditions in place does not guarantee teams will be successful, but if those conditions are absent, the process of becoming a PLC becomes much more difficult.

2. Many of the resources necessary to support collaborative teams are available in every school; however, teams may not understand how to use those resources most efficiently to promote high levels of collaboration.

3. How a school supports teams (providing the right resources and creating the necessary conditions) says a lot about what the school values.

Important Vocabulary and Terms

Designated and protected time: This is the sacred time set aside during the regular school day for teams to meet and respond to the four critical questions of learning.

Common language: This is an agreed-on glossary of important words, terms, and phrases that form the basis of how collaborative teams communicate about the PLC process.

Meaningful teams: This is a group of educators who share responsibility for teaching the same class, course, or grade level, and who work together to ensure high levels of learning for all.

Section II: During the Learning

Preparation—Time and Materials

Complete this module in fifty minutes. Preferably, participants have seating at tables. Each table group chooses a facilitator, timekeeper, recorder, and reporter. The ideal small-group size is four participants, but the activity will work equally well with three to six participants in a group. Necessary materials include 3 × 5-inch index cards and sentence strips. If sentence strips are not readily available, the person delivering the professional development can cut chart paper into four-inch strips and distribute one per person. Participants will also need the following page from *Energize Your Teams.*

- "Conditions to Consider Before Establishing Teams" (page 55)

Step 1: Getting Ready to Learn—You Might Be a Team if . . . Activity (Fifteen Minutes)

Teachers will be asked to think of a simile that describes the team meetings they attend. An example might be, "My team is like a roller coaster, lots of ups and downs" or "Our team meetings are like a first date, everyone is on their best behavior." Distribute a standard 3 × 5-inch note card to each participant and follow this process.

1. Ask participants to respond to the following statement on the front of their index card: When we are meeting, our team is like . . . (two minutes)

2. Ask each person to respond to the following statement on the back of their index card: When I am in our team meeting, I am like . . . (two minutes)

3. Ask the participants to share (while working within their small groups) the statements on the front and back of the index cards and reach consensus on one statement from each side of the cards to share publicly. The reporter for each small group will share the chosen similes with the large group. (six minutes)

4. Ask as many groups as time allows to publicly share their statements from each side of the card. Write the quotes on chart paper and post them on the wall. (five minutes)

Step 2: Interactive Strategy, Protocol, or Activity—Surfacing Significant Ideas (Thirty-Five Minutes)

1. **Read the article:** Ask participants to read "Conditions to Consider Before Establishing Teams" (page 55) and highlight at least two quotes or passages that represent the article's significant ideas. (eight minutes)

2. **Choose a quote or passage:** As everyone finishes reading, each participant should write one quote or passage on a sentence strip (or chart paper). Post sentence strips on the wall. (two minutes)

3. **Surface significant ideas:** With participants working as small groups, ask one participant to present his or her most significant idea and explain the implications

the idea has on his or her work. Other group members may then comment on the idea. (five minutes)

4. **Repeat the process:** Repeat the previous step until all participants in the table group have an opportunity to "surface" at least one significant idea. If one person's idea is the same or similar to another person's idea, place the sentence strips (or strips of chart paper) adjacent to each other. (fifteen minutes)

5. **Closure:** After completing the activity, give each small group an opportunity to summarize and reach consensus on what participants learned together. (five minutes)

Step 3: Personal Reflection (Five Minutes)

Have teachers reflect on the implications of today's learning for teams in their school. Which of the conditions in the article is strongest or weakest for teams in your school? Are there any conditions that should be added? What questions are you still wrestling with, and what do you want to learn more about? Teachers should record and retain their reflections until the section III debrief session with a coach.

Section III: After the Learning

Next Steps and Follow-Up for Coaching Teams

The first task is to understand how schools (principals and teacher leaders) create the conditions teams need to succeed. Your goal as the coach for this debriefing should be to focus attention on how time was set aside for teams to meet, how teachers were assigned to teams, and how teams develop common language around their PLC process. Coaches should be listening for suggestions (or an emerging consensus) that teams need additional work on any or all of the conditions to be successful. Possible questions or tasks for teams to consider might include the following.

1. Using a round-robin approach, give each participant a chance to share his or her biggest takeaway from the professional development activity. Each participant should identify the *one* thing he or she believes should definitely be a priority with the faculty.

2. Review the questions members generated during step 3, the personal reflection. Are there any patterns? Is there a consensus on any of the questions? Are there particular topics the team wants or needs to learn more about?

3. Ask the team to cite evidence of the conditions the section Five Strategies to Make Time for Collaboration presents. Identify any other conditions that have become barriers to more effective teaming and discuss the team's next steps for overcoming the barriers, with whom, and by when.

4. Ask team members to determine how they might address any questions teachers generate during their personal reflection in step 3 of the module.

5. Establish a timeline for the team to implement its plan for moving forward at the next collaborative team meeting where members will analyze student assessment data.

Conditions to Consider Before Establishing Collaborative Teams

By Thomas W. Many

> Those who hope to improve student achievement by developing the capacity of staff to function as a PLC must create and foster the conditions that move educators from mere work groups to high-performing collaborative teams.
>
> —Richard DuFour, Rebecca DuFour, Robert Eaker, Thomas W. Many, and Mike Mattos

There are several conditions administrators and teacher leaders should consider as they contemplate establishing collaborative teams. Teachers will inevitably ask questions like: "Why was the team established? What is the team's purpose? When will the team meet? How will the team communicate? Who will be on the team?" All of these are important questions to consider, and if principals, coaches, and teacher leaders answer as many of these questions as possible during the early phases of implementing the PLC process, they greatly enhance the chances of a successful launch.

We already established *why* collaborative teams are important. If we, as educators, believe the fundamental purpose of schools—and by extension, collaborative teams—is learning, not teaching, and if we acknowledge teachers are better able to fulfill that purpose when they collaborate, then it is not complicated; working together is more effective than working alone.

Designated and protected time for teams to meet during the regular school day is one of the critical conditions that must be in place before establishing teams. According to Mary Anne Raywid (1993), "Collaborative time for teachers to meet to undertake and sustain school improvement may be more important than equipment, facilities, or even staff development" (p. 30).

When will teams find time to collaborate? is really the wrong question. It's unlikely leaders will *find* any more time, so it's important that schools *make* time for teams to collaborate on a high priority when designing the master schedule. Time is a resource, and how (and on what topics) time is spent reflects what schools value.

As teams' PLC practice develops, the way teachers use time shifts. They find they need less time *learning about* the work and more time *working on* the work. Researchers Gary D. Watts and Shari Castle (1993) identify five strategies school leaders can use to make time for

Five Strategies to Make Time for Collaboration

1. **Free up time:** This strategy involves relieving teachers of nonteaching responsibilities so time can be set aside for collaborative team meetings. Administrators, other teachers, instructional aides, or even volunteers can assume some of the routine tasks, freeing up time for teachers to collaborate on their instructional practice.

2. **Purchase time:** Schools can budget funds to pay for substitutes or release time for teachers to collaborate during the regular school year. Some schools have been successful paying teachers additional stipends for time collaborating on Saturdays or during the summer months.

3. **Restructure or reschedule time:** Some schools and districts schedule late arrival or early dismissal so teachers have the opportunity to collaborate on a regular basis. A similar strategy—*banking time*—has been successful, and some districts are moving to a four-day week for students to release one day a week for teacher collaboration.

4. **More efficient use of existing time:** Other schools are conducting time audits and launching into careful reviews of the way educators use time to accomplish operational tasks. These schools are finding ways to use technology to simplify and streamline procedures to find time to reinvest in teacher collaboration.

5. **Schedule common planning time:** Planning time is not a new or novel idea, but the daily schedule can be designed in new and different ways to allow teachers from the same class, course, or grade level to have planning time at the same time during the day.

Source: Adapted from Watts & Castle, 1993.

collaboration (see the sidebar for more information). Leaders need to understand that as teacher roles shift from working in isolation to working in collaboration with others, so too must the way that schools use time.

Building common language is the best way to respond to questions about *how* teams will communicate, and schools should address it during the process of establishing teams. As teachers begin collaborating with colleagues, they discover the need for greater clarity around the definition and meaning of important words, terms, and phrases. Teams naturally develop common language around their practice; however, it is more efficient and effective to be intentional about the development of common language. Regardless of the strategy used to develop a PLC vocabulary (like playing PLC vocabulary bingo or using more sophisticated mental models like the Frayer Model), teachers find it very beneficial to focus on common language.

Teachers can participate in workshops, read relevant articles, or participate in book studies as they begin to learn about the PLC process. Occasionally, teams with more experience find it necessary to engage in professional development to refocus the PLC process in their school. Whether beginner or advanced, W. Richard Smith (2015), former deputy superintendent of the Sanger Unified School District in California, believes creating a districtwide glossary of PLC terms using these kinds of activities offers great opportunities to develop common language.

Smith (2015) suggests the faculty engage in a simple but powerful process to build common language (see the sidebar for a description of the process). Note that starting the process differs for those new to PLCs and those with experience; but regardless, building common language is essential to the successful implementation of the PLC process.

Finally, teachers must be members of *meaningful* teams. Some argue that factors such as access and proximity to other team members during the regular school day should be considered when creating teams, but the single most critical factor in deciding *who* should be on a team is based on the answer to a relatively straightforward question: "Do team members have a shared responsibility for responding to the four critical questions in ways that enhance student learning?" (DuFour et al., 2016, p. 60). If the answer is *yes*, the leaders have identified right team members.

Creating highly effective teams is a deliberate process, and consideration of each of these conditions enhances the odds that a school's efforts to establish teams will succeed.

Building Common Language

For teams beginning their PLC journey, each member of the team should create a list of twenty-five to thirty words they believe are essential to understanding the PLC process. At the end of a professional development activity (training, reading, observing), participants write down a few more words, terms, or phrases they think are especially important. If they read an article, they add a word or two to their list. If they participate in a workshop, they add a few more words to their list. When they hear a word during a conversation they believe is important, they add it to the list.

For teams with more experience with the PLC process, the initial step is slightly different. In these schools, individuals should write down twenty-five to thirty words, terms, or phrases they believe are important *but* at this time, are confusing or unclear to the faculty and staff. Next, teachers work in pairs, compare their lists, and reach consensus on a common list of twenty-five to thirty words, terms, or phrases both agree are important.

After the first step, the process is the same regardless of the group's experience level. In the next step, each pair writes their words on sticky notes—one word per note. The entire group engages in an affinity process to uncover any patterns or highlight any areas of agreement. Then the participants group the sticky notes by the same or similar words, terms, or phrases and compile them into a final list of key terms. This list becomes the district's working glossary.

Teams identify terms for the working glossary, clarify meaning, and create a common understanding of each word, term, or phrase. During the next part of the process, teachers working in small groups work on subsets of the glossary to write working definitions for their part of the document. The small groups can take several weeks to draft their working definitions.

The next step takes place when the faculty reconvenes. The draft definitions are posted on chart paper. The group then engages in a gallery walk leaving feedback, suggestions, or possible revisions for each draft definition on sticky notes. After collection of the feedback, small working groups finalize the definitions.

The last step in the process is to celebrate, share the agreed-on definitions, and publish the glossary of key PLC terms with all the teams in the school.

Source: Smith, 2015.

References

Carroll, T. (2009). The next generation of learning teams. *Phi Delta Kappan, 91*(2), 8–13.

DuFour, R., DuFour, R., Eaker, R., Many, T. W., & Mattos, M. (2016). *Learning by doing: A handbook for Professional Learning Communities at Work* (3rd ed.). Bloomington, IN: Solution Tree Press.

Raywid, M. A. (1993). Finding time for collaboration. *Educational Leadership, 51*(1), 30–34.

Smith, W. R. (2015). *How to launch PLCs in your district*. Bloomington, IN: Solution Tree Press.

Watts, G. D., & Castle, S. (1993). The time dilemma in school restructuring. *Phi Delta Kappan, 75*(4), 306–310.

How Do Teams Operationalize the Five Key Elements of Effective Team Meetings?

Section I: Before the Learning

Rationale—Why It Matters

In our work in schools, time and again we see teachers becoming anxious, disillusioned, and resentful of the PLC process when team meetings are inefficient and ineffective. Team meetings should result in team members experiencing an *energy gain—not an energy drain.* Coaching helps teachers articulate and promote the specific behaviors that result in more productive meetings.

Outcomes

The purpose of this module is to help teams *get better at getting better.* After completing this module, teachers will understand and can articulate the keys to effective meetings. Coaches can support collaboration by maximizing the productivity of team meetings. Our experience shows the more precise a team's professional practice is around the keys to productive team meetings, the more efficient and effective collaboration will be.

SIG and Pathways

SIG prerequisite one (page 239) and the Pathways for Prerequisite One (1.1–1.5; page 243)

Key Coaching Points

1. Emphasize that while all teams are different (just like people), there are some common elements that consistently impact a team's performance. Teams can operationalize the five keys in different ways, but productive teams work to ensure all are in place.

2. There is no right or wrong place to begin; each key is important in different ways for different reasons. Encourage teams to reflect on the biggest barriers to better team meetings, identify one, and focus on improving that element of the teaming process.

3. Improving the productivity of team meetings is an ongoing process that requires regular and routine attention. The goal is not to master one particular key to effective team meetings, but rather to embrace the habit of continuously improving all of them.

Important Vocabulary and Terms

Focus: This is a clearly understood and articulated purpose that describes the desired outcomes of the work. Focus keeps results of team meetings front and center.

Structure: The tools teams use or create to accomplish their work. Examples of structures include SMART goals, agendas, timelines, calendars, norms, and protocols.

Roles and responsibilities: These are the different duties and assignments individual team members accept to foster high levels of collaboration; common roles and responsibilities include, but are not limited to, a facilitator, process observer, recorder, and timekeeper.

Relationships: These are the personal and professional commitments and behaviors team members make and exhibit toward one another that support high levels of collaboration.

Process: The specific and purposeful strategies, tactics, and activities teams use to encourage participation, promote ownership, and engage team members in the work of a PLC

Section II: During the Learning

Preparation—Time and Materials

Complete this module in fifty to sixty minutes. The ideal size of the working groups is five, and preferably, have seating at tables. Begin by choosing roles (a facilitator, timekeeper, recorder, and reporter). The small groups will need access to chart paper and markers. Provide participants with the following handouts per the instructions in step 2.

- "Focus: A State or Condition Permitting Clear Perception and Understanding" (page 62)
- "Structures: The Building Blocks of Collaboration" (page 65)
- "Clarifying Roles and Responsibilities: A Critical Task When Forming Collaborative Teams" (page 68)
- "Investments in High-Trust Relationships Produce Big Dividends for Collaborative Teams" (page 71)
- "Connoisseurs of Interactive Tools and Strategies: How Teams Use Process to Achieve Results" (page 74)

Step 1: Getting Ready to Learn—Write a Movie Review Activity (Ten Minutes)

Ask each participant to think of the best team meeting he or she ever attended. Next, have teachers imagine they have just watched a movie and ask them to write a review; but instead of a movie review, the review will be a description of the ideal team meeting. The review should reflect the things participants think and feel are important. Writing the review should take five minutes. Once participants complete the task, give the participants another five minutes for everyone to share their reviews within their small group.

Step 2: Interactive Strategy, Protocol, or Activity—Jigsaw (Forty-Five to Fifty Minutes)

Before beginning this activity, assign each reproducible article in this module a number between one and five. Write each number on an individual piece of chart paper, and post the numbers around the room.

Ask participants to count off by five, and assign them the corresponding numbered article. Explain that after reading their article, each participant will gather at the number that corresponds to the number of their article.

1. **Read the article:** Ask participants to read the article that corresponds to their number. While reading, they should highlight three ideas they believe are significant, labeling one *aha*, the next one *atta boy*, and the last one *amen*. (six minutes, maximum)

2. **Convene by the article:** Tell participants to gather by their number, meet in pairs for two minutes, then reconvene in groups of four for three more minutes. Agree on what is significant in the article and brainstorm ideas about how to share the big ideas when participants return to their tables. (five or six minutes)

3. **Share important, *ahas*, *atta boys*, and *amens* with colleagues:** Beginning with article one, each participant describes what aspect of the article is important to him or her and why. (three minutes per article, maximum; fifteen minutes total)

4. **Closure:** After completing the activity, provide the group with an opportunity to summarize what they learned together. (ten minutes)

5. **Summarizing the learning:** Ask each group to use a piece of chart paper to capture their biggest takeaways from the activity and post their summaries around the room. (five minutes)

Step 3—Personal Reflection (Five Minutes)

Have participants take a moment and reflect on the implications the five keys of productive meetings have for the collaborative teams in your school. Which keys are strongest, and which are the weakest for your team? Does the team regularly (at least once a quarter) review the team's levels of productivity (efficiency and effectiveness)? After thinking about the level of productivity of your team, are there any keys that should receive more attention or be a higher priority to promote more productive meetings? Based on what you know, rate your team on each key, compile the ratings, and discuss the ratings amongst the team. Have participants record and retain their reflections until the debrief with a coach in section III of this module.

Focus	1	2	3	4	5
Structures	1	2	3	4	5
Roles and responsibilities	1	2	3	4	5
Relationships	1	2	3	4	5
Process	1	2	3	4	5

Ask participants to record their thoughts about the keys to productive team meetings. Ask, did anything in this module make you reconsider how your team approaches this topic? What questions are you still wrestling with, and what do you want to learn more about?

Section III: After the Learning

Next Steps and Follow-Up for Coaching Teams

The coach's goal during the debrief is to identify the team's current reality about the keys of productive team meetings, set some goals, and identify potential next steps for moving forward. Possible questions or tasks for the team to consider might include the following.

1. Check for agreement on a definition for each of the keys of productive team meetings.

2. Ask individual team members to work with a partner and discuss whether their vision of an effective team meeting has changed, and, if so, in what way?

3. Refer to the SIG for prerequisite one (page 239) and Pathways for Prerequisite One (1.1–1.5; page 243) to help the team determine its current reality, set a specific improvement goal, and identify some possible next steps.

4. Agree on a plan for moving forward, establish a timeline to implement the plan, and check on progress at the beginning of the next team meeting.

MODULE
4.3

Focus: A State or Condition Permitting
Clear Perception and Understanding

By Thomas W. Many and Susan K. Sparks

Adapted from Texas Elementary Principals & Supervisors Association's TEPSA News, May/June 2015, Vol. 72, No. 3, www.tepsa.org

Teachers on effective and ineffective teams both put forth effort; indeed, teachers on effective and ineffective teams often engage in the very same kind of work. So, why is it that some teams are able to embrace the kind of work that leads to high levels of learning for all while other teams struggle to find their focus? The answer to this question begins with *clarity*, *coherence*, and *precision*.

"Schools that function as professional learning communities are characterized by an academic focus that brings clarity, coherence, and precision to every classroom."

—Jonathon Saphier

One of the key questions teams must answer is, "What will be the focus of our work while we're together?" According to PLC experts Richard DuFour, Rebecca DuFour, Robert Eaker, Thomas W. Many, and Mike Mattos (2016), "The pertinent question is not 'Are they [teachers] collaborating?' but rather, 'What are they [teachers] collaborating about?'" (p. 59). What has become increasingly clear is the most effective teams create an unrelenting focus on learning.

Teachers in traditional schools have gathered together for generations. In the best of times, they discuss grading practices and gigabytes. In the worst of times, they struggle through awkward conversations about problems outside their control. These teams gravitate toward discussions related to teaching, and while issues such as dress codes, field trips, and tardy policies may be school related, it is not the kind of work DuFour and his colleagues (2016) envisioned for highly effective teams.

Contrast this with what effective teams discuss in high-performing PLCs. In these schools, teachers come together to clarify what students should know and be able to do, create common assessments, engage in constructive conversations about data, and design systematic pyramids of intervention for students who need more time and support to learn (Buffum, Mattos, & Malone, 2018). These teams focus on learning by concentrating their efforts on responding to the critical questions of learning.

Heather Clifton provides a good way to determine if schools have the right focus on their teams. Clifton says, "A lot of schools think they're doing PLCs and are happy holding meetings, but the work teachers are doing in these meetings does not impact student achievement and thus it cannot be characterized as the work of professional learning communities" (H. Clifton, personal communication, April 26, 2011).

Clifton continues, "The definition of what is and is not PLC work is relatively simple; if the work does not impact student achievement it cannot be characterized as the work of a professional learning community" (H. Clifton, personal communication, April 26, 2011).

In the most effective schools, teams ask and answer the questions, What do we want our students to know and be able to do? How will we know they have learned it? What will we do if they don't learn it? What will we do when they do learn it? (DuFour et al., 2016). Let's examine how some teams use clarity, coherence, and precision to create an unrelenting focus on learning.

Effective teams seek clarity around best practice: The most effective teams create clarity and make meaning of their practice by seeking to understand why certain instructional practices are more effective than others.

Teachers on both effective and ineffective teams talk about issues related to teaching and learning, but teachers on effective teams regularly engage in the kind of facilitated dialogue designed to promote the sharing of best practice. These teams gather evidence of student learning and seek out the kind of honest, growth-oriented feedback that creates greater clarity.

In contrast, less-effective teams favor the kind of polite, superficial conversations that protect adult relationships. Teachers on ineffective teams tolerate random discussions, talk about topics unrelated to improving student learning, and sanction the hoarding of best practice.

Effective teams create coherence around their practice: The most effective teams build coherence and continuously search for deeper levels of understanding around how to improve instructional practices in their schools.

Teachers on both effective and ineffective teams do what school or district leaders ask of them, but teachers on effective teams reject the precedent of past practice and commit to understanding how best to improve their practice. Teachers on these teams value collaboration and view meetings as precious opportunities to sharpen their pedagogy and deepen their content knowledge.

Teachers on less-effective teams comply with school or district leaders' requirements and expectations. These teachers just want to be left alone, and meetings remain an excruciating exercise in compliant behavior as teachers dutifully attend but quietly wonder how long it will be until they can return to their classroom, shut the door, and *get back to work*!

Effective teams strive for precision around their practice: The most effective teams seek to create a high level of precision and clear agreement on what instructional practices will promote higher levels of learning in their schools.

For example, effective and ineffective teams both acknowledge the standards, but teachers on effective teams invest time and energy in an organized and purposeful process to determine the essence of what each standard is asking students to learn. These teams work to identify precisely what every student must know and be able to do.

Teachers on less-effective teams also acknowledge the standards but engage in erratic and sometimes haphazard procedures to choose which standards to teach. They make (and post) long lists of standards based on personal preferences, the availability of materials, or what the district's pacing guide reflects.

"When you have a very clear focus, you recognize what's important and all the other stuff becomes not important."

—Anthony Alvarado

Jonathon Saphier's elegant observation at the beginning of this article (as cited in DuFour & Marzano, 2011) highlights the importance of clarity, coherence, and precision in developing the right focus for collaborative teams. As teams engage in the process of continuous improvement together, they seek greater clarity around *the why* behind their instructional practices. As clarity improves, teachers construct deeper levels of coherence about how to improve their instructional practice. And finally, as teams achieve higher levels of clarity and coherence, they naturally develop more expertise and become increasingly precise about what is the best way to improve their instructional practice.

References

Bradley, A. (1993). *N.Y.C.'s District 2 gives top priority to educators' learning*. Accessed at www.edweek.org/education/n-y-c-s-district-2-gives-top-priority-to-educators -learning/1993/07 on June 7, 2021.

Buffum, A., Mattos, M., & Malone, J. (2018). *Taking action: A handbook for RTI at Work.* Bloomington, IN: Solution Tree Press.

DuFour, R., DuFour, R., Eaker, R., Many, T., & Mattos, M. (2016). *Learning by doing: A handbook for Professional Learning Communities at Work* (3rd ed.). Bloomington, IN: Solution Tree Press.

DuFour R., & Marzano, R. (2011). *Leaders of learning: How district, school, and classroom leaders improve student achievement*. Bloomington, IN: Solution Tree Press.

Structures: The Building Blocks of Collaboration

By Thomas W. Many

Adapted with permission from Texas Elementary Principals & Supervisors Association's TEPSA News, March/April 2015, Vol. 72, No. 2, www.tepsa.org

---

"Professional Learning Communities require organizational structures and supports to be successful."

—Jonathan A. Supovitz and Jolley Bruce Christman

Certain structural conditions are necessary for a school to become a highly effective PLC (DuFour, DuFour, Eaker, Many, & Mattos, 2016; Louis, Kruse, & Bryk, 1995); thus, it's useful to understand how the right structures can promote collaboration in schools.

The most effective principals embrace structures such as a master schedule that provides time for teams to meet during the regular school day. Other structures in highly collaborative schools include the regular and routine use of protocols to promote richer conversations about instructional strategies, team norms to manage members' behavior resulting in more effective team meetings, and common assessments to generate data about teaching and learning. To understand how structure impacts collaboration, following are five key points to remember about structure.

First, structure should maximize a school's resources. The best way to understand how structure promotes collaboration is to focus first on how a resource might enhance or inhibit the effectiveness of collaborative teams. Once leaders and teacher teams ask and answer that initial question, they can design a structure or structures to maximize the positive effect of a resource on collaboration.

Second, structure reflects a school's priorities. The fastest way to identify what is important to a faculty is to look at the structures that school employs. The structures that a school designs and supports make a statement about what the faculty values.

Third, structure evolves as a school's practice evolves. Educators must be able to articulate why a structure exists, but structures can fall victim to the precedent of past practice. Too many schools continue to embrace outdated structures that do not support best practice simply because "that's the way it's always been."

Fourth, schools control the structures in their buildings. Similar to the previous key point, some leaders and teachers may feel powerless to make changes and thus continue using outdated and ineffective structures or dismiss newer and more effective structures because "that is out of our control." In many cases, putting the right structures in place simply requires a little creativity or fresh perspective.

And finally, the presence or absence of structure impacts collaboration. The right structure can encourage, facilitate, and encourage collaboration. Likewise, the wrong structure will certainly discourage, inhibit, or derail a team's efforts to collaborate. For example, a school designs a form to record minutes of team meetings. Originally intended to serve as a record of a team's work and as a tool to promote communication between the team and principal, the form eventually becomes nothing more than an accountability tool. This negative outcome results in the team focusing on completing and submitting the form quickly as the priority rather than using the tool to facilitate collaboration. Because of this, the structure actually inhibits meaningful conversations on the team.

"As odd as it sounds, simple, well-known strategies and structures drive improvement in any organization."

—Jeffrey Pfeffer and Robert I. Sutton

Structures maximize a school's resources: Schools that are most successful develop a structure after understanding how a resource will support collaboration.

Consider the many templates for meeting agendas. One of the most effective examples utilizes the four critical questions of a PLC (DuFour et al., 2016) to create a graphic organizer teams use when creating meeting agendas. To create this type of agenda, team members fold a piece of chart paper in half and then in half again to form four quadrants. Each quadrant is labeled with one of the four PLC critical questions. As team members suggest potential topics for the meeting, they also try to categorize each topic under one of the four questions. If the topic does not fit under any of the four questions, it is not a topic for the collaborative team meeting. This type of agenda helps teams focus on the four critical questions of a PLC and promotes more effective team meetings.

Structures reflect a school's priorities: It doesn't take long; a quick review of the structures a school supports and implements illustrates what that school values.

For example, if designated and protected time during the regular school day is not clearly evident on the master schedule, collaboration is not a school priority. On the other hand, when a school creates a pyramid of interventions that allows students access to additional time and support without missing direct instruction in a core subject, the staff are demonstrating the importance they place on the belief that all students can learn if they receive enough opportunities and the right instructional strategies. This same school might emphasize the routine use of protocols as a way to promote dialogue. On these teams, teachers value feedback from their peers around teaching and learning as a powerful way to improve their instructional practice. The use of protocols reflects the priority teachers place on the kinds of conversations and dialogue that lead to openly sharing best practice.

Structures evolve as a school's practice evolves: Just as best practice continues to evolve, so too must a school's structures.

During the 1980s and 1990s, many districts implemented the *middle school concept*; educators made a conscious effort to create interdisciplinary teams by assigning one teacher from each subject area to a classroom in the same hallway. To this day, despite the fact that the benefits of the middle school model never fully materialized, schools across the United States assign teachers to classrooms that reflect the structure of interdisciplinary teams. In contrast, the more effective schools organize teachers into content-alike teams and assign them to classrooms in close physical proximity to one another to facilitate collaboration. Clearly, location of the classroom to which a teacher is assigned can enhance or inhibit a team's efforts to collaborate, and being cognizant of that illustrates how important it is for structure to evolve along with best practice.

The school controls the structures: In his work with schools and his many keynote presentations, Robert Eaker describes a visit to one comprehensive high school where the staff explained there simply wasn't time for collaboration inside the regular school day; he was told point blank that, "The schedule just wouldn't allow it."

Eaker asked if the school ever created alternative schedules to accommodate special circumstances such as assemblies, testing, or sporting events. When given an entire notebook of alternative schedules, Eaker asked what would happen if we changed the name of this schedule from *assembly schedule* to *collaboration schedule*, looked at repurposing the advisory period, or explored a late-start model as possibilities to support increased opportunities for teacher collaboration? Obviously, the design of the school's master schedule was influencing the way, and for what purpose, the school allocated time, and just as a teacher's room assignment was within the control of the school, so too was the design of the master schedule.

Finally, the presence or absence of structure impacts collaboration: The absence of the right kinds of structure prevents schools from developing more collaborative cultures.

Most would agree that designated and protected time for teams during the regular school day enhances the effectiveness of team meetings. Likewise, there is little argument that reflecting on data from common assessments improves a teacher's instructional practice or that access to more time and support helps improve student learning. But, if the right structural conditions are missing or ineffective, teachers cannot leverage these powerful resources in ways that promote collaboration.

"Collaborative teams must carefully design the format of their work."

—Mike Schmoker

Expecting teachers to collaborate without providing the necessary structures is a recipe for failure. According to Richard DuFour (2004), "Educators who are building a professional learning community recognize that they must work together to achieve their collective purpose of learning for all. Therefore, they create structures to promote a collaborative culture."

References

DuFour, R. (2004). What is a professional learning community? *Educational Leadership*, *61*(8), 6–11. Accessed at www.ascd.org/publications/educational-leadership/may04/vol61 /num08/What-Is-a-Professional-Learning-Community%C2%A2.aspx on March 9, 2021.

DuFour, R., DuFour, R., Eaker, R., Many, T., & Mattos, M. (2016). *Learning by doing: A handbook for Professional Learning Communities at Work* (3rd ed.). Bloomington, IN: Solution Tree Press.

Louis, K. S., Kruse, S. & Bryk, A. S. (1995). Professionalism and community: What is it and why is it important in urban schools? In K. S. Louis, S. Kruse, & Associates, *Professionalism and community: Perspectives on reforming urban schools*. Long Oaks, CA: Corwin.

Pfeffer, J., & Sutton, R. I. (2000). *The knowing-doing gap: How smart companies turn knowledge into action*. Boston: Harvard Business School Press.

Schmoker, M. (2001). *The results fieldbook: Practical strategies from dramatically improved schools*. Alexandria, VA: Association for Supervision and Curriculum Development.

Supovitz, J. A., & Christman, J. B. (2003). Developing communities of instructional practice: Lessons from Cincinnati and Philadelphia. *CPRE Policy Brief*. Accessed at https:// repository.upenn.edu/cpre_policybriefs/28 on March 2, 2021.

MODULE 4.3

Clarifying Roles and Responsibilities: A Critical Task When Forming Collaborative Teams

By Thomas W. Many and Susan K. Sparks

Adapted from Texas Elementary Principals & Supervisors Association's TEPSA News, *August 2015, Vol. 72, No. 4, www.tepsa.org*

There is no definitive list of which roles must be present on a collaborative team. At a minimum, most teams designate one person as team leader or facilitator. Teams will often have a recorder or note taker and usually a timekeeper. Many teams assign the role of air traffic controller or process observer with the task of monitoring the level of participation or observing how the meetings are conducted. Teams may even add task-specific roles such as summarizer or "most responsible person" in hopes of making their team meetings more effective.

Some teams may decide it's best to separate roles. For example, a team might decide to establish distinct responsibilities for both the facilitator and team leader. Others may decide to combine roles like the recorder and timekeeper. The number of roles often depends on the size and sophistication of the team, but one of the most important roles on any team is that of team leader.

"Just as district success depends on the leadership capability of superintendents and school success depends to a great degree on the leadership of principals, the success of collaborative teams depends on the leadership capacity of team leaders."

—Robert Eaker and Janel Keating

There are many ways to organize the leadership of collaborative teams. Some schools designate a single person who is responsible for facilitating all team meetings; the authors have used the term *designated facilitator* to describe this approach. Robert J. Garmston (2007) refers to this approach as the *professional facilitator*. When schools organize their teams using a designated facilitator, they provide extensive training for that one person. Professional or designated facilitators manage team processes and outcomes without bringing content into the conversation. They remain neutral and focus on team dynamics and process.

The authors have used the term *rotating facilitator* or *citizen facilitator* (Garmston, 2007) to describe another approach many schools use. With rotating facilitators, a different team member serves as facilitator for each meeting. When schools organize their teams using rotating or citizen facilitators, everyone receives some training and shares the responsibility for ensuring productive team meetings. Rotating or citizen facilitators are active participants in meetings, bring their own voice into the conversation, and contribute ideas and content while simultaneously managing and monitoring the team's dynamics and process. We encourage teams to foster a sense of interdependence between and among members, so in PLCs, most grade-level or content-area teams utilize the citizen-facilitator approach as a way to encourage everyone's involvement as active participants in team meetings.

With either approach, the team leader has similar responsibilities. Team leaders are typically responsible for developing the agenda, establishing the purpose at the beginning of the meeting, referring to the products or expected results, recommending procedures for accomplishing the task, and engaging every member in the process. They are also responsible for protecting the norms and summarizing who is doing what and by when at the end of each meeting.

Other important responsibilities of team leaders include serving as the link between the team and the principal, helping the team develop new ways of collaborating more effectively, and maintaining the focus on accomplishing the team's goals around student learning. Of all the team leader's responsibilities, perhaps the most important one is ensuring members are clear on their roles and responsibilities. Each team member should understand what his or her role is, what the responsibilities of that role entail, and how that role contributes to the success of the team.

To be most effective, team leaders should review roles and responsibilities on a regular basis. Occasionally, individuals take a back seat or expect others to complete important tasks, but team leaders can prevent this and enhance the likelihood that members will fulfill their responsibilities when they clearly and carefully define the expectations for each role. The phrase *first define, then assign* are words to live by when establishing roles and responsibilities; if the team cannot define what someone in a role is responsible for doing or how the existence of the role is beneficial to the team, then the role is probably not needed.

"The most effective teams have identified roles and responsibilities that help team members avoid confusion and resentment. If team roles and responsibilities are not defined when teams begin working, the effectiveness of team meetings suffers."

—Susan Sparks

Team roles can change throughout the year—even from one project to the next—but for a team's most critical activities, effective team leaders can use a RASCI responsibility matrix to clearly articulate who is responsible for what (Management Mania, n.d.).

Each letter of the RASCI acronym represents a different responsibility (Management Mania, n.d.). The letter *R* designates who is responsible for a specific task, while the letter *A* identifies who has overall responsibility for the team's productivity. An *S* indicates which team members will be expected to provide active support, and *C* clarifies who must be consulted on the task. Finally, the letter *I* indicates who must be informed of the status of the work (typically this is reserved for the principal or department chair). The following chart is an example of a RASCI matrix for a school.

Name	Alexis	Mary	Mike	Sam	Juan	Jada
Assignment	Teacher	Teacher	Teacher	Teacher	SPED	Principal
Team Role	Facilitator	Recorder	Timekeeper	Member	Member	Ex officio
Team Task or Project						
Agenda	A	S	S	S	S	I/C
Minutes	A/R	R	S	S	S	I/C
Norms	A/R	S	S	S	S	I/C
SMART goals	A/R	S	S	S	S	I/C
Learning targets	A/S	R	S	S	S	I
Assessments	A/S	S	R	S	S	I
Interventions	A/S	S	S	R	C	I

In a PLC, everyone shares responsibility and is mutually accountable for the work, but in reality, one person usually assumes the primary responsibility for completion of a project, task, or activity. Teams can create multiple matrices—one for the roles in team meetings and others for the roles associated with a specific task or activity—but the matrix identifies who is in charge, who is filling a helping role, who needs to know the status of the project, and so on. The process of completing a RASCI matrix compels the team to articulate who is responsible for what and helps team leaders accomplish the important task of clarifying team roles and responsibilities.

"When team members are unclear about their roles and responsibilities, even the best teams find themselves off track and less productive."

—Susan Sparks

For collaborative teams to be successful, it is critical that team members have clearly defined roles within the team structure. It is also important that team members understand, respect, and effectively carry out the responsibilities of their role. Using a RASCI matrix to establish roles and responsibilities helps team leaders enhance productivity of team meetings.

References

Eaker, R., & Keating, J. (2009, July 22). *Team leaders in a professional learning community* [Blog post]. Accessed at www.allthingsplc.info/blog/view/54/team-leaders-in-a-professional-learning-community on February 28, 2021.

Garmston, R. J. (2007). Collaborative culture. *Journal of Staff Development, 28*(3), 57–58. Accessed at https://learningforward.org/wp-content/uploads/2007/06/garmston283.pdf on March 9, 2021.

Management Mania. (n.d.). *RASCI responsibility matrix*. Accessed at https://managementmania.com/en/rasci-responsibility-matrix on March 9, 2021.

Sparks, S. (2015). Study: RTI practice falls short of promise. *Education Week*. Accessed at www.edweek.org/ew/articles/2015/11/11/study-rti-practice-falls-short-of-promise.html on January 26, 2021.

Investments in High-Trust Relationships Produce Big Dividends for Collaborative Teams

By Thomas W. Many and Susan K. Sparks

Adapted from Texas Elementary Principals & Supervisors Association's TEPSA News, *September/ October 2015, Vol. 72, No. 5, www.tepsa.org*

"Building a culture of trust in a given school may require time, effort, and leadership, but the investment is likely to bring satisfying returns."

—Megan Tschannen-Moran

In their seminal study of trust in schools, Anthony S. Bryk and Barbara Schneider (2002) establish a clear connection between the level of relational trust in a school and improved student learning. Bryk and Schneider (2002) argue that "relational trust is the connective tissue that binds individuals together to advance the education and welfare of students" (p. 44).

There is a robust body of evidence supporting the relationship between trust and high levels of learning. Since Bryk and Schneider's (2002) early work, Tschannen-Moran (2014) found that high-trust cultures are associated with higher levels of student achievement, "*even when taking into account the socioeconomic status of students*" (p. 146). Other researchers reported similar results confirming that high levels of relational trust are associated with high levels of student achievement (Goddard, Tschannen-Moran, & Hoy, 2005; Louis & Wahlstrom, 2011; Moses, 2019). While these studies shine light on the positive effect trust has on student achievement, what has received far less attention is the positive impact trust has on collaborative teams.

"Trust is the foundation for collaboration, and collaboration is what makes organizations great."

—Jane Modoono

Researchers have that found trust and collaboration are reciprocal, mutually reinforcing, and closely linked. Tschannen-Moran (2014) observes that the level of collaboration in a school is related to the level of trust present in the school. According to Paul S. Sutton and Andrew W. Shouse (2016), "Collaboration builds teacher trust and expertise and enables schools to implement changes in instruction with greater ease and comfort" (p. 69). Miesner and colleagues (2019) report that "when teachers trust their colleagues, they are likely to collaborate more often *even if the time for collaboration is not allocated during the regular school day*" (emphasis added). Clearly trust and collaboration are closely linked to one another.

In addition to promoting higher levels of collaboration in general, trust also promotes other, more specific benefits that support development of collaborative cultures. In high-trust schools, teams are more highly motivated, better able to adapt to challenges, and more likely to achieve school goals (Louis & Wahlstrom, 2011). In cultures where trust is high, teams demonstrate higher levels of engagement and self-efficacy and more effective problem solving (Miesner et al., 2019), exhibit a greater commitment to the success of students (Brewster & Railsback, 2003; Modoono, 2017), and are more willing to take risks. The consensus is, "While trust alone does not guarantee success, schools with little or no trust have almost no chance of improving" (Brewster & Railsback, 2003, p. 7).

MODULE 4.3

> "The latest work on trust in schools ties the growth of trust to gains in school [teacher] productivity and increased school [student] achievement."
>
> —Julie Reed Kochanek

Principals certainly set the tone for building high-trust relationships, but they cannot accomplish the task alone. Trusting relationship experts and coauthors Cori Brewster and Jennifer Railsback (2003) argue that "The responsibility for building trust among teachers falls on the shoulders of principals and teachers alike" (p. 15). Brewster and Railsback (2003) suggest, "Identifying the specific causes of mistrust in the school and making a sincere commitment to address them is the first and probably most important step" (p. 11).

One excellent way to begin building (or rebuilding) trust is to gather data. Several authors and experts have developed surveys that can be helpful in identifying the specific causes for the lack of trust in a school (Kochanek, 2005; Sanderson, 2005; Tschannen-Moran, 2014). Utilizing these surveys, teachers can generate data and establish specific goals around improving the level of trust in their schools and on their teams. Data from the surveys also help principals identify and celebrate the specific behaviors that build trust while simultaneously minimizing those that erode trust. The following process will produce a set of measurable goals to improve the level of relational trust in a school.

- **Step 1:** Teachers complete a survey that measures the level of trust in schools. Experience has shown that gathering the data anonymously will create a safer environment and encourage participation.

- **Step 2:** The completed surveys are turned in to a trusted member of the faculty who, working with the principal, compiles the results anonymously. What we have learned is that compiling the data anonymously will generate even more comfort among the faculty. The resulting data create a *trust profile* for the school.

- **Step 3:** Publicly share the school's trust profile during a faculty meeting where teachers, working together in teams, identify trends or reoccurring patterns of behavior that contribute to high or low levels of trust. Reflect on the level of trust at the school and on the team.

- **Step 4:** Teacher teams use the data to establish specific goals to promote the development of higher levels of relational trust on their teams and in their schools.

As Brewster and Railsback (2003) correctly observe, "If relationships between teachers are to change significantly, teachers themselves must work to identify barriers to trust within the faculty and take the initiative to improve, repair, and maintain relationships" (p. 15).

> "Just as the tax created by low trust is real, measurable, and extremely high, so the dividends of high trust are also real, quantifiable, and incredibly high."
>
> —Stephen M. R. Covey

Leadership expert and author Stephen M. R. Covey (2006) argues that all organizations either "pay a tax" or "collect a dividend" based on the level of trust in their culture. In low-trust schools, the *trust tax* is high and negatively affects the productivity of collaborative teams. In high-trust schools the opposite is true; the *trust dividend* is high, and the level of trust enhances the productivity of collaborative teams. The most effective principals are intentional around their efforts to avoid taxes and increase dividends in their schools.

Energize Your Teams © 2022 Solution Tree Press • SolutionTree.com
Visit **go.SolutionTree.com/PLCbooks** to download this free reproducible.

The bottom line is that creating healthy relationships based on high levels of relational trust requires an investment of time and energy. It can be challenging but the payoff—*the return on investment*—is improvement in both student achievement and the productivity of collaborative teams.

References

Brewster, C., & Railsback, J. (2003, September). *Building trusting relationships for school improvement: Implications for principals and teachers*. Portland, OR: Northwestern Regional Educational Laboratory. Accessed at https://educationnorthwest.org/sites /default/files/trust.pdf on March 1, 2021.

Bryk, A. S., & Schneider, B. (2002). *Trust in schools: A core resource for improvement*. New York: Russell Sage Foundation.

Covey, S. M. R. (2006). *The speed of trust: The one thing that changes everything*. New York: Free Press.

Goddard, R. D., Tschannen-Moran, M., & Hoy, W. K. (2001). Teacher trust in students and parents: A multilevel examination of the distribution and effects of teacher trust in urban elementary schools. *Elementary School Journal, 102*(1), 3–17.

Kochanek, J. R. (2005). *Building trust for better schools*. Thousand Oaks, CA: Corwin Press.

Louis, K., & Wahlstrom, K. (2011). Principals as cultural leaders. *Kappan Magazine, 92*(5), 52–56.

Miesner, H. R., Blair, E. E., Packard, C. C., Velazquez, M., Macgregor, L., & Grodsky, E. (2019). *Collaborating in context: Relational trust and collaborative structures at eight Wisconsin elementary schools*. Accessed at www.wcer.wisc.edu/publications/working on May 21, 2021.

Modoono, J. (2017). The trust factor. *Educational Leadership, 74*(8), 30–34.

Moses, L. (2019). *How trusting relationships advance school culture and influence student achievement*. Accessed at www.ascd.org/blogs/how-trusting-relationships-advance -school-culture-and-influence-student-achievement on March 9, 2021.

Sanderson, B. E. (2005). *Talk it out! The educator's guide to successful difficult conversations*. Larchmont, NY: Eye on Education.

Sutton, P. S., & Shouse, A. W. (2016). Building a culture of collaboration in schools. *Kappan Magazine, 97*(7), 69–73.

Tschannen-Moran, M. (2014). *Trust matters: Leadership for successful schools*. San Francisco: Jossey-Bass.

Connoisseurs of Interactive Tools and Strategies: How Teams Use Process to Achieve Results

By Thomas W. Many and Susan K. Sparks

Adapted from Texas Elementary Principals & Supervisors Association's TEPSA News, *November/ December 2015, Vol. 72, No. 6, www.tepsa.org*

> "The process of becoming a PLC is designed to achieve a very specific purpose: to continuously improve the collective capacity of a group to achieve intended results. Therefore, it is incongruous to engage in elements of the process and ignore results."
>
> —Richard DuFour, Rebecca DuFour, Robert Eaker, Tom Many, and Mike Mattos

We couldn't agree more with Richard DuFour and his colleagues (2006, 2016); any process that teams engage in should be purposeful and lead to results. We do not support arbitrary process or random activities; process for the sake of process only creates resentment on a team. Instead, we recommend teachers be intentional and use process to improve the productivity of their teams.

The right kinds of processes—ones that engage team members in a collective effort to improve their practice—greatly increase the likelihood that teams will reach their goals. The best teams are results oriented, but those teams are also mindful that without a solid grasp of how to use process effectively, they will struggle to achieve the kind of results they seek. Simply put, the key to achieving results is effective process.

> "One of the key skills or attributes of a quality principal is expertise in group process."
>
> —John Gooden, Garth Petrie, Patricia Lindauer, and Michael Richardson

Ensuring teams use process to achieve their goals is the responsibility of principals and teacher leaders alike; schools can encourage more effective process in three important ways.

First, teachers benefit from training on how to use process effectively. If leaders expect teams to use process well, it just makes sense to show them how and develop their capacity to match the right process with the right task. Second, as part of teacher evaluation and performance appraisal, principals should ask individual teachers to assess the impact of their team's process on improving teaching and learning and identify ways they personally contribute to making that process more effective. Finally, the only way teachers will know leaders value that process is for leaders to confront individuals who do not meaningfully engage in process and hold them accountable for their actions.

> "Process must match intended outcomes and help you accomplish your goals. Be deliberate and focused on results when determining what process will work best for you."
>
> —Susan K. Sparks

There are a variety of interactive tools and strategies teams use to strengthen process on collaborative teams. Most fall under the headings of rituals and routines, interactive tools, interactive activities, or protocols. The key is to match the choice with the task at hand.

Rituals and Routines

Teams use rituals and routines to highlight what is important, celebrate what the school values, and provide the encouragement necessary to continue improving. Rituals and routines are also terrific ways to enhance communication and create greater comfort and predictability on teams.

Beginning each meeting with a quick check-in is an example of using rituals and routines effectively. *Check-ins* can be something as simple as answering a question the team leader poses or an activity like WHIP (without hesitation invite participation). WHIP is a simple, easy-to-use interactive strategy where the team leader goes from one person to the next asking each in rapid succession to share a word, phrase, thought, or question related to the day's topic. There is no judgment, and no comments or questions are allowed about what is shared.

Teams can also use rituals and routines to honor and celebrate success. Team members often begin meetings with a statement like, "I would like to recognize one of my teammates," followed by two or three sentences specifically describing the colleague's good work or extra effort. Using rituals and routines in this way recognizes the importance of celebration.

Another ritual and routine teams find useful is to close each meeting with a quick summary of the work or an answer to the question "What are our next steps?" When used regularly, this technique signals the end of the meeting and reminds everyone what the leader expects of them.

Interactive Tools

Teams use a variety of tools such as planning templates, data-gathering forms, and graphic organizers to augment their process. For example, each chapter of *Learning by Doing* (DuFour, DuFour, Eaker, Many, & Mattos, 2016) includes a continuum describing the development of important PLC concepts. Teams use tools like these continuums and the planning templates that follow to explore their current reality and identify what next steps the team will take to improve.

When teams have limited time and resources, they often rely on a simple form to collect data. Using a single, standardized form to gather everyone's data in one central place makes teams more efficient and moves teachers from looking at "data from *my* students" to looking at "data from *our* students."

Finally, graphic organizers increase understanding, maximize organization, and promote professional learning. Graphic organizers are great tools to link content and show the relationship of past, present, and future work. For example, write agendas as graphic organizers to help lead teams through their meetings.

Interactive Activities

Interactive activities promote everyone's involvement. Use them to gather information, define and clarify problems, generate ideas and possibilities, categorize and narrow options, or prioritize and evaluate alternatives.

Examples of interactive strategies range from something as simple as *Turn to a Partner* to more sophisticated strategies like a *Criteria Matrix* in which teams identify specific criteria or important characteristics, list all the possibilities, and rate each possibility against each criterion. More than anything, interactive activities promote engagement.

Protocols

Protocols are the most powerful interactive strategy teams use to improve their practice. A *protocol* is a set of agreed-on guidelines for a conversation about teaching and learning. Lois Brown Easton (2009) identifies four major categories of protocols, and while they share some similarities, protocols in each category serve a different purpose. The four categories include

page 2 of 3

(1) protocols for looking at professional reading, (2) protocols for looking at issues and concerns, (3) protocols for looking at student work, and (4) protocols for looking at professional practice.

"Process is a method of conducting meetings and engaging participants. It is a series of actions that move teams closer to their goals."

—Susan Sparks

We believe collaborative teams are most effective when they balance effective process and a strong results orientation. Furthermore, we argue teams must be intentional with process. Team members should consider themselves connoisseurs who collect a variety of interactive tools and strategies and use them to accomplish their goals. Regardless of which they choose, the purpose of process is to engage teams in a cycle of continuous improvement to achieve results.

References

Easton, L. B. (2009). *Protocols for professional learning: The professional learning community series*. Alexandria, VA: Association for Supervision and Curriculum Development.

DuFour, R., DuFour, R., Eaker, R., & Many, T. (2006). *Learning by doing: A handbook for Professional Learning Communities at Work* (1st ed.). Bloomington, IN: Solution Tree Press.

DuFour, R., DuFour, R., Eaker, R., Many, T. W., & Mattos, M. (2016). *Learning by doing: A handbook for Professional Learning Communities at Work* (3rd ed.). Bloomington, IN: Solution Tree Press.

Gooden, J., Petrie, G., Lindauer, P., & Richardson, M. (1998). Principals' needs for small-group process skills. *NASSP Bulletin, 82*(596), 102–107.

Sparks, S. K. (2008). Creating intentional collaboration. In *The collaborative teacher: Working together as a professional learning community* (pp. 31–55). Bloomington, IN: Solution Tree Press.

Sparks, S. K., & Many, T. W. (2015). *How to cultivate collaboration in a PLC*. Bloomington, IN: Solution Tree Press.

CHAPTER 5

Guaranteed and Viable Curriculum

Prerequisite two: *Collaborative teams implement a guaranteed and viable curriculum, unit by unit (DuFour & Reeves, 2016).*

The second prerequisite of a PLC, implementing a guaranteed and viable curriculum or *GVC*, requires all students to have the opportunity to learn the same rigorous curriculum. A GVC involves much more than publishing a list of standards in a binder or on a website; it takes time, commitment, and a concerted faculty effort.

In a PLC, creating a GVC manifests itself as teams respond to critical question one, "What knowledge, skills, and dispositions should every student acquire as a result of this unit, this course, or this grade level?" (DuFour et al., 2016, p. 36). Collaborative teams learn and work together to reach agreement on precisely what teachers will teach and students will learn. Once teams achieve consensus on the essential standards, they commit to one another—and to their students—that before the students move on to the next class, course, or grade level, they will learn the essential standards. It is the teachers' commitment to teach what is essential that matters most.

As teams respond to critical question one, they engage in a three-step process involving standards, learning targets, and *I can* statements. While all three structures share some common characteristics, "The biggest difference among a standard, a learning target, and an 'I can' statement is the intended audience and how each can promote high levels of learning" (Mattos, DuFour, DuFour, Eaker, & Many, 2016, p. 76). The overarching goal of this process is to create greater clarity, coherence, and commitment around the GVC, but it is only after completing all three steps of this process that teachers can truly respond to the first critical question of a PLC with confidence.

Teacher teams begin the process of responding to the first critical question by prioritizing the standards to identify those absolutely essential for all students to learn. Educators sometimes refer to *power standards*, *priority standards*, or *promise standards* (which all mean basically the same thing) as the standards students *need to know* as opposed to standards that are *nice to know*. Prioritizing standards does not mean eliminating standards; rather, it acknowledges that while all standards are important, they're not all *equally* important. Prioritizing standards is a crucial first step, "However, the prioritization of standards alone does not ensure clarity around what students are expected to understand and do" (Clayton, 2017, p. 1). Clarity is the primary goal of the next step: unwrapping the priority standards.

Teams unwrap the essential standards to identify the highest-leverage learning targets. All standards consist of multiple learning targets; unwrapping, unpacking, or deconstructing the standards helps create more clarity and precision in the planning for and assessment of student learning. Researchers and coauthors Connie M. Moss, Susan M. Brookhart, and Beverly A. Long (2011) explain, "Instructional objectives [learning targets] are about instruction, derived from content standards, written in teacher language, and used to guide teachers during a lesson or across a series of lessons" (p. 67). Regardless of whether the state, province, county, or district previously prioritized the standards, teams must unwrap them to understand exactly what the standard is asking teachers to teach and students to learn.

The process concludes with the final step, as teacher teams collaborate to translate the learning targets into *I can* statements (sometimes called *student learning targets*) that help make expectations for the lesson clear to students. According to Clayton (2017), these *I can* statements "describe in student-friendly language the learning to occur in the day's lesson" (p. 1). She continues explaining that *I can* statements are "written from the students' point of view and represent what both the teacher and the student are aiming for during the lesson" (p. 1). Students are better able to track their own progress, assess their own learning, and set specific goals for improvement when they understand exactly what teachers expect them to learn.

Synopsis of Chapter 5 Modules

The modules in this chapter support the second prerequisite of a PLC which states, *Collaborative teams implement a guaranteed and viable curriculum, unit by unit* (DuFour & Reeves, 2016). The professional development activities in this chapter explore several important aspects of the GVC, such as why teams should ensure students have access to a GVC, what a GVC is and is not, and how teacher teams can operationalize the GVC in their school.

Module 5.1: Why Should Teams Establish a Guaranteed and Viable Curriculum?

A GVC promotes clarity for teachers and equity for all students. According to Marzano, Warrick, Rains, & DuFour (2018):

> A guaranteed and viable curriculum means all teachers teach the same content for the same course or grade level. With a guaranteed and viable curriculum, a student in one second-grade class is taught the same content as a student in a different second-grade class, or a student in one ninth-grade English class is taught the same content as a student in a different ninth-grade class. (p. 116)

The effort of creating a GVC promotes teachers' deeper and more thorough understanding of what is most essential for all students to know and be able to do.

Module 5.2: What Is a Guaranteed and Viable Curriculum?

The *guaranteed* dimension of a GVC requires all educators accept responsibility for ensuring all students enrolled in the same class, course, or grade level are exposed to the same rigorous curriculum. The *viable* aspect recognizes *teaching* the curriculum and *covering* the curriculum are two very different things, and while teachers can cover lots of content, to teach the curriculum requires students learn what teachers teach. If the amount of content teachers are responsible for exceeds what they can reasonably teach within the time allotted, the curriculum is not viable. For a curriculum to be both guaranteed and viable, teachers must have a common understanding of the curriculum and a commitment to teach it.

Module 5.3: How Do Teams Identify the Essential Standards?

The question is not, Will teachers prioritize the standards? but *How* will teachers prioritize the standards? The sheer number of standards forces teachers to prioritize and, in the absence of an organized approach, teachers will choose standards based on criteria unique to each individual teacher; however, a far better approach is to coordinate the process. Using the R.E.A.L. criteria to prioritize the standards produces a number of benefits principals, coaches, and teacher leaders can leverage to improve teaching and learning in their schools.

Module 5.4: How Do Teams Unwrap Essential Standards and Identify High-Leverage Learning Targets?

Standards are complex, and each contains multiple learning targets. Deconstructing standards to identify the learning targets provides teachers with more clarity around what to teach, how to assess whether students have learned, and when to intervene. This module introduces a process teams can use to unwrap the priority standards and identify the highest-leverage learning targets.

Module 5.5: How Do Teams Use I Can *Statements to Maximize Learning?*

The level of student engagement increases when teachers create *I can* statements and use them in classrooms. The use of *I can* statements to explain specific learning targets in student-friendly language provides students with greater clarity and allows them to understand where they are at this moment, where they need to go in the learning progression, and what they need to do to achieve mastery on each learning target.

These modules are best thought of as (1) an opportunity for teachers to learn together or (2) as a starting point for further exploration and investigation. We intentionally designed the modules to be flexible; they can be delivered to individual teams or the entire faculty. The modules can be delivered in order, within a chapter or the entire book, or they can be delivered as stand-alone modules to provide teams with just-in-time job-embedded professional development.

Most importantly, teams need differentiated support, so those coaching teams should match the learning (the modules) with what the team needs to work on. Asking teams, "What would you like to work on?" or "What would you like feedback on?" will make teams *feel* better, but these are the wrong questions. The right questions to ask teams are, "What do the data indicate that you need to work on?" or "What do the data indicate that you need feedback on?" which will make teams *do* better. Those who coach teams need to decide whether they want their teams to *feel* better or to *do* better.

Knowing what the team needs to do to improve should guide the choice of module. We believe that the decision of what teams should work on or get feedback on must reflect what the data indicate is the teams' greatest area of need (GAN), not their greatest area of comfort (GAC). The authors' goal is to provide the right information to the right people in the right settings at the right time.

Why Should Teams Establish a Guaranteed and Viable Curriculum?

Section I: Before the Learning

Rationale—Why It Matters

Students and teachers benefit from a focused, cohesive, and well-articulated curriculum. The premise is that students will learn more if teachers clearly define the learning expectations, if students know the criteria for meeting those expectations, and if the instructional strategies and assessment practices support those expectations. A well-articulated GVC helps improve teaching and learning by clarifying what teachers should teach and students should learn.

Outcomes

Teachers can articulate *why* it is important for all students to have access to a GVC.

SIG and Pathways

SIG prerequisite two (page 239) and the Pathways for Prerequisite Two (2.1–2.5; page 244)

Key Coaching Points

1. Instead of asking teachers to identify what they should teach, teachers should describe what their students should learn. The process of answering critical question one, "What knowledge, skills, and dispositions should every student acquire as a result of this unit, this course, or this grade level?" (DuFour et al., 2016, p. 36) should reflect a focus on learning, not teaching, by identifying the GVC.

2. An important benefit of creating a GVC is it shifts the conversation at the school, team, grade level, or department from teaching to learning.

3. Another benefit of identifying a GVC is teachers become more comfortable with the idea that their students are not missing something.

4. Finally, establishing a GVC identifies *what*—not *how*—teachers should teach and in no way infringes on teachers' academic freedom in choosing methods of instruction.

Important Vocabulary and Terms

Guaranteed: This means that regardless of who teaches a given class, course, or grade level, every student will have an opportunity to learn the same rigorous curriculum.

Viable: The size and scope of the standards allow teachers to adequately address all essential standards in the time available, and students can master the essential standards when they receive an appropriate amount of additional time and support.

Section II: During the Learning

Preparation—Time and Materials

Complete this module in one hour. The ideal group size is four to six teachers per group seated at tables. In addition to the person responsible for delivering the session, the activity requires four cofacilitators. (During the second half of the session, the cofacilitators will each be assigned to a different easel and will be responsible for keeping the conversation flowing.)

Before the meeting, create stations by setting up easels with chart paper and markers in the four corners of the room. Write one of the following questions on each easel:

1. How guaranteed is our curriculum? What evidence do we have that all students have access?

2. How viable is our curriculum? What evidence do we have that teachers can teach all the standards students need to know in the time allotted?

3. What are the implications of a GVC for students? Why is a GVC important for students to be successful?

4. What are the implications of a GVC for teachers? Why is a GVC important for teachers to be successful?

Participants will also need the following handouts.

*   "Why Should We Ensure Students Have Access to a Guaranteed and Viable Curriculum?" (page 84)

*   "Are We Making a List or Delivering on a Promise? The Unintended Consequences of Believing All Standards Are Equal" (page 86)

Step 1: Getting Ready to Learn—Block Party Activity (Twenty Minutes)

This adapted Block Party activity is a warm-up and follows this process.

1. Ask participants to count off by nine, and direct their attention to the "Why Should We Ensure Students Have Access to a Guaranteed and Viable Curriculum?" handout, which contains nine research quotes on the importance of a GVC. Ask each participant to find the quote that matches his or her number and reflect on its meaning and implications for his or her work. (three minutes)

2. Next, ask participants to find a partner from another table and share his or her thinking about their quote (two minutes). With their partner, teachers then form groups of four and share again (four minutes). Groups mix one last time, forming groups of six, and repeat the process (six minutes). The mixing and sharing last twelve minutes, and when finished, teachers return to their original small groups seated at tables.

3. The entire group then talks about any relevant insights and observations raised in the small-group conversations. Accomplish this using either a popcorn or round-robin approach. (five minutes)

Step 2: Interactive Strategy, Protocol, or Activity— "Conver-Stations" (Forty Minutes)

Muir (2019) created the Conver-Stations protocol for this activity. To begin, cofacilitators go to their preassigned station (easel) and everyone counts off by four. This will create mixed groups of participants from different tables.

1. **Read the article:** Ask participants to read and highlight key points in the article "Are We Making a List or Delivering on a Promise?" (six minutes)

2. **Respond to the questions:** Direct participants to convene at the station (easel) that matches their number and respond to the questions written on the easels. After four minutes (at this point, no consensus is required), the person responsible for delivering the professional development announces that it is time for everyone to move to the next easel. The cofacilitators remain at their easel while the group rotates clockwise to the next station and repeats the same process with a new question. (twenty minutes)

3. **Debrief the learning:** Participants return to their original table and, using a round-robin approach, share what they discussed during the Conver-Stations activity. (ten minutes)

Step 3: Personal Reflection (Five Minutes)

Before the next team meeting, participants record and retain their thoughts about what they learned during this professional development until the section III debrief with a coach. Ask participants to respond to the questions, "How do we view the standards? Are we making a list or delivering on a promise?"

Section III: After the Learning

Next Steps and Follow-Up for Coaching Teams

A GVC promotes both excellence and equity by ensuring all students have access to the same rigorous curriculum while simultaneously promoting clarity among teachers about *what* to teach, so their time and energy focus on *how* to teach it well. The coach's goal for this module is to help teams reflect on their beliefs around responding to critical question one of a PLC, "What knowledge, skills, and dispositions should every student acquire as a result of this unit, this course, or this grade level?" (DuFour et al., 2016, p. 36).

Using a T-chart, ask teams to identify the policies, practices, and procedures that support the notion of *guaranteed* and *viable*. Participants can develop a second T-chart to explore whether teachers feel standards are a list to cover or a promise teachers make to students. Other questions or tasks for the team to consider might include the following.

1. What can the faculty do to promote a GVC? What things can teams do to clarify what is essential for teachers to teach and students to learn?

2. Refer to the SIG for prerequisite two (page 239) and the Pathways for Prerequisite Two (2.1–2.5; page 244) to help determine the team's current reality, identify some possible next steps, and agree on a plan for moving forward.

3. Establish a timeline for teams to implement their plan at the next collaborative team meeting where members will analyze student assessment data.

Why Should We Ensure Students Have Access to a Guaranteed and Viable Curriculum?

To improve student achievement, educators must determine the *power standards*—learning standards that are most essential because they possess the qualities of endurance, leverage, and readiness for success at the next level; "the first and most important practical implication of power standards is that leaders must make time for teachers to collaborate within and among grade levels to identify the power standards" (Reeves, 2002, p. 54).

"The staff in the effective school accepts responsibility for the students' learning of the *essential curricular goals*" (Lezotte, 2002, p. 4, emphasis added).

Professional learning communities are characterized by an academic focus that begins with a set of practices that bring clarity, coherence, and precision to every teacher's classroom work. Teachers work collaboratively to provide a rigorous curriculum that is crystal clear and includes a compact list of learning expectations for each grade or course and tangible exemplars of student proficiency for each learning expectation (Saphier, 2005).

The first step in curriculum development is to "identify desired results. What should students know, understand, and be able to do? What content is worthy of understanding? What 'enduring' understandings are desired? What essential questions will be explored? [This step] calls for clarity about priorities" (Tomlinson & McTighe, 2006, pp. 27–28).

One of the keys to improving schools is to ensure teachers "know the learning intentions and success criteria of their lessons, know how well they are attaining these criteria for all students, and know where to go next in light of the gap between students' current knowledge and understanding and the success criteria"; this can be maximized in a safe and collaborative environment where teachers talk to each other about teaching (Hattie, 2009, p. 239).

"Implementing a strategy of common, rigorous standards with differentiated resources and instruction can create excellence and equity for all students" (Childress, Doyle, & Thomas, 2009, p. 133).

A high-reliability school provides students with a guaranteed and viable curriculum focused on enhancing student learning. The curriculum is focused enough that it can be adequately addressed in the time available to teachers. All students have the opportunity to learn the critical content of the curriculum. Individual teachers do not have the option to disregard or replace content that has been designated as essential (Marzano, Warrick, & Simms, 2014).

"The only way the curriculum in a school can truly be guaranteed is if the teachers themselves, those who are called upon to deliver the curriculum, have worked collaboratively to do the following:

- Study the intended curriculum.
- Agree on priorities within the curriculum.
- Clarify how the curriculum translates into student knowledge and skills.
- Establish general pacing guidelines for delivering the curriculum.
- Commit to one another that they will, in fact, teach the agreed-upon curriculum" (DuFour & Marzano, 2011, p. 91).

"If we want to mobilize concerted action and a deep shift in practice then governments, districts, and schools need to develop clarity of outcomes and build shared understanding of these by educators, students, and parents" (Fullan & Quinn, 2016, p. 83).

page 1 of 2

References

Childress, S. M., Doyle, D. P., & Thomas, D. A. (2009). *Leading for equity: The pursuit of excellence in Montgomery County Public Schools*. Cambridge, MA: Harvard Education Press.

DuFour, R., & Marzano, R. J. (2011). *Leaders of learning: How district, school, and classroom leaders improve student achievement*. Bloomington, IN: Solution Tree Press.

Fullan, M., & Quinn, J. (2016). *Coherence: The* right *drivers in action for schools, districts, and systems*. Thousand Oaks, CA: Corwin Press.

Hattie, J. (2009). *Visible learning: A synthesis of over 800 meta-analyses relating to achievement*. New York: Routledge.

Lezotte, L. W. (2002). *Revolutionary and evolutionary: The effective schools movement*. Accessed at www.effectiveschools.com/images/stories/RevEv.pdf on January 10, 2010.

Marzano, R. J., Warrick, P., & Simms, J. A. (2014). *A handbook for high reliability schools: The next step in school reform*. Bloomington, IN: Marzano Research.

Reeves, D. B. (2002). *The leader's guide to standards: A blueprint for educational equity and excellence*. San Francisco: Jossey-Bass.

Saphier, J. (2005). *John Adams' promise: How to have good schools for all our children, not just for some*. Acton, MA: Research for Better Teaching.

Tomlinson, C. A., & McTighe, J. (2006). *Integrating differentiated instruction and understanding by design*. Alexandria, VA: Association for Supervision and Curriculum Development.

Are We Making a List or Delivering on a Promise? The Unintended Consequences of Believing All Standards Are Equal

By Thomas W. Many

Adapted from Texas Elementary Principals & Supervisors Association's TEPSA News, *November/ December 2014, Vol. 71, No. 6, www.tepsa.org*

> "If everything is important then nothing is important."
>
> —Patrick Lencioni

When school administrators express the belief that every standard is equally important (thus, teachers must teach every standard), they create unanticipated consequences for their schools.

Educators hope a benefit of adopting consistent state, national, or provincial standards is better alignment and a more coherent curriculum. Educators expect a common set of standards to generate greater consistency around what teachers teach from grade to grade and school to school. Unfortunately, rigid adherence to the belief that every standard is equally important and teachers must teach every standard is actually creating opportunities for more—not less—variance in a classroom curriculum.

Teachers recognize not all standards are equally important, and they routinely make decisions about what to teach and what not to teach. However, since most school districts do not sanction or support the practice of prioritizing standards, teachers are left to figure things out on their own and approach this task without the benefit of consistent criteria. According to educational consultant and author Larry Ainsworth (2013):

> Left to their own professional opinions when faced with the task of narrowing a voluminous number of student learning outcomes [standards], educators naturally "pick and choose" those they know and like best, the ones for which they have materials and lesson plans or activities, and those most likely to appear on state tests. (p. 16)

The practice of prioritizing or identifying the most important standards based on unique and individually created criteria leads to inconsistent teacher choices, undermines the consistency of what students experience in the classroom, and creates exactly the opposite effect of what educators hope for when they adopt various state and national standards.

The reality is that while all the standards are important, some are more important than others. Teachers can begin to make an important shift by acknowledging what they already intuitively know and support the collective efforts of collaborative teams to identify the most important, high-priority standards in systemic and systematic ways. (See Module 5.3, page 94, for a description and activity for how to prioritize the standards using R.E.A.L. criteria.)

> "Learning has little or nothing to do with what a teacher covers. Learning has everything to do with what students can accomplish."
>
> —Harry Wong and Rosemary T. Wong

Any reasonable definition of *teaching* incorporates the notion that students learn. The purpose of teaching the standards is to ensure students learn the knowledge, skills, and

page 1 of 3

dispositions the standards describe. So by definition, *teaching* the standards is different from *covering* the standards.

Quantity Versus Quality

Despite successful efforts to refine and improve standards, most teachers continue to believe there are still too many standards to teach. An unbending belief that every standard is equally important, and teachers must teach them all, forces teachers to abandon the deep, meaningful mastery of the most important standards in exchange for the broad, superficial coverage of all the standards.

In some districts, administrators enacted policies and procedures that require teachers to document when and where they address each and every standard. This policy sends the wrong message and places the emphasis on quantity rather than quality. (A far better approach would be to identify and track mastery of the high-priority standards.) While many teachers will do their best to cover all the standards, most will not be able teach all the standards to mastery.

Because people support what they help create, the question to answer is, "Have you been involved in deciding which standards you should teach and students should learn, or have administrators handed you a list of standards already designated and decided?" Even the exceptional teacher who covers all the standards will find it difficult to adequately assess them all and will be even more challenged to remediate them all. When administrators insist teachers teach every standard, regardless of a standard's relative importance to the student or other standards, they promote compliance to district policies instead of a commitment to student learning.

Teaching Versus Covering

Collaborative teams must exercise sound professional judgment and focus on teaching—as opposed to covering—the most important standards. Educators must reject the notion that covering the standards is an acceptable alternative to teaching the standards.

Another consequence of believing that every standard is equally important and must be taught is school leaders often require teachers teach all the standards without the opportunity to thoroughly understand the standards. If standards truly define what teachers should teach and students should learn, teachers should engage in a process of prioritizing and then unwrapping the most important standards. According to assessment expert and author Nicole Dimich (personal communication, January 20, 2020), "The purpose of unwrapping standards is not to create another standards document; instead, it is to get at the heart, at the very essence of what we expect in student learning." By understanding the essence of each standard, teachers can create engaging and effective classroom lessons.

Author and researcher Douglas Reeves (personal communication, January 28, 2020) suggests the only time the argument that every standard is equally important makes sense is when every student is working at or above grade level, and therein lies the problem. It would be rare indeed to find a class, school, or district where every student was working at or above grade level. Teachers know they must constantly adjust and prioritize. They recognize it makes no sense to teach a standard when students lack the necessary prerequisite skills. The best teachers formatively assess their students, identify their instructional level, plan lessons that address the missing prerequisite skills, and remediate any gaps in student learning before moving on to teaching the grade-level standards.

A Collaborative Process

The most successful teams engage in a collaborative process to promote deep understanding of the rigor, content, and connection of one standard to another. Arguing that every standard is equally important and must be taught only discourages teachers from taking the time to understand the standards so crucial to student success.

"You are not making a list; you are making a promise. This is the information we promise our students will learn."

—Tim Brown

Whether state and national standards result in higher levels of student learning will depend, in large part, on the beliefs administrators, coaches, and teacher leaders hold regarding the implementation of the standards. Will standards be used to guide instruction, or will they be measures of accountability with consequences for individual teachers, students, and schools?

Educational consultant and former principal Tim Brown (personal communication, July 30, 2018) asks educators to reflect on what they believe about state or national standards. On one hand, if teachers look at standards as the content school leaders require them to cover during a particular class, course, or grade level, they will likely generate a list of standards to post on the walls of their classrooms. On the other hand, if teachers look at standards as a promise they make, they will more likely make the commitment to ensure students master the standards.

As to whether educators are making a list or delivering on a promise—the answer will go a long way to resolving some of the unintended consequences the belief that every standard is equally important and must be taught created.

References

Ainsworth, L. (2013). *Prioritizing the Common Core: Identifying the specific standards to emphasize the most*. Englewood, CO: Lead + Learn Press.

Lencioni, P. (2006). *Silos, politics, and turf wars: A leadership fable about destroying the barriers that turn colleagues into competitors*. San Francisco: Jossey-Bass.

Wong, H. K., & Wong, R. T. (2018). *The first days of school: How to be an effective teacher* (5th ed.). Mountain View, CA: Author.

What Is a Guaranteed and Viable Curriculum?

Section I: Before the Learning

Rationale—Why It Matters

You won't find a GVC in a notebook or on a website; rather, it exists within the teacher team's commitment to teach what the team agrees is essential. For this commitment to be meaningful, teachers must understand what a GVC is and is not.

Outcomes

Teachers can define what a GVC is and is not.

SIG and Pathways

SIG prerequisite two (page 239) and the Pathways for Prerequisite Two (2.1–2.5; page 244)

Key Coaching Points

1. The most effective principals, coaches, and teacher leaders acknowledge the only person who can ensure all students have access to a GVC is the classroom teacher who delivers the curriculum.

2. As the faculty works to collectively establish a GVC, teacher teams engage in a process to build shared knowledge and a common understanding of what all students should know and be able to do.

3. Once teacher teams reach agreement on what to include in the GVC, school leaders expect individual teachers to honor their commitment to the team. Individual teachers do not have the authority to independently add or delete, ignore or discount, or substitute or supplant content from the agreed-on curriculum.

Important Vocabulary and Terms

Build shared knowledge: By definition, members of a PLC learn together. Working in collaborative teams, teachers seek to ascertain the impact that current policies, practices, and procedures have on teaching and learning in their schools and districts.

Collective inquiry: This is the process of building shared knowledge by clarifying the questions a group will explore together (Mattos et al., 2016).

Section II: During the Learning

Preparation—Time and Materials

Complete this module in forty-five to fifty minutes. The ideal group size is four to six teachers per group seated at tables. Each group should choose a facilitator, timekeeper, recorder, and reporter. Groups will need chart paper and markers. Participants will need the following handout.

- "A Guaranteed and Viable Curriculum Is Not a Proper Noun" (page 92)

Step 1: Getting Ready to Learn—T-Chart Activity (Fifteen Minutes)

Prepare for this part of the training by asking each group to write *Guaranteed and Viable Curriculum* at the top of a piece of chart paper and then draw a T-chart under the title, leaving about three inches of space between the title and the T-chart. Groups should then label the left-hand column *A GVC is . . .* and the right-hand column *A GVC is not . . . .* (less than a minute)

1. Ask the groups to (a) discuss what the words *guaranteed* and *viable* mean for teachers and students, (b) identify the attributes of a GVC, and (c) describe what it would look and sound like if a GVC were in place and working well. From that brief conversation, have each group develop its own definition of a GVC and write it on the paper between the title and the T-chart. (five minutes)

2. Conclude step 1, Getting Ready to Learn, by having the group complete, *A GVC is . . .* and *A GVC is not . . . .* Encourage group members to contribute ideas that fit into one column or the other. (five minutes)

3. Ask each group to present its chart to the larger group. This warm-up activity ends after everyone has two minutes to add any ideas they've learned since their initial brainstorming. (five minutes)

Step 2: Interactive Strategy, Protocol, or Activity—Making Meaning Protocol (Thirty Minutes)

This protocol will help participants make meaning of a text while identifying broader implications for their professional practice.

1. **Read the article:** Ask participants to silently read "A Guaranteed and Viable Curriculum Is Not a Proper Noun" (page 92) and take notes or highlight particular points of interest. (six minutes)

2. **Share facts:** Ask the group, "What did you see when you read this article that is and is not aligned with the team's current professional practice?" Participants then share their factual and nonjudgmental observations about the text.

3. **Ask questions:** Ask the group, "What questions does this text raise for you?" Record participant answers for follow-up at a later time.

4. **Speculate about the meaning or significance of the text:** Ask the group, "What is significant or important about this article?" During this time, the group is *making meaning* by identifying any insights, problems, or issues the article raises.

5. **Discuss the implications:** Invite participants to share any thoughts they have about ways this article might impact, influence, or inspire the professional practice of their team or themselves as individual teachers.

Step 3: Personal Reflection (Five Minutes)

Ask each member of the group to take five minutes and silently reflect on the following questions: "How guaranteed is the curriculum; do all students have access to the same rigorous curriculum? How viable is our curriculum; are we able to teach the curriculum given the time we have available to us?" Ask participants to record and retain their comments; their reflections will be used during the section III debrief with a coach.

Section III: After the Learning

Next Steps and Follow-Up for Coaching Teams

The goal for this part of the module is to extend participants' thinking. First, ask team members to review the working definition of a GVC they developed in step 1 of this module. Ask the participants if they would make any changes after participating in the previous training session.

Next, ask participants to discuss their level of involvement in identifying what is essential (or what all students should know and be able to do). Are external voices (textbook publishers or state departments of education) driving the curriculum, or is what's essential an internal decision within the purview of teams? Or is the decision a balance of external and internal interests?

Finally, explore how the team feels about each member's commitment to teach what the team agrees is essential without adding or deleting content. Do participants think the GVC makes what students should learn clear while leaving the decision of how to teach it to members of the faculty and staff?

Refer to the SIG for prerequisite two (page 239) and the Pathways for Prerequisite Two (2.1–2.5; page 244) to help determine the team's current reality, identify some possible next steps, and agree on a plan for moving forward.

MODULE

5.2

A Guaranteed and Viable Curriculum Is Not a Proper Noun

By Thomas Many

Adapted from Texas Elementary Principals & Supervisors Association's TEPSA News, *August 2016, Vol. 73, No. 4, www.tepsa.org*

"One of the most powerful things a school can do to help enhance student achievement is to guarantee that specific content is taught in specific courses and grade levels."

—DuFour and Marzano, 2011, p. 89

When researcher and author Robert J. Marzano (2003) introduced the term *guaranteed and viable curriculum* into the lexicon of educational best practice, he identified one of the most powerful ways to improve schools.

The *guaranteed* aspect of a guaranteed and viable curriculum (GVC) requires all students enrolled in the same class, course, or grade level *be* exposed to the same rigorous curriculum regardless of the teacher to whom they are assigned. If what teachers teach is different from one classroom to the next, the curriculum is not guaranteed.

The *viable* aspect of a GVC recognizes that *teaching* the curriculum and *covering* the curriculum are two very different things. While teachers can cover a lot of content, to *teach* the curriculum requires *students learn* what teachers teach. If the amount of content for which teachers are responsible exceeds what they can reasonably teach within the time allotted, the curriculum is not viable.

To establish a curriculum that is both guaranteed and viable, teams of classroom teachers must engage in a process to build a common understanding of what students should know and be able to do.

"If schools are to establish a truly guaranteed and viable curriculum, those who are called upon to deliver it must have both a common understanding of the curriculum and a commitment to teach it."

—Richard DuFour and Robert Marzano

Marzano (2003) recommends districts begin by providing "clear guidance to teachers regarding the content to be addressed in specific courses and at specific grade levels" (p. 24). The key word is *guidance*, and the implication is teachers will work together in a collaborative process to identify the essential standards with the support of district-level leaders and content-area specialists.

This guidance might come in the form of training, coaching, and providing extended opportunities for in-depth analysis of the standards. As teachers work together to understand the essence of what they should teach and students must learn, teams build the kind of shared knowledge and common understandings so essential to creating a guaranteed and viable curriculum.

Marzano (2003) maintains that a guaranteed and viable curriculum also means that "Individual teachers do not have the option to disregard or replace assigned content" (p. 24). Some districts—those where administrators contend teachers are unwilling or unable to identify the essential standards—use Marzano's admonition to justify publishing curriculum documents filled with long lists of standards content-area specialists at the state and local levels select. Once district leaders publish and distribute them to teachers, these documents become *the* GVC.

Unfortunately, the secret to creating a GVC is not more lists or another document; and while schools and districts should never return to the days when what a teacher teaches depends on his or her individual interests, talents, or expertise, mandating a specific set of standards absent any meaningful classroom teachers' input will prove to be an equally ineffective approach.

Others believe the key to a GVC is as simple as holding teachers accountable for teaching their ⅟₁₃ of the curriculum (the teachers' portion of the students' thirteen years of schooling). These educators believe publishing the GVC ensures teachers will know the level of learning to expect and maintain that if teachers would simply take responsibility for teaching the ⅟₁₃ of the curriculum for their class, course, or grade level, there won't be a problem.

This ⅟₁₃ solution might be more reasonable if—and it's a big if—all students in the classroom are functioning at grade level and ready to learn. That condition does not exist in most schools. When students are not ready to learn grade-level content, teachers will go beyond, sometimes far beyond, the boundaries their ⅟₁₃ of the curriculum establishes to meet students' needs. It makes no sense to deliver lessons to students who lack the prior knowledge or prerequisite skills necessary to be successful in the unit. It makes far more sense for teachers to use a consistent and coherent process for identifying the most essential standards and teach what they themselves identify as essential.

The most effective schools recognize the only way to develop a GVC is to engage teachers—with district-level leaders' and content-area specialists' support—in a collaborative process to identify what is essential for each class, course, or grade level. It is the combination of the expertise of district-level content-area specialists, coupled with the building of shared knowledge among teachers at the classroom level, that is essential to creating a GVC. It is not one or the other; it's both.

"We have a problem when the guaranteed and viable curriculum is viewed as a proper noun."

—Tanya Batzel, Staff Developer, Cherry Creek Colorado

A GVC is not a proper noun; it is not a concrete object. It is not something that is contained within a notebook or available online. A GVC is the commitment between and among teachers to teach what the team has agreed are the essential standards.

In order to be successful, principals, coaches, and teacher leaders must recognize that creating a GVC is not a static, one-time event. It is a dynamic, ongoing process of building shared knowledge about what students should know and be able to do. To ensure a common understanding of and a commitment to a GVC, those coaching collaborative teams must commit to training and supporting teachers as they do the work.

The only person who can ensure all students have access to a GVC is the teacher who delivers the curriculum in the classroom. Those who are involved in coaching collaborative teams recognize that engaging teachers in a process to identify what is essential for all students to learn is the best way—perhaps the only way—to establish a GVC.

References

DuFour, R., & Marzano, R. J. (2011). *Leaders of learning: How district, school, and classroom leaders improve student learning*. Bloomington, IN: Solution Tree Press.

Marzano, R. J. (2003). *What works in schools: Translating research into action*. Alexandria, VA: Association for Supervision and Curriculum Development.

page 2 of 2

How Do Teams Identify What's Essential?

Section I: Before the Learning

Rationale—Why It Matters

There are simply too many standards to teach to mastery; more and more teachers find themselves prioritizing the standards to decide what they will and won't teach. Without a common and consistent approach to prioritizing the standards, teachers use their own individual criteria, which runs counter to the notion of a GVC. It just makes sense to support a consistent, research-based approach to identifying the essential standards.

Outcomes

This module introduces a process using the *R.E.A.L. criteria* to prioritize the standards and identify what is essential for students to know and be able to do. When teams collectively identify the essential standards, they foster consistency around what is important for teachers to teach and students to learn.

SIG and Pathways

SIG prerequisite two (page 239) and the Pathways for Prerequisite Two (2.1; page 244)

Key Coaching Points

1. When collaborative teams prioritize standards, it promotes greater clarity and ownership of the GVC and represents a priceless opportunity for job-embedded professional development.

2. Prioritizing standards (a) is one of the most effective and efficient ways teachers can sharpen their pedagogy and deepen their content knowledge, (b) provides teachers with greater clarity around what knowledge, skills, and dispositions each standard addresses, (c) encourages teachers to embrace more rigorous instruction and more effective instructional practices, and (d) leads to better lessons, enhanced assessments, and more targeted support for students who do or do not learn.

Important Vocabulary and Terms

Readiness: This is when the standard provides essential knowledge and skills necessary for the next class, course, or grade level.

Endurance: This is when the standard supports knowledge and skills useful beyond a single test or unit of study.

Assessed: This is when the standard is likely to appear on upcoming state and national exams.

Leverage: This is when the standard covers knowledge and skills of value in multiple disciplines.

Section II: During the Learning

Preparation—Time and Materials

Complete this module in fifty minutes. The ideal small group size is between four and six teachers per group seated at tables. Before beginning, each group will need chart paper and markers and should choose a facilitator, timekeeper, recorder, and reporter. Each individual teacher will need a sheet of standard lined notebook paper and the following handouts.

- "Prioritizing the Standards Using R.E.A.L. Criteria" (page 97)
- "Is It R.E.A.L. or Not?" (page 100)

Step 1—Getting Ready to Learn: Give-and-Go Activity (Fifteen Minutes)

Give-and-Go is a high-energy, interactive activity designed to promote the generating, sharing, and transferring of ideas about a topic of interest to the group.

1. Ask participants to fold a piece of notebook paper in half lengthwise, write *How Do I Decide Where to Begin?* across the top of the page, and number the page vertically, 1 through 10 on the left-hand side. (three minutes)

2. For the first part of the Give-and-Go activity, read the following scenario and ask participants to write their answers in the form of words or phrases, one word or phrase per number, to the question, How do I decide where to begin? in the left-hand column of their paper. (six minutes)

   A teacher expressed fear she would not be able to cover all the material in the curriculum to her principal. She said, "The list of what I am supposed to cover just seems to grow and grow. More than that, what is important today is different than what was important yesterday. How am I supposed to know where to begin?"

3. The second part of the Give-and-Go activity is energetic, almost frenetic, and requires teachers to quickly share their thinking with a colleague. After participants record their own ideas in the left-hand column, ask them to find a partner and share their thinking. Each partner writes one new idea from his or her partner in the right-hand column of the paper. With the person responsible for leading the session tracking the time, have participants switch partners every thirty seconds and continue meeting with colleagues until teachers have captured ten new ideas. Once the warmup activity is complete, teachers return to their tables and get ready to begin step 2 of the module. (six minutes)

Step 2—Interactive Strategy, Protocol, or Activity: First Word (Thirty-Five Minutes)

While the Give-and-Go activity promotes the rapid-fire sharing of new ideas, the First Word protocol prompts teachers to think more deeply about the process of prioritizing standards using the R.E.A.L. criteria (readiness, endurance, assessed, and leverage). Note this is an acrostic, and this activity has participants create their own acrostic.

1. **Read the article:** Ask participants to read the article "Prioritizing the Standards Using the R.E.A.L. Criteria" and highlight three or four important ideas. (six minutes)

2. **Brainstorm:** Ask each group to write the word *PRIORITIZE* in all capital letters vertically down the side of a piece of chart paper and begin brainstorming words or phrases related to an important aspect or outcome of the prioritizing process. Each letter of *prioritize* must have a word or phrase whose first letter corresponds or matches it to form an acrostic. After ten minutes, encourage participants to visit other groups to look for additional ideas before returning to their seats to complete their work. (twenty minutes)

3. **Share:** Each group then shares its acrostic. The reporter should highlight the group's favorite word or phrase and briefly explain why. Each group should post their chart paper on the wall after sharing their product. (five minutes)

Step 3—Personal Reflection (Five Minutes)

Ask participants to write down and reflect on any new insights they have after the training session on prioritizing the standards. Ask, "How might what you learned change your practice or the team's approach to identifying the essential standards?" Have the teachers retain their step 3 personal reflection until section III when the team will debrief the module with a coach.

Section III: After the Learning

Next Steps and Follow-Up for Coaching Teams

The goal of this section of the module is to build the capacity of teams around the process of prioritizing the standards to the point where teams begin the planning of their units by identifying which standards students must absolutely know and be able to do at the unit level.

To move the prioritizing process from learning to doing, coaches should practice the following process of prioritizing standards with teams.

1. Begin by checking in with teams and clarifying any misunderstandings or misconceptions from the previous professional development session.

2. Once teams understand the R.E.A.L. criteria, ask them to select three to five standards from an upcoming unit of study and engage in some deliberate practice using the "Is It R.E.A.L. or Not?" reproducible (page 100). By looking at standards through the lens of the R.E.A.L. criteria, teacher teams can answer the question, "Are the skills, concepts, and dispositions contained within this standard something students will need to know in order to be successful?"

3. Establish a timeline for individual teams to implement their plans at the next collaborative team meeting. Choose an upcoming unit—far enough in advance to allow the team to work without feeling time pressure—and, as a team, have members begin prioritizing the standards for that unit.

4. Refer to the SIG for prerequisite two (page 239) and the pathways tool (page 244) to help determine the team's current reality, identify some possible next steps, and agree on a plan for moving forward. Optional: Ask members to determine how they might address the question they generated during the reflection (step 3) of the module.

Prioritizing the Standards Using R.E.A.L. Criteria

By Thomas W. Many and Ted Horrell

Adapted from Texas Elementary Principals & Supervisors Association's TEPSA News, *January/ February 2014, Vol. 71, No. 1, www.tepsa.org*

"In the absence of an agreed-upon set of criteria for prioritizing the standards . . . , educators will, out of necessity, make up their own."

—Larry Ainsworth

Regardless of their state, province, or district, teachers routinely ask themselves the same questions: "Are some standards more important than others? Which standards will students need in the next class, course, or grade level? Will all the standards be tested?"

Consider this scenario. During a team meeting, the team leader gives teachers a sample unit plan and asks them to identify what is important for students to learn before an upcoming assessment. Teachers embrace the task, but as they work to identify the requisite standards for the upcoming unit, it becomes obvious that each individual teacher is using his or her own unique criteria to prioritize what is essential for students to learn. The result is several different and competing sets of standards based on the teachers' contrasting views. Agreement on the unit's essential outcomes remains an elusive goal.

Educational consultant and author Larry Ainsworth (2013) argues this experience is not unique to a single district, school, or team. He suggests:

> Left to their own professional opinions when faced with the task of narrowing a voluminous number of student learning outcomes, educators naturally "pick and choose" those they know and like best, the ones for which they have materials and lesson plans or activities, and those most likely to appear on state tests. (p. 16)

Reaching consensus on a unit's essential outcomes is important, but many teachers wonder where to begin the task of prioritizing an overwhelming number of standards. Without consensus around what students should know and be able to do (PLC critical question 1) and the development of valid and reliable assessments (PLC critical question 2), development of a systematic and schoolwide pyramid of interventions (critical questions 3 and 4) becomes more difficult.

Using R.E.A.L. Criteria to Prioritize Standards

In response to this dilemma, Ted Horrell and his colleagues in Shelby County, Tennessee, translated criteria Ainsworth (2013) developed into an easy-to-remember acronym. Using the R.E.A.L. criteria (readiness, endurance, assessed, and leverage), teachers collaborate as to whether they should consider a particular standard a priority. An example for each of the four categories follows.

Readiness

The *R* stands for *readiness*. This standard provides students with essential knowledge and skills necessary for success in the next class, course, or grade level. Here is an example of a readiness standard for algebra 1: *Manipulate formulas and solve literal equations*.

Student proficiency in this standard is necessary for success in subsequent mathematics classes, including geometry and algebra 2. Students who cannot demonstrate these skills are ready to advance to the next level of instruction.

Endurance

The *E* represents *endurance*. This standard provides students with knowledge and skills useful beyond a single test or unit of study. Here is an example of an endurance standard for English 9–10: *Determine a central idea of a text and analyze its development over the course of the text, including how it emerges and is shaped and refined by specific details; provide an objective summary of the text.*

Students will require this standard, in particular, the skill of providing an objective summary of written passages, for future high school and college courses. It is also likely to be an essential skill in many professions and in everyday life. The standard has a high degree of endurance.

Assessed

The *A* stands for *assessed*. Upcoming state and national exams will assess this standard. Here is an example of a standard reflecting the assessed criteria for algebra 1: *Order and classify rational numbers.*

Although ordering numbers is a vital part of the mathematics curriculum that most students master at an early age, the skill of classifying rational numbers is not an essential building block for understanding future concepts, nor does it have much practical application outside the mathematics curriculum. However, there are questions on the ACT and PSAT that require students to use this specific skill—a fact teams should consider when prioritizing this standard.

Leverage

The *L* refers to *leverage*. This standard provides students with the knowledge and skills that will be of value in multiple disciplines. Here is an example of a standard reflecting the leverage criteria for physical science: *Choose, construct, and analyze appropriate graphical representations for a data set.*

Though it is part of the physical science curriculum, this standard has significant leverage. Teachers expect students to apply these skills in future science classes, as well as in other content areas such as social studies, career and technical education, and mathematics.

Should Teachers Prioritize the Standards?

Educators on both sides make passionate arguments for and against the idea of prioritizing standards. Whether educators acknowledge it or not, the truth is teachers are prioritizing standards all the time. Collaboratively prioritizing the standards creates greater clarity around what teachers should teach and students should learn. Many teachers find the process of prioritizing standards allows them to see how one standard overlaps with other standards. Furthermore, prioritizing the standards sharpens the focus on what students should learn, which promotes development of better assessments and helps identify which students need more time and support. This kind of knowledge fosters more efficient planning and more efficient sharing of resources.

Prioritizing the standards also encourages teachers to embrace more effective instructional practices by reducing the pressure to simply cover the material. According to Ainsworth (2004), the consensus among educators "is that in-depth instruction of 'essential' concepts and skills is more effective than superficially 'covering' every concept in the textbook" (p. 7).

Perhaps the biggest argument in favor of prioritizing standards is the positive effect the process has on sharpening teachers' pedagogy and deepening their content knowledge. Teams that prioritize the standards recognize that in many ways, the process is as important as the product. Carefully analyzing the standards, debating the merits of individual standards, and coming to consensus on the most essential standards help everyone gain a more thorough understanding of what teachers should teach and students should learn.

If Everything Is Important, Then Nothing Is Important

So the question is not whether teachers should prioritize standards, but rather how will teachers prioritize the standards? Will teachers work in isolation to form a unique set of criteria individually, or will they prioritize the standards based on a common and agreed-on set of criteria their collaborative team develops? The goal is to create clear, consistent, and coherent commitments among the faculty around what *all* students must know and be able to do. This is accomplished by examining the standards, one at a time, through the lens of the R.E.A.L. criteria. Only after examining the standards together can teams be confident that the standards they choose to focus on represent what is most important for all students to know and be able to do.

The answer is to embrace collective responsibility and decide together what is most important for students to know and be able to do.

References

Ainsworth, L. (2004). *Power standards: Identifying the standards that matter the most.* Englewood, CO: Advanced Learning Press.

Ainsworth, L. (2013). *Prioritizing the Common Core: Identifying the specific standards to emphasize the most*. Englewood, CO: Lead + Learn Press.

Marzano, R. J., Yanoski, D. C., Hoegh, J. K., & Simms, J. A. (2013). *Using Common Core standards to enhance classroom instruction and assessment*. Bloomington, IN: Marzano Resources.

Is It R.E.A.L. or Not?

By Thomas W. Many

Teams that prioritize the standards they teach learn the process is as important as the product. Carefully analyzing the standards, debating the merits of individual standards, and coming to a consensus on the most essential standards help everyone gain a more thorough understanding of what teachers should teach and what students should learn.

Identifying the essential standards for every subject and every course is at the heart of the work PLCs do when they answer the first critical question, "What knowledge, skills, and dispositions should every student acquire as a result of this unit, this course, or this grade level?" (DuFour, DuFour, Eaker, Many, & Mattos, 2016, p. 36).

Here's one strategy teams can use to aid in this important work. Ted Horrell and his colleagues at Germantown High School in Germantown, Tennessee, created the R.E.A.L. criteria to determine if a standard is essential, drawing on the work of educational consultant and author Larry Ainsworth (2004) in *Power Standards: Identifying the Standards That Matter the Most*.

The four R.E.A.L. criteria are:

1. **Readiness:** The standard may be essential if it provides students with essential knowledge and skills necessary for success in the next class, course, or grade level.

   An example of a standard meeting this criterion for algebra 1—*Manipulate formulas and solve literal equations*. Students will need this skill for geometry or algebra 2.

2. **Endurance:** The standard may be essential if it provides students with knowledge and skills useful beyond a single test or unit of study.

   An example of a standard meeting this criterion for English 9–10—*Determine a central idea of a text and analyze its development over the course of the text, including how it emerges and is shaped and refined by specific details; provide an objective summary of the text*. Knowing how to write an objective summary of written passages is necessary for many high school and college courses, as well as many professions.

3. **Assessed:** The standard may be essential if upcoming state and national exams are likely to assess it.

   An example of a standard meeting this criterion for algebra 1—*Order and classify rational numbers*. Questions on the ACT and PSAT require students to use this skill, which might make this a priority standard.

4. **Leverage:** The standard may be essential if it provides students with knowledge and skills of value in multiple disciplines.

   An example of a standard meeting this criterion for physical science—*Choose, construct, and analyze appropriate graphical representations for a data set*. Teachers expect students to apply these skills in future science classes, as well as in other content areas such as social studies, career and technical education, and mathematics.

   If a standard aligns with these criteria, teachers should consider it an essential standard and teach it to mastery.

References

Ainsworth, L. (2004). *Power standards: Identifying the standards that matter the most*. Englewood, CO: Advanced Learning Press.

DuFour, R., DuFour, R., Eaker, R., Many, T., & Mattos, M. (2016). *Learning by doing: A handbook for Professional Learning Communities at Work* (3rd ed.). Bloomington, IN: Solution Tree Press.

Is This Standard R.E.A.L?

Proposed standard: _____

Readiness: If students meet this standard, will it prepare them for the next class, course, or grade level? What classes or courses might expect students to have the knowledge they acquire by meeting this standard?

_____

_____

_____

_____

Endurance: If students meet this standard, will they have knowledge and skills to serve them beyond a single test or one unit of study? What knowledge and skills will students acquire by meeting this standard?

_____

_____

_____

_____

Assessed: Will students benefit from having met this standard when they take an upcoming state exam or a college-readiness exam?

- Upcoming state exams?   Yes   No
- College-readiness exams, such as the SAT or ACT?   Yes   No

_____

_____

_____

_____

Leverage: By meeting this standard, will students have knowledge and skills they need in multiple disciplines?

- What knowledge and skills would students acquire by meeting this standard?

_____

_____

_____

_____

Source: Many, T. W. (2016, Summer). Is it R.E.A.L. or not? PLC Magazine, *p. 34–35.*

How Do Teams Unwrap Essential Standards and Identify High-Leverage Learning Targets?

Section I: Before the Learning

Rationale—Why It Matters

The goal of PLC critical question one is to ensure all students have access to the same rigorous curriculum. To do this requires teacher teams to reach consensus on what is essential for all students to know and be able to do. Prioritizing the standards is the first step, but teams must commit to the unwrapping process to identify the highest-leverage learning targets.

Outcomes

Teacher teams understand how unwrapping the priority standards is a critical step that leads to the creation of greater clarity and precision in the teaching and learning process.

SIG and Pathways

SIG prerequisite two (page 239) and the Pathways for Prerequisite Two (2.2; page 244)

Key Coaching Points

1. Standards contain multiple learning targets, and the unwrapping process provides an opportunity to understand the standard and identify the learning targets that matter most.

2. There is widespread agreement on the importance of unwrapping the standards, and teams can utilize any number of simple, straightforward approaches to accomplish the task.

3. Unwrapping the standards results in increased clarity and precision around critical question one by helping teacher teams deepen their content knowledge and sharpen their pedagogy.

4. If standards are not unwrapped, teachers are more likely to interpret them differently and, thus, are more likely to teach and test them differently.

Important Vocabulary and Terms

Standards: This is a general description of the most important outcomes (knowledge, skills, and dispositions) that identify what students should know and be able to do.

Learning targets: A subset or specific statement written by teachers for teachers that is taken directly from a larger standard of what students will need to know and be able to do

Unwrapping: Also called *unpacking* or *deconstructing*, this process promotes greater clarity and deeper understanding of precisely what teachers will teach and students will learn.

Section II: During the Learning

Preparation—Time and Materials

Complete this module in forty-five minutes. The ideal small group size is four participants per group seated at tables, but the activity works with small groups of between three and six. Each group will need a facilitator, timekeeper, recorder, and reporter; chart paper and markers; and a 4-ounce package of M&M's® candies. Participants need copies of the following handout.

- "Unwrapping the Standards: A Priceless Professional Development Opportunity" (page 105)

Step 1: Getting Ready to Learn—M&M's and Essential Standards (Ten Minutes)

This part of the module is designed to prompt reflection on the part of teacher teams. Ask participants how essential standards are like a bag of M&M's candies. For example, the M&M's bag is a wrapper that contains multiple chocolate candies, just as a standard is a statement that contains multiple skills and concepts. Or a bag of M&M's candies contains chocolate pieces of many different colors just like a standard contains many different skills and concepts.

In a two-part conversation, ask each table group to first brainstorm at least five ways a bag of M&M's candies is like an essential standard. Next, ask each group to reach agreement on how unwrapping standards is beneficial. The recorder should capture the group's thinking to both questions and share the comments with the larger group.

Step 2: Interactive Strategy, Protocol, or Activity—Text-Rendering Activity (Thirty-Five Minutes)

1. **Read the article:** As the participants read the article "Unwrapping the Standards: A Priceless Professional Development Opportunity" (page 105), ask them to highlight key ideas from the text by underlining one sentence, drawing a box around one phrase, and circling one word; the sentence, phrase, and word must all be from separate sentences. (six minutes)

2. **Share:** Using a round-robin approach, ask each individual to share their sentence, phrase, and word with other members of their small group while they listen for commonalities but do not comment. (ten minutes)

3. **Reach consensus:** After individuals share, members of the small group identify any common themes or insights. Members may ask others to clarify or explain the reasons for their choice. The recorder writes key insights and agreements on chart paper. Each small group posts its chart, and the large group works to reach consensus on one key sentence, one key phrase, and one key word from the article. (fifteen minutes)

Step 3: Personal Reflection—Summarize Your Thinking (Five Minutes)

Ask participants if their thinking has changed after the workshop on unwrapping the standards. Ask them to write down their biggest takeaways and think about how the experience impacts their perspective or their team's professional practice regarding unwrapping the priority standards as a tool for creating greater clarity, consistency, and commitment to the idea of ensuring all students have access to a GVC. Teachers should record and retain their reflections until the section III debriefing session with a coach.

Section III: After the Learning

Next Steps and Follow-Up for Coaching Teams

Your goal as the coach is to support the team with deliberate practice around unwrapping the standards. Write the following standard where all members can see it and ask the team to work in pairs and unwrap the standard using the process the article outlines.

"Determine a theme or central idea of a text and how it is conveyed through particular details; provide a summary of the text distinct from personal opinions or judgments" (RL.6.2; National Governors Association Center for Best Practices & Council of Chief State School Officers, 2010).

This standard contains at least three separate and distinct learning targets.

- **Learning target 1:** Determine the central idea of a text.

- **Learning target 2:** Determine how particular details convey a central idea of a text.

- **Learning target 3:** Provide a summary of a text distinct from personal opinions or judgments.

Using the example standard, a teacher would instruct students on how to determine a text's central idea before exploring different ways authors use details to convey a central idea. Afterward, the teacher may deliver a separate lesson on how to use a text's central idea to develop an objective summary. Teaching these separate learning targets allows the teacher to individually assess each target. If a student does not clearly understand how to identify a central idea, that student will struggle to write an effective summary. If a teacher delivers a formative assessment on central ideas before beginning instruction on writing summaries, the teacher can identify struggling students and intervene before moving on.

Many standards are bundles of skills and concepts students need to know and understand to attain mastery. Unwrapping the standards to reveal individual learning targets helps teachers plan direct instruction and design formative assessments that provide useful information about student learning. Just like opening a bag of M&M's candies to reveal those delicious, colorful treats, unwrapping standards and intentionally teaching to the learning target level ensure students receive the instruction they need to master the standards.

Unwrapping the Standards:
A Priceless Professional Development Opportunity

By Thomas W. Many

Adapted from Texas Elementary Principals & Supervisors Association's TEPSA News, *November/ December 2020, Vol. 77, No. 6, www.tepsa.org*

"Unwrapping the standards will provide [educators] with a first step to better focus instruction on the concepts and skills students need for success."

—Larry Ainsworth

At its core, responding to PLC critical question one is about creating a faculty *commitment* that all students will master the most essential learning outcomes. To operationalize the answer to question one, teams must engage in a three-step process of prioritizing the standards to identify the most essential learning outcomes; unwrapping, unpacking, or deconstructing the standards to pinpoint the highest-leverage learning targets; and translating and rewriting the learning targets into *I can* statements using student-friendly language.

Whether educators call them *power standards*, *priority standards*, or *promise standards*, these statements represent what is absolutely essential all students know and be able to do. They represent a subset of the larger list of standards and help educators distinguish between those standards that students *need to know* from those *nice to know*.

One of the benefits of local, state, or national standards is that they promote the development of a guaranteed and viable curriculum by reducing the amount of variability from one teacher to the next regarding what students are expected to know and be able to do. However, many standards are written in complex ways using confusing language that is open to interpretation. When individual teachers interpret standards differently and emphasize different aspects of the standards during instruction, it is virtually impossible to guarantee all students will have access to the same rigorous curriculum.

Interpreting the standards differently defeats the purpose of answering critical question one, which is to create clear, consistent, and coherent commitments among the faculty around what *all* students must know and be able to do. The only way to mitigate the potential for variance in the process is to unwrap the standards as a team and identify the highest-leverage learning targets within each standard.

"There is the added challenge of really understanding what the standard means. It's one thing to read a standard and get a general sense of what it's about. It's another thing to thoroughly understand what it explicitly and implicitly indicates."

—Larry Ainsworth

The need for clarity, or *collective clarity*, and the precision it creates necessitates all team members share a common understanding of the *meaning* of each standard. When teams are clear on the meaning of the standard, there is no ambiguity around what students must learn. Thus, the purpose of unwrapping the priority standards is threefold: (1) to clearly identify what knowledge, skills, and dispositions all students must know and be able to do, (2) to ensure teachers clearly understand the level of cognitive demand (*rigor*) and the learning tasks the standard expresses explicitly or implicitly, and (3) to support identification of prerequisite skills, academic vocabulary, instructional practices, and assessment strategies, as well as any opportunities for intervention and extension.

page 1 of 3

"The goal is clarity—and by having that structured conversation that answers the question "What do they really mean by this standard?" every teacher will be enlightened and informed on an equal basis."

—Kim Bailey, Chris Jakicic, and Jeanne Spiller

There are many variations of the unwrapping process, but all follow a similar sequence of steps. Coauthors Kim Bailey and Chris Jakicic (2012) share an effective and efficient approach that consists of a few simple steps.

First, focus on key words. Bailey and Jakicic (2012) suggest teams start by circling the verbs (what students should be able to do), underlining the nouns (what students should know), and bracketing or double underlining any context clues. Some teams prefer to substitute highlighters of different colors for the verbs, nouns, and context clues.

Next, map out the unwrapped standard. Transfer the highlighted verbs, nouns, and context clues to an unwrapping template (see Bailey & Jakicic, 2018, pp. 75–76; visit **go.SolutionTree .com/PLCbooks** to find a link to an unwrapping template), which will allow for a closer examination of the learning targets within the standard. The key is to study the standard and reach agreement on what the standard is *really* trying to say. Charting the unwrapped standard ensures the teams identify all of the explicit and implicitly stated targets.

Finally, reach consensus on the targets. At this point, teams should intentionally slow the process down and carefully analyze the learning targets to (1) decide if any of the targets are more important than others (Which targets must students master to be successful?) and (2) determine what level of rigor (*cognitive demand*) is the best match for each target. These last conversations allow teams to concentrate on teaching the highest-leverage learning targets to mastery and help with planning the best approach to instruction and assessment.

The most effective way to become comfortable with the unwrapping process is to practice using it!

We recommend teams unwrap *only* the essential standards. Whether educators call them *power standards*, *priority standards*, or *promise standards*, the team should focus its limited time and energy on the most important and impactful standards. If the team is able to unwrap all the *need to know* standards, they can turn their attention to the *nice to know* standards at a later date.

"By unwrapping the standards as a team, each member walks back to his or her classroom with the same picture of what students should know and be able to do, and, consequently, the same expectations for student learning."

—Kim Bailey and Chris Jakicic

Teams should look at the unwrapping process as an opportunity to deepen their content knowledge and sharpen their pedagogy. A lot of learning happens during the unwrapping process so regardless of who (the state, district, or team) decides what is essential, teams should unwrap the standards. Invariably after unwrapping the standards, teachers share they feel they know exactly what they want their students to learn, at what level of rigor, using which instructional strategy, and which assessment approach. Those insights into teaching and learning are priceless!

References

Ainsworth, L. (2003). *Unwrapping the standards: A simple process to make standards manageable*. Englewood, CO: Advanced Learning Press.

Ainsworth, L. (2015, March 25). *Unwrapping the standards: A simple way to deconstruct learning outcomes* [Blog post]. Accessed at https://edweek.org/education/opinion-unwrapping-the-standards-a-simple-way-to-deconstruct-learning-outcomes/2015/03 on March 1, 2021.

Bailey, K., & Jakicic, C. (2012). *Common formative assessment: A toolkit for Professional Learning Communities at Work.* Bloomington, IN: Solution Tree Press.

Bailey, K., & Jakicic, C. (2018). *Make it happen: Coaching with the four critical questions of PLCs at Work.* Bloomington, IN: Solution Tree Press.

Bailey, K., Jakicic, C., & Spiller, J. (2014). *Collaborating for success with the Common Core: A toolkit for Professional Learning Communities at Work.* Bloomington, IN: Solution Tree Press.

How Do Teams Use *I Can* Statements to Maximize Learning?

Section I: Before the Learning

Rationale—Why It Matters

The research is pervasive and persuasive; when students are clear about the expectations for learning, they do better. While prioritizing and unwrapping standards are productive tasks that benefit *teachers* and their practice, carefully crafted *I can* statements teachers write in student-friendly language have a significant and positive impact on *students* and their learning.

Outcomes

Teachers understand the positive impact the effective use of *I can* statements has on student learning. Teachers also learn how to write measurable *I can* statements in student-friendly language that students use to track their own progress.

SIG and Pathways

SIG prerequisite two (page 239) and the Pathways for Prerequisite Two (2.3; page 244)

Key Coaching Points

1. Unwrapped standards are written for teachers by teachers for the benefit of teachers. *I can* statements are written for students by teachers for the benefit of students.

2. Well-written *I can* statements have many benefits; they create clarity, allow students to track their own progress, and encourage students to become more independent learners.

3. Whether educators call them *I can statements*, *learning intentions*, *shared learning targets*, or *student learning targets*, these statements clarify student learning expectations.

4. The collaborative team derives *I can* statements directly from their previously prioritized and unwrapped standards.

5. To be effective, an *I can* statement should be measurable, written in student-friendly language, express the outcome for the upcoming lesson, and contain a limited number of targets; students should use an *I can* statement to measure and monitor their own learning.

Important Vocabulary and Terms

***I can* statement:** A statement written in student-friendly language that communicates to students the learning expectations for the upcoming lesson

Section II: During the Learning

Preparation—Time and Materials

Complete this module in fifty minutes. The ideal group size is four teachers per group seated at tables. The group should choose a facilitator, timekeeper, recorder, and reporter. Each member will also need notebook paper, access to chart paper and markers, and the following reproducible.

- "Crafting *I Can* Statements: A Practice Worth Pursuing" (page 111)

Step 1: Getting Ready to Learn—Promissory Note Activity (Ten Minutes)

Explain that participants will use notebook paper to write themselves a *promissory note* (a written promise or commitment to oneself) outlining what they intend to do as a result of what they learn about using *I can* statements to impact student learning. Encourage participants to be specific about what they will do and by when. Once finished, have teachers fold their promissory note and write their name on the outside. At this point, the person leading the session will collect the promissory notes and return them as the final part of the protocol in step 2.

Step 2: Interactive Strategy, Protocol, or Activity: "Four A" Text Protocol (Forty Minutes)

1. **Read the article:** Ask participants to read the article "Crafting *I Can* Statements: A Practice Worth Pursuing" (page 111). As the group reads the article silently, participants should annotate the text using the "Four A" text protocol (eight minutes). They should make notes in the margins using the following.

   - A plus (+) sign for topics they Agree with
   - A minus (–) sign for statements they would Argue with
   - A question mark (?) for matters they want to Ask about
   - A star (*) for ideas they Aspire to achieve with their team

2. **Share thinking:** Once the group is finished reading and annotating the selection, the facilitator should use a round-robin approach to have each participant in the small group share his or her thinking. In a series of four rounds, each member of the small group (without comment or discussion at this point) quickly shares one thing they:

   - Agree with (round one)
   - Argue with (round two)
   - Ask about (round three)
   - Aspire to (round four)

   Record key words or phrases from each round. (five minutes)

3. **Summarize:** In a fifth and final round, while still working in the small groups, participants should summarize their thinking (six minutes) before sharing any agreements or consensus with the larger group. (four minutes)

4. **Review and reach consensus:** Working as a large group, ask the participants to review what they recorded, identify common themes, and reach consensus on any takeaways. (five minutes)

5. **Reflect and update:** Return the promissory notes to each participant. Allow everyone a few moments to silently reflect on what they learned and update their note based on this module's learning. Ask for volunteers to share their notes with the group. (five minutes)

Step 3: Personal Reflection—Summarize Your Thinking (Five Minutes)

Ask participants to consider the following question: "What about your thinking changed after the workshop on using *I can* statements?" Participants should record and retain any new insights and reflect on how this experience might change their beliefs or their team's professional practice. The reflections will be used during the section III debrief with a coach.

Section III: After the Learning

Next Steps and Follow-Up for Coaching Teams

1. This is a good opportunity for some guided practice. Using one of the targets the team unwrapped in Module 5.4, ask participants to draft several *I can* statements. If the team did not complete Module 5.4, they may choose any target they have already unwrapped. Once finished, help participants analyze their work to ensure the *I can* statement (1) links to the learning target for the lesson, (2) contains a limited number of skills, (3) is written in student-friendly language, and (4) can be used by students to track their own progress toward mastery.

2. Ask participants to bring their promissory notes and use them to plan the next steps for using *I can* statements on their team. Making the promissory note activity actionable is an opportunity for the team to design and implement a PDSA cycle to study the impact using *I can* statements on student learning.

3. Refer to the SIG for prerequisite two (page 239) and the pathways tool (page 244) to help the team determine its current reality, identify some possible next steps, and agree on a plan for moving forward.

In the next chapter, teachers will have an opportunity to learn how teams use what they have learned in this chapter to design and deliver valid and reliable common assessments. Teams will recognize the important role PLC critical question 1, What should students know and be able to do? (and especially their practice with learning targets) plays in the development of common formative and summative assessments to answer PLC critical question 2, How do we know if students have learned it?

Crafting *I Can* Statements: A Practice Worth Pursuing

By Thomas W. Many

Adapted from Texas Elementary Principals & Supervisors Association's TEPSA News, *January/ February 2021, Vol. 78, No. 1, www.tepsa.org*

"The learning target [of the lesson] can be made visible and accessible to students through the use of student-friendly language and the words "I can . . . " to begin each learning target statement."

—Heather Clayton

One of the most unambiguous conclusions practitioners can draw from the research is that clarity around a lesson's learning target can help boost student achievement. When used consistently and in ways that reflect best practice, researchers find translating learning targets into *I can* statements benefits students and their teachers.

Renowned author and researcher John Hattie (2009) reports on the importance of communicating "the intentions of the lessons and the notion of what success means for those intentions" (p. 125). Likewise, coauthors Susan M. Brookhart and Connie M. Moss (2014) identify eight separate studies between 1995 and 2011 that find teaching students the learning targets and success criteria for a lesson has a positive effect on learning. The terminology may vary, but regardless of whether educators call them *learning targets*, *student learning targets*, *shared learning targets*, *learning intentions*, or *I can statements*, all help students learn to higher levels.

"To be effective, the language we use must be descriptive, specific, developmentally appropriate and written in student-friendly language."

—Connie M. Moss and Susan M. Brookhart

One of the distinctive characteristics of *I can* statements is they are narrow by design. In practice, teachers write *I can* statements in student-friendly language and describe precisely what they expect students to learn during a particular lesson. For example, "*I can* explain the difference between a first- and secondhand account of an event in my own words." Teachers might use this kind of *I can* statement in a social studies class where students are working to understand the importance of primary sources.

An *I can* statement represents a small part of a much larger learning progression and helps students maintain their trajectory toward mastery of essential learning targets. When done well, *I can* statements help students understand what the lesson is about, why it is important, how teachers expect them to learn, and what they need to do to demonstrate what they have learned. These *I can* statements also convey the progression of learning by connecting lessons from yesterday, today, and tomorrow.

Finally, *I can* statements enable students to do a better job of self-assessing their progress by empowering them to answer the following three questions about their learning.

1. "Where do I need to go?"

2. "Where am I right now?"

3. "What do I need to do to close the gap between where I need to go and where I am right now?"

Blogger and teacher Jody Waltman (n.d.a) provides a step-by-step guide for creating *I can* statements. Waltman (n.d.a) encourages teams to begin by agreeing on the learning target (or targets) for the upcoming lesson. Once in agreement, the team divides the target into smaller bits of information. This initial conversation helps the team build shared knowledge about exactly what should be the outcome of the upcoming lesson (or lessons).

Next, Waltman (n.d.a) encourages teams to "write a series of statements, each beginning with the words 'I can,' that outline the path that students will follow and each of the skills that the students will obtain by the end of the instructional period." Waltman (n.d.a) encourages teams to avoid crafting *I can* statements in isolation; she believes it is better to reflect on what students will experience over a series of lessons during the course of an upcoming unit.

Finally, Waltman (n.d.a) recommends teachers "write these 'I can' statements at the target level," stating just a simple, singular goal for a single lesson or set of lessons. This helps narrow the focus of the *I can* statement, which makes it easier for students to understand, facilitates alignment of the team's common assessments, and expedites the tracking of student progress.

> "The 'I can' statements frame the standards and goals in a student-friendly way. This allows them [students] to take ownership of their own learning to track and monitor their progress towards the learning targets."
>
> —Jody Waltman

Mindfulness educator Melanie Black (2017) describes additional benefits when students use *I can* statements to track their progress:

> Students who track their grades regularly, not just at midterms and finals, take ownership of their learning, and are more likely to persevere in the face of challenges and take steps to proactively meet their goals. Tracking their progress empowers students to be independent and successful, which will not only benefit them in school but in any future endeavor.

According to author Robert J. Marzano (2010), "The strategy of tracking student progress on specific learning goals is well supported" (p. 86). Marzano (2010) reports researchers found a 26-percentile point gain in student achievement when teachers tracked student progress using visual displays of formative assessment results. Even more significant, researchers found a 32-percentile point gain in student achievement when students tracked their own progress using visual displays of formative assessment results.

What Marzano (2010), Black (2017), and others are saying is in addition to higher levels of student achievement, clearly communicating the intent of a lesson to students generates a host of other noteworthy benefits such as greater ownership of their learning, increased intrinsic motivation, and the development of more self-directed learners.

> "When students understand exactly what they're supposed to learn and what their work will look like when they learn it, they're better able to monitor and adjust their work, select effective strategies, and connect current work to prior learning."
>
> —Susan M. Brookhart and Connie M. Moss

There is more to the effective use of *I can* statements than simply writing them on the board or posting them on the wall. The level of learning improves in classrooms where teachers embrace the expert advice of Brookhart and Moss (2014), Hattie (2009), Marzano (2010), and others who show time and again that using *I can* statements to clearly communicate the intent of a lesson is a practice worth pursuing.

References

Black, M. (2017). *Helping students track their own progress.* Accessed at https://studentfutures
.org/college-planning/helping-students-track-their-own-progress on September 16, 2019.

Brookhart, S. M., & Moss, C. M. (2014). Learning targets on parade. *Educational Leadership,*
72(2), 28–33.

Clayton, H. (2017). Learning targets. *Making the standards come alive! VI*(1). Alexandria,
VA: Just Ask. Accessed at https://justaskpublications.s3.amazonaws.com/Learning
_Targets_5.pdf on March 10, 2021.

Crockett, H. (2013). *How I can statements can work for you.* Accessed at www.theartofed
.com/2013/02/21/how-i-can-statements-can-work-for-you on September 14, 2020.

Hattie, J. (2009). *Visible learning: A synthesis of over 800 meta-analysis relating to*
achievement. New York. Routledge.

Marzano, R. (2010). When students track their progress. *Educational Leadership, 67*(4), 86–87.

Mattos, M., DuFour, R., DuFour, R., Eaker, R., & Many, T. W. (2016). *Concise answers to*
frequently asked questions about Professional Learning Communities at Work.
Bloomington, IN: Solution Tree Press.

Moss, C. M., & Brookhart, S. M. (2012). *Learning targets: Helping students aim for*
understanding in today's lesson. Alexandria, VA: Association for Supervision and
Curriculum Development.

Moss, C. M., Brookhart, S. M., & Long, B. A. (2011). Knowing your learning target. *Educational*
Leadership, 68(6), 66–69.

Waltman, J. (n.d.a). *I can statements* [Video file]. Accessed at https://sophia.org/tutorials
/i-can-statements-2 on September 25, 2020.

Waltman, J. (n.d.b). *Why should students track their own progress?* [Video file]. Accessed at
https://sophia.org/tutorials/why-should-students-track-their-own-progress-2 on March
9, 2021.

CHAPTER 6

A Balanced and Coherent System of Assessment

Prerequisite three: *Collaborative teams monitor student learning through an ongoing assessment process that includes frequent, team-developed, common formative assessments (DuFour & Reeves, 2016).*

Those coaching teacher teams understand one of the most effective ways to build collaboration among teachers is to task them with operationalizing common assessments. Crafting valid and reliable common assessments is a powerful professional development opportunity, and when teachers co-create common assessments, they engage in conversations around all four of the critical questions of a PLC (DuFour et al., 2016). Simply put, creating, administering, and reviewing common assessments provide a context for implementing all four of these questions.

DuFour and his colleagues (2010) articulate it well: "team-developed common assessments used for formative purposes are so powerful that no team of teachers should be allowed to opt out of creating them" (p. 76). Those words describe exactly what teams must understand about the third prerequisite of a PLC.

The first word teams should consider is *common*. It doesn't say assessments should be 75 percent or 80 percent common. Nor does it advocate that assessments be kind of common, mostly common, or predominantly common; it says *common*, which means the assessment is the same for all students enrolled in the same class, course, or grade level. It also means individual teachers do not customize the assessments by adding "a few of my favorite things" or "extra problems for extra points" at the end. An assessment consistent across the team furthers its validity and reliability, and the commonness enables teachers to accurately analyze results.

Understanding the phrase *team-developed* is critical to the third prerequisite. Some teams delegate assessment development to one person or rotate responsibility among all team members. When this happens, the person creating the assessment is the only one who is learning what and how to assess the standards or developing any ownership of the results. It may sound like a good idea but, delegating or rotating responsibility for creating common assessments actually inhibits team development.

Next, teams should examine the implications of the word *frequent* on their practice. Teams need to talk about how often they should administer common assessments and, while the answer is dependent on the instruction taking place in the classroom, research suggests the most effective and efficient frequency is about every three weeks. Marzano (2007) reports on a meta-analysis by Robert L. Bangent-Drowns, James A. Kulik, and Chen-Lin C. Kulik (1991) where researchers found that the *frequency* of formative assessment had a positive impact on student achievement. In particular, their analysis showed that five assessments in a fifteen-week period created the best balance between impact on learning and frequency of assessment. There is nothing magic about *exactly* three weeks (student achievement continues to improve with more frequent assessment, albeit at a slower and slower rate), but teams whose members argue they cannot create, administer, and review the results of an assessment any more frequently than every six or eight weeks are engaging in malpractice or simply being resistant.

Finally, while it is arguable that the commonness of an assessment is more important to developing highly effective collaborative teams than whether assessments are formative or summative, DuFour and his colleagues' (2010) quote clearly indicates teams should embrace *formative* as the primary form of assessment. What determines if an assessment is *formative* or *summative* depends on how teachers use it, but when the goal is improved teaching and learning, it is widely accepted that formative assessment is more impactful than summative assessment.

This chapter provides coaches with the *why*, *what*, and *how* of common assessments. *Common*, *team-developed*, *frequent*, and *formative* are all key words or phrases those supporting collaborative teams should be familiar with, but there is one more important part of DuFour and his colleagues' (2010) quote coaches and teams should not overlook.

DuFour and colleagues (2010, 2016) argue regular and routine use of valid and reliable common formative and summative assessments must be among the tight aspects for any team, at any school, and in any district seeking to become a fully functioning PLC.

Synopsis of Chapter 6 Modules

The modules in this chapter explore the third prerequisite condition of a PLC, which states *Collaborative teams monitor student learning through an ongoing assessment process that includes frequent, team-developed common formative assessments* (DuFour & Fullan, 2013). The activities in this chapter focus on how to develop and use valid and reliable common formative and common summative assessments. This chapter concludes with a conversation about the importance of using preassessments to maximize opportunities for student learning.

Module 6.1: What Is the Secret to Success?

Common assessments function as a lynchpin for the four critical questions of a PLC by creating a bridge between question one ("What knowledge, skills, and dispositions should every student acquire as a result of this unit, this course, or this grade level?") and questions three and four ("How will we respond when students do not learn?" and "How will we extend the learning for students who are already proficient?"; DuFour et al., 2016, p. 36). Teams begin creating common assessments by agreeing on what is essential (question one). Then, as the team reviews assessment results, they naturally talk about which students are and are not proficient (questions three and four). This module helps teams understand why common assessments are so critical to the PLC process.

Module 6.2: What Does a Balanced and Coherent System of Assessment Look Like?

Formative and summative assessment are both legitimate when teachers use them properly; however, the authors believe schools are testing too much. By this, we mean traditionally, teams rely too heavily on summative and not nearly enough on formative assessments. To operationalize a balanced and coherent system of assessment, teachers must understand the purpose of formative and summative assessment and make an effort to ensure they use the right mix of both. This module presents teacher teams with a mental model they can use to look at the range of assessments in a systemic and systematic way.

Module 6.3: How Do We Design Valid and Reliable Assessments?

Many teachers do not believe they have the expertise necessary to craft valid and reliable assessments, but that simply is not true; teacher teams often create assessments that align more with the guaranteed and viable curriculum than those publishers or external psychometricians (who have little knowledge of the context teachers teach) create. This module provides teams with a four-step process to develop valid and reliable common formative and summative assessments.

Module 6.4: How Do We Use the Power of Distractors to Improve Student Learning?

Common assessments are the lynchpin of the PLC process. When teachers use them with purpose, data from common assessments help teams identify struggling students, uncover problems with the curriculum, and reveal the impact of specific instructional strategies. This module emphasizes the importance of the design and analysis of student responses to selected-response items by guiding teams through the process of writing distractors, which provide valuable information about student learning.

Module 6.5: What Is the Purpose of Preassessments?

Preassessments are beneficial if—and that's a big if—teachers design and use them properly. This module makes the case for shifting the focus of preassessments to a broader, more comprehensive effort to gauge a student's readiness to learn. To assess a student's level of readiness, teachers should focus their preassessments on (1) prior knowledge, (2) mastery of prerequisite skills, and (3) understanding of important academic language *in addition to* what he or she may know about the content from the upcoming unit. Without the necessary prerequisite skills or understanding of academic language, a student may not be able to access even the finest lessons teachers may deliver in the classroom.

These modules are best thought of either as an opportunity for teachers to learn together or as a starting point for further exploration and investigation. We intentionally designed the professional development activities in this chapter to be flexible; they can be delivered to individual teams or the entire faculty. The modules can be delivered in order within a chapter or through the entire book, or they can be delivered in a way that provides just-in-time embedded professional development for collaborative teams. The authors' goal is to provide the right information to the right people in the right settings at the right time.

Most importantly, teams need differentiated support, so those coaching teams should match the learning (as reflected in the modules) with what the team needs to work on. Asking teams, "What would you like to work on?" or "What would you like feedback on?" will make teams *feel* better, but these are the wrong questions. "What do the data indicate that you need to work on?" or "What do the data indicate that you need feedback on?" will make teams *do* better and are the right questions those who coach teams should be asking.

Those coaching collaborative teams need to decide whether they want their teams to *feel* better or to *do* better. We believe that the decision of what teams should work on or receive feedback on must reflect what the data indicate is the teams' greatest area of need (GAN), not their greatest area of comfort (GAC). Knowing what teams need to improve their professional practice should guide the choice of module.

What Is the Secret to Success?

Section I: Before the Learning

Rationale—Why It Matters

The article "The Secret to Success" (page 123) introduces the importance of common assessments. As DuFour notes, "people don't really start to think and act like a learning community until they are engaged in a collaborative effort to answer the question, 'How do we know our students are learning?'" (personal communication, July 30, 2005). In this module, teams explore the role of common assessments in a PLC.

Outcomes

After completing this module, teachers can articulate the benefits of common assessments and identify some of the implications regular use of common assessments will have on their professional practice, including higher levels of student achievement.

SIG and Pathways

SIG prerequisite three (page 240) and the Pathways for Prerequisite Three (3.1–3.5; page 245)

Key Coaching Points

1. Developing common assessments provides the context for collaborative teams to learn together (collective inquiry), improve their craft (continuous improvement), and promote collaboration by working together on a common task.

2. Common assessments are a great starting place for teams as they respond to the four critical questions of a PLC—"What knowledge, skills, and dispositions should every student acquire as a result of this unit, this course, or this grade level? How will we know when each student has acquired the essential knowledge and skills? How will we respond when students do not learn? and How will we extend the learning for students who are already proficient?" (DuFour et al., 2016, p. 36). In fact, asking teams to begin their response to the critical questions of learning by designing common assessments creates a tangible product based on a practical goal for the team's collaboration energy.

Important Vocabulary and Terms

Common assessment: A common assessment is "collaboratively designed by a grade level or department [and is] administered to students by each participating teacher periodically throughout the year" (Ainsworth & Viegut, 2006, p. 3).

Professional dissonance: This is a state of psychological discomfort experienced when new learning conflicts or is inconsistent with past practice or what is currently considered best practice.

Section II: During the Learning

Preparation—Time and Materials

Complete this module in fifty minutes. The ideal group size is four participants per group seated at tables, but the activity works with three to six participants. Groups will need chart paper and markers and should choose roles including a facilitator, timekeeper, recorder, and reporter. Each participant should have a copy of the following handouts.

- "Why Should We Use Common Assessments?" (page 122)
- "The Secret to Success" (page 123)

Step 1: Getting Ready to Learn—Quotation Mingle Activity (Twenty Minutes)

1. Begin by having small groups quickly brainstorm at least five reasons why teams should use common assessments, record the ideas on chart paper, and save them for for later. (three minutes)

2. Have the entire group count off by seven and turn to the handout, "Why Should We Use Common Assessments?" which contains seven quotes. Participants should locate the quote that corresponds to their number, read the quote silently, underline or highlight relevant words or phrases, and make notes about why the quote is important. (three minutes)

3. When the group is ready, ask each participant to find a partner with a different quote. Once everyone has a partner, each person explains why his or her quote is important. These are quick conversations, so keep the participants moving. Rotate every three minutes until each participant has talked with three other participants, each time with a different quote. (three minutes per conversation; nine minutes total)

4. Participants return to their original tables and update the original brainstorming session on why teams should use common assessments to reflect the new learning. (five minutes)

Step 2: Interactive Strategy, Protocol, or Activity—Unpacking Luggage (Forty-Five Minutes)

This protocol will help participants raise questions and identify implications that a new process or procedure may have on their professional practice. Using a series of three categories and a short article, coaches prompt participants' thinking about a change in practice.

While the participants read the article, create a visual model of the three categories on chart paper. Fold the paper into three sections lengthwise and title each section as one of the three categories: *Successes*, *Challenges*, and *Questions*. Post the model on the wall.

1. **Read the article:** Ask the group to silently read "The Secret to Success" on page 123. (seven minutes)

2. **Respond to the three statements:** After participants finish reading, ask each table group to respond to the idea of implementing common assessments by reaching

consensus on three (or more) comments for each statement. The participants should write their comments on the chart paper. The comments can be as simple as single words or lengthier celebrations and aspirations related to some aspect of implementing common assessments. (ten minutes)

3. **Record thinking:** Once they finish, ask each table group to share its thinking, beginning with successes. All groups share their comments regarding successes before moving on to the next statement. Repeat the same process for challenges and questions. (five minutes per statement; fifteen minutes total)

4. **Reach consensus on *one* success, challenge, and question per group:** After sharing all the participants' comments, ask each small group to choose the one comment that best represents their thinking for each statement, circling it on their chart paper. Post the charts and do a quick gallery walk to look for any emerging themes. (five minutes)

5. **The final task:** Ask each group to reach agreement on the main idea of the "Secret to Success" article and cite supporting evidence from the article. (three minutes)

Step 3: Personal Reflection (Five Minutes)

Ask participants to take five minutes to reflect on the questions, "Why should our team use common assessments?" and "Why are common assessments beneficial to teachers and students?" and record their thinking. Have each person record and retain their personal reflections until the debriefing session in section III.

Section III: After the Learning

Next Steps and Follow-Up for Coaching Teams

This module provides an opportunity to explore teachers' beliefs about the important role common assessments play in developing a high-performing collaborative team.

1. Gather any questions the team has about what it takes to implement common assessments. Allow teachers the opportunity to talk about the effect that committing to the regular and ongoing use of common assessments will have on their professional practice. The questions and concerns provide an excellent place to begin coaching teams. Teachers can refer to their personal reflections for questions.

2. Refer to the SIG for prerequisite three (page 240) and Pathways for Prerequisite Three (3.1–3.5; page 245) to help the team determine its current reality, identify some possible next steps, and agree on a plan for moving forward.

3. Establish a timeline for the team to implement its plan at the next collaborative team meeting where members will analyze student assessment data.

Why Should We Use Common Assessments?

Reviews of accountability data from hundreds of schools reveal the schools with the greatest gains in achievement consistently employ common assessments, nonfiction writing, and collaborative scoring by faculty (Reeves, 2004).

Powerful, proven structures for improved results are at hand. "It starts when a group of teachers meets regularly as a team to identify essential and valued student learning, develop common formative assessments, analyze current levels of achievement, set achievement goals, and then share and create lessons and strategies to improve upon those levels" (Schmoker, 2004, p. 84).

The schools and districts that doubled student achievement added another layer of testing—common formative or benchmark assessments. These assessments were designed to provide detailed and concrete information on what students know and do not know with respect to specific learning targets (Odden & Archibald, 2009).

The key to improved student achievement was moving beyond an individual teacher looking at his or her classroom data. Instead, it took getting same-grade teacher teams to meet, analyze the results of each interim assessment to understand what concepts in the curriculum were posing difficulty for students, share ideas, figure out the best interventions, and actually follow up in their classrooms (Christman et al., 2009).

In schools that help students burdened by poverty achieve remarkable success, teachers work in collaborative teams to build common formative assessments and use the data to identify which students need help and which need greater challenges. But they also use data to inform teachers' practice, to discuss why one teacher is having success in teaching a concept and others are not, and what the more successful teacher can teach his or her colleagues (Chenoweth, 2009).

"High-growth schools and districts use frequent, common short-cycle assessments—at least every three to six weeks. Teachers create formative assessments before developing their lessons for a unit and clarify success criteria. The importance of focusing the attention of teachers on formative assessment practices and developing and using short-cycle common assessments was one of the most consistent findings of the study" (Battelle for Kids, 2015).

One of the most effective ways educators can use formative assessments is by collaboratively creating common formative assessments with grade-level or course-level colleagues . . . to assess student understanding of the particular learning intentions and success criteria currently in focus within a curricular unit of study. Common formative assessments afford teacher teams a clear lens through which to see their instructional impact on student learning (Ainsworth, 2014).

References

Ainsworth, L. (2014). *Common formative assessments 2.0: How teacher teams intentionally align standards, instruction, and assessment* (2nd ed.). Thousand Oaks, CA: Corwin Press.

Battelle for Kids. (2015). *Five strategies for creating a high-growth school.* Accessed at www .battelleforkids.org/docs/default-source/publications/soar_five_strategies_for_creating _a_high-growth_school.pdf?sfvrsn=2 on September 10, 2015.

Chenoweth, K. (2009). It can be done, it's being done, and here's how. *Phi Delta Kappan, 91*(1), 38–43.

Christman, J. B., Neild, R. C., Bulkley, K., Blanc, S., Liu, R., Mitchell, C., et al. (2009, June). *Making the most of interim assessment data: Lessons from Philadelphia.* Philadelphia: Research for Action. Accessed at www.researchforaction.org/making-the-most-of-interim-assessment-data-lessons -from-philadelphia on January 10, 2010.

Odden, A. R., & Archibald, S. J. (2009). *Doubling student performance . . . and finding the resources to do it.* Thousand Oaks, CA: Corwin Press.

Reeves, D. B. (2004). *Accountability for learning: How teachers and school leaders can take charge.* Alexandria, VA: Association for Supervision and Curriculum Development.

Schmoker, M. (2004). Learning communities at the crossroads: A response to Joyce and Cook. *Phi Delta Kappan, 86*(1), 84–89.

The Secret to Success

By Thomas W. Many

Adapted from Texas Elementary Principals & Supervisors Association's TEPSA News, *August 2010, Vol. 67, No. 4, www.tepsa.org*

Teacher teams in PLCs respond to the four critical questions of learning: "What knowledge, skills, and dispositions should every student acquire as a result of this unit, this course, or this grade level? How will we know when each student has acquired the essential knowledge and skills? How will we respond when students do not learn? and How will we extend the learning for students who are already proficient?" (DuFour, DuFour, Eaker, Many, & Mattos, 2016, p. 36). Collaborative teams in PLCs design common assessments to answer these questions.

Common assessments provide teams with a concrete way to connect the four PLC critical questions of learning. As Richard DuFour notes:

> The questions of a learning community really flow up and down from collaboratively developed common formative assessments. We have found that people don't really start to think and act like a learning community until they are engaged in a collaborative effort to answer the question "How do we know our students are learning?" (personal communication, July 30, 2005)

Why is this so? Perhaps it is because people learn best by *doing*, and when teachers collaboratively develop a common assessment, they make meaning of their work and introduce a healthy dose of professional dissonance into the process.

Professional Dissonance and Making Meaning

The concept of *cognitive dissonance* is a psychological phenomenon that refers to the discomfort an individual feels when presented with new information or a different approach discrepant from what the individual already knows or believes. Psychologists have long understood that the act of resolving dissonance actually promotes learning. Teachers can use cognitive dissonance as a tool to increase motivation in learning. For instance, if a student is stuck on an incorrect belief about something, his or her teacher can use the dissonance as motivation to help the student find out the correct fact in order to deal with the psychological discomfort that he or she is feeling (PsycholoGenie, n.d.).

Starting with common assessments, which require teachers to work together on a common task, fosters what the authors call *professional dissonance*. By definition, the content of a *common assessment* is common to all members of a team who teach the same class, course, or grade level; thus, working together to develop a common assessment promotes the kind of collaborative relationships so fundamental to a PLC.

When agreeing on which topics or targets to include on a valid and reliable assessment, teachers begin by articulating what they hope all students will know and be able to do as a result of the class, course, or unit of instruction. Teachers then must identify what they actually taught during the unit. The final step is to compare what teachers actually taught with what the team agreed all students should learn. The answers to this question—What should students learn and what have teachers taught?—do not always align. Reconciling the professional dissonance these different answers cause can enhance teachers' knowledge of both their content and pedagogy.

A Powerful Practical Context

Common assessments also provide a powerful and practical context for teachers to make meaning of their work. Even when teachers agree on what all students should learn and be able

page 1 of 2

to do, standards and learning targets remain abstract and theoretical until teachers translate them into changes in classroom practice. Teachers can return to their classroom and teach what they always have unless there is some concrete way to analyze the degree to which all students in the same class, course, or grade level are able to learn what teachers expect. As Sam Redding (2006) says, the task of creating common assessments provides "an operational definition of the standards in that they [the common assessments] define in measurable terms what teachers should teach and students should learn."

As teams examine their collaboratively developed common assessment data, they inevitably discover some students have learned and others have not. Once teachers gather data about which students did and did not learn, the natural inclination is to reflect on the results of their instruction and ask, "What do we do now?" Teams begin to dialogue about ways to help those students who are not learning. Likewise, teachers will seek out ways to extend and enrich the learning of those students who are proficient.

Begin With Common Assessments

Some might think it impractical to write common assessments before teachers reach consensus on what they expect students to learn. Others might argue it is impossible to target interventions until teachers have evidence of what students did or did not learn. But, as teacher teams work to write a common assessment, they must reconcile any differences teachers have about what all students should learn and what each teacher teaches. Resolving that kind of dissonance among and between teachers is healthy.

Beginning with common assessments also provides a practical context for teachers to make meaning of their work. Teachers might believe they should identify the essential outcomes before designing a common assessment, but, in practice, it is more effective to roll up your sleeves and dig into the work. As teachers approach the task of writing a common assessment, they create an operational definition of the standards.

Engaging in work that requires the resolution of important questions while helping to make meaning of the work is a powerful way to promote the kind of *learning by doing* that can transform a school. The secret to success is simple: teachers can enhance the effectiveness of their collaborative teams by collaboratively developing common assessments.

References

Atherton, J. S. (2009). *Learning and teaching; Cognitive dissonance and learning*. Accessed at www.learningandteaching.info/learning/dissonance.htm on July 29, 2021.

DuFour, R., DuFour, R., Eaker, R., Many, T. W., & Mattos, M. (2016). *Learning by doing: A handbook for Professional Learning Communities at Work*. Bloomington, IN: Solution Tree Press.

PsycholoGenie. (n.d.). *Examples and practical application of cognitive dissonance*. Accessed at https://psychologenie.com/examples-practical-applications-of-cognitive-dissonance on May 21, 2021.

Redding, S. (2006). *The mega system: A handbook for continuous improvement within a community of the school*. Des Plaines, IL: Academic Development Institute. Accessed at http://adi.org/mega on May 21, 2021.

What Does a Balanced and Coherent System of Assessment Look Like?

Section I: Before the Learning

Rationale—Why It Matters

The consensus is clear and conclusive; there is nearly universal agreement that the regular and routine use of common formative and summative assessments promotes higher levels of student learning. The effective use of common assessments represents one of the most effective improvement strategies within the purview of teams.

Outcomes

After completing this module, teachers will appreciate the importance of a balanced *and* coherent assessment system. The term *balanced* means the teams' assessment practices reflect an appropriate balance between formative and summative assessments; *coherent* means teachers have a current and comprehensive understanding of best assessment practice.

SIG and Pathways

SIG prerequisite three (page 240) and the Pathways for Prerequisite Three (3.1–3.5; page 245)

Key Coaching Points

1. An assessment itself is neither formative nor summative; it is what teams do with the results of an assessment that makes it summative or formative. The best teams understand the most appropriate way to use each type of assessment to promote learning.

2. Educators often misunderstand the terms *formative* and *summative*. One form of assessment (formative or summative) is not inherently better than the other, but teams need to understand the differences in use and the effect each type of assessment has on learning.

3. There is a role for both formative and summative assessments; however, teams should make greater use of formative assessments and rely less on summative assessments.

4. Whether an assessment is formative or summative is less important than whether the assessment is common. Developing an assessment as a team promotes collaboration.

Important Vocabulary and Terms

Formative assessment: An assessment *for* learning (Stiggins, 2002) educators use to advance and not merely monitor each student's learning; a formative assessment informs the teacher regarding the effectiveness of his or her instruction and the individual student regarding his or her progress in becoming proficient.

Summative assessment: An assessment *of* learning (Stiggins, 2002) educators use to provide a final measure to determine if each student has met his or her learning goals (Ainsworth & Viegut, 2006). Summative assessments yield a dichotomy: pass or fail, proficient or not proficient. Additional time and support after a summative assessment are typically not forthcoming (DuFour et al., 2016).

Section II: During the Learning

Preparation—Time and Materials

Complete this module in fifty minutes. The ideal group size is four teachers per group seated at tables. Each small group will need a facilitator, timekeeper, recorder, and reporter, plus access to chart paper and markers, and a copy of *Energize Your Teams*. Each participant should have a copy of the following reproducible:

- "A Balanced and Coherent System of Assessment" (page 128)

Step 1: Getting Ready to Learn—Reflection on a Word Activity (Fifteen Minutes)

This warm-up involves three cycles of interaction between participants.

1. Direct participants to find a partner *not* from their table, introduce themselves, and take three minutes to share their understanding of the term *common assessment*. (three minutes)

2. Participants should then switch partners, introduce themselves, and for three minutes share their understanding of the term *formative assessment*. (three minutes)

3. Participants switch partners one final time, introduce themselves, and share their understanding of the term *summative assessment*. (three minutes)

4. When finished, direct participants to return their table and use a T-chart to record their consensus on the characteristics of formative and summative assessments. Post the charts around the room. (six minutes)

Step 2: Interactive Strategy, Protocol, or Activity—Text on Text Protocol (Thirty-Five Minutes)

This protocol will help teams identify and reflect on their assessment practices. To prepare for the activity, paste a copy of the article "A Balanced and Coherent System of Assessment" (page 128) in the center of a piece of chart paper, leaving wide margins. Working in groups of three or four, teachers should position themselves in a U-shape around the article and within reach of the chart paper. Ensure each person has a different colored marker.

1. **Read the article:** Ask the reporter to read the article, "A Balanced and Coherent System of Assessment" aloud while other participants follow along. Once finished, the group *silently* rereads or skims the article as each participant, using his or her colored marker, comments on different words, phrases, or sentences in the margins around the article. This is not time for discussion, however; participants should feel free to comment in writing on what others are writing. (fifteen minutes)

2. **Gallery walk:** Post the charts and conduct a gallery walk. Be sure to take along some sticky notes so you and the participants can leave comments, ask questions, or ask for clarifications on what others have written. (ten minutes)

3. **Share:** Reconvene and talk about what the participants noticed about the way other groups interpreted the article; look for themes or patterns. (five minutes)

Step 3: Personal Reflection (Five Minutes)

Ask teachers to take five minutes before the next team meeting and reflect on the question, "Is our assessment system balanced and coherent?" Teachers should record and retain their comments until the section III debriefing session with a coach.

Section III: After the Learning

Next Steps and Follow-Up for Coaching Teams

The goal is to help the team reflect on the current reality of assessment practice (1) on their team, (2) at their school, and (3) in the district. Each team will need chart paper and three different-colored markers.

1. Divide a sheet of chart paper into four columns lengthwise; label the columns to match the four categories of assessment the article discusses (that is, *Classroom, Common, District Level,* and *External*).

2. Ask participants to identify and write *specific examples* of assessments their team uses to measure student progress through the curriculum in each column. Switch colors and ask the team to do the same thing for assessments teachers use at the school level, and using a third color, identify assessments they use at the district level.

3. Once the process of identifying the various assessments by level is complete, the team should make some observational statements about the system of assessment on the team, at the school, and in the district. Is the system balanced? Is it coherent?

4. Allow teachers the opportunity to talk about what they have learned and if this new knowledge warrants any realignment of resources and priorities. Encourage teachers to reflect on how any changes would impact the way they currently use assessments. Record any comments, questions, and concerns.

5. Refer to the SIG for prerequisite three (page 240) and Pathways for Prerequisite Three (3.1–3.5; page 245)to help the team determine its current reality, identify some possible next steps, and agree on a plan for moving forward.

6. Establish a timeline for teams to implement their plan at the next collaborative team meeting where members will analyze student assessment data.

MODULE

6.2

A Balanced and Coherent System of Assessment

By Thomas W. Many

Adapted from Texas Elementary Principals & Supervisors Association's TEPSA News, *March/April 2010, Vol. 67, No. 2, www.tepsa.org*

> "As we look to the future, we must balance annual, interim or benchmark, and classroom assessment. Only then will we meet the critically important information needs of all instructional decision makers."
>
> —Rick Stiggins

The assessment system a school embraces should reflect a balance of both formative and summative assessments. A second and equally important priority is to ensure teachers understand the purpose of each assessment. Both priorities are essential to create a balanced and coherent assessment system.

Here are four categories of assessment.

1. Classroom assessments (the most formative)
2. Common assessments (more formative)
3. District benchmark assessments (more summative)
4. External assessments (the most summative)

All are valuable, but each serves a distinctly different purpose.

Classroom assessments	Common assessments	District-level assessments	External assessments
Most Formative	More Formative	More Summative	Most Summative

Daily	Weekly	Unit	Monthly	Semester	Annual

Classroom assessments	Common assessments	District-level assessments	External assessments
Ongoing student and teacher formative assessment Diagnostic and prescriptive	Collaboratively developed CFAs Identify students eligible for support in pyramid of interventions	Collaboratively developed DBAs Calibrate and pace the curriculum.	Annual state-mandated summative assessment Ranks and benchmarks Entrance and exit criteria

Source: Kildeer Countryside Community Consolidated School District 96, Buffalo Grove, Illinois.

Four Categories of Assessment

The first category of a balanced and coherent assessment system is *most formative.* Ongoing, daily, sometimes in the moment, these classroom-level assessments align directly with what teachers teach. Sam Redding (2006) describes this first category of *most formative* class-room assessments as "quick diagnostic tests used to prescribe appropriate learning activities for a student or group of students" (p. 87). He elaborates, "These tests may be pencil-and-paper tests, oral quizzes, or 'show-me' assessments that a teacher can quickly and conveniently administer to determine each student's level of mastery of the lesson's objectives" (p. 87).

At the opposite end of the continuum are most summative assessments. The best example of an assessment in the *most summative* category is the once-a-year, high-stakes state exam-inations so prevalent in U.S. public schools. Emeritus professor in the UCLA Graduate School of Education and Information Studies, W. James Popham (2008), observes that, "there is no evidence that these district-developed or state-developed assessments boost student achieve-ment" (p. 10).

Within the category of *most summative* assessment, Redding (2006) includes "state assess-ments and norm-referenced achievement tests that provide an annual assessment of each student's and the school's progress by subject area and grade level" (p. 88). These assessments help individual schools or districts target areas in which groups of students may be under-performing; however, these most summative assessments do not provide information timely enough to assist teachers in making instructional decisions to help individual students learn. Teachers know receiving feedback on student progress only once a year—no matter how valid or reliable—simply is not often enough.

Assessments from the *most formative* and *most summative* categories are common in most schools; it is the interim assessments in the middle two categories of *more formative* and *more summative* that offer teachers and principals the biggest opportunity to impact student learning.

Redding (2006) maintains that teachers should administer more summative assessments in each class, course, or grade level two to four times a year. These periodic benchmark assess-ments "enable teacher teams to see how students are progressing towards mastery of standards that will be included on state assessments" (p. 88). Most important, "the periodic assessments help bring a closer alignment between instruction and annual standards-based assessments" (p. 88). Monitoring student performance on a periodic basis with these *more summative* assess-ments allows teachers to predict which students will be successful with the core curriculum and which will require additional time and support. On a very practical level, the more summative category assessments help calibrate the curriculum and pace of instruction.

While practitioners find periodic data the more summative benchmark assessments generate more useful than the once-a-year autopsy data the most summative assessments generate, the more summative assessments are not generated timely enough to guide a teams' day-to-day instructional decision making. Teachers need more frequent and formative assessments at the building level to effectively monitor student learning.

Using more formative common assessments embedded in the teaching and learning process fills this need. The primary purpose of these common assessments is to provide teachers with frequent information about student learning. Redding (2006) describes these more formative assessments as "learning activities aligned to objectives with criteria for mastery which enable a teacher to check mastery within the context of instruction" (p. 87). Redding (2006) contin-ues, "by completing these assigned activities, students demonstrate a level of mastery of the objectives the activities are designed to teach or to reinforce" (p. 87).

Teams of teachers design more formative common assessments at the building level, which provides them greatest leverage because these assessments so closely link to what the teachers are teaching in the classroom. These assessments generate timely results that allow

page 2 of 3

teachers to adjust the sequence of instruction. As educator, author, and speaker Carol Ann Tomlinson (2007) reports, "Assessments that came at the end of a unit—although important manifestations of student knowledge, understanding, and skill—were less useful to me as a teacher than were assessments that occurred during a unit of study."

It is clear that for teachers to be successful, they need information about student learning from a variety of sources. PLC at Work architects Richard DuFour, Rebecca DuFour, Robert Eaker, Thomas W. Many, and Mike Mattos (2016) caution that relying on any one model of assessment is a seriously flawed assessment strategy. Balanced assessment systems must include both summative and formative assessments.

Formative and summative assessments are not in and of themselves inherently better or worse than the other. What is important is that teachers understand the purpose of each assessment they use in their classroom. As Tomlinson (2007) observes, "The greatest power of assessment information lies in its capacity to help me [the teacher] see how to become a better teacher."

References

DuFour, R., DuFour, R., Eaker, R., Many, T. W., & Mattos, M. (2016). *Learning by doing: A handbook for Professional Learning Communities at Work* (3rd ed.). Bloomington, IN: Solution Tree Press.

Popham, W. J. (2008). *Transformative assessment*. Alexandria, VA: Association for Supervision and Curriculum Development.

Redding, S. (2006). *The mega system—Deciding. Learning. Connecting: A handbook for continuous improvement within a community of the school*. Lincoln, IL: Academic Development Institute. Accessed at http://adi.org/mega on March 21, 2021.

Stiggins, R. (2007). Five assessment myths and their consequences. *Education Week, 27*(8), 28–29.

Tomlinson, C. A. (2007/2008). Learning to love assessment. *Educational Leadership, 65*(4), 8–13. Accessed at www.ascd.org/publications/educational-leadership/dec07/vol65/num04/Learning-to-Love-Assessment.aspx on March 21, 2021.

How Do We Design Valid and Reliable Assessments?

Section I: Before the Learning

Rationale—Why It Matters

Teachers have been writing assessments in the form of classroom quizzes and tests for generations, yet many teachers feel they lack the expertise necessary to write valid and reliable common assessments; this simply is not true. When teams engage in the process of authoring assessments, they deepen their content knowledge, sharpen their pedagogy, and generate more confidence in and ownership of the results. More important, teams are better able to ensure the assessment aligns with the content and the context of their classroom. With proper training and opportunities for practice, teams produce valid and reliable assessments often more beneficial than commercially developed assessments.

Outcomes

This module introduces teams to a process they can use to design valid and reliable common assessments. The goal of this module is to encourage teacher teams to create and use locally developed common formative and summative assessments more frequently.

SIG and Pathways

SIG prerequisite three (page 240) and the Pathways for Prerequisite Three (3.4; page 245)

Key Coaching Points

1. Designing common assessments is not a burden, nor is it a task that an external, third party could better perform. In fact, creating common assessments is one of the best ways to provide teams with ongoing, job-embedded professional development.

2. Benefits of authoring common assessments at the team level include a deeper understanding of what students should know and be able to do, greater clarity around instructional strategies, better alignment of assessment and instruction, more timely and reliable data for designing interventions, and more ownership of the results of the assessment itself, all of which support the four critical questions of a PLC.

3. Locally developing common assessments also provides teams with a concrete task that promotes collaboration and creates the context for collective inquiry, continuous improvement, and reflection on the four critical questions of a PLC.

Important Vocabulary and Terms

Validity: Understand validity by responding affirmatively to the following questions: "Does the assessment measure what I want it to measure? Does it measure what I taught? Will it tell me whether or not the students learned the material I expected them to learn?"

Reliability: Answer the question of reliability by responding to the following questions: "Can I rely on the data to make decisions about what to do next for my students? Do the data tell me with confidence whether a student is ready to move on or if he or she needs more time and support?"

Depth of Knowledge (DOK): Sometimes educators refer to this as *rigor* or *cognitive demand*. Teachers use this system to determine the kind and level of thinking they require students to successfully engage with and solve a task. It is the way students interact with content.

Section II: During the Learning

Preparation—Time and Materials

Complete this module in an hour or split the session into two separate professional development opportunities. The ideal group size is four participants per group seated at tables. Each group should select roles (facilitator, timekeeper, recorder, and reporter). Groups will need chart paper and markers, and each participant will need copies of the following handouts.

- "Four Steps to Creating Valid and Reliable Common Assessments" (page 135)
- "Evaluating the Quality of an Assessment" (page 137)

Step 1: Getting Ready to Learn—ABC Conversations Activity (Twenty Minutes)

This warm-up activity consists of three rounds of interviews. Direct participants to form triads with others *not* from their table, introduce themselves, and choose a letter (*A*, *B*, or *C*). Person *A* is the questioner, person *B* is the respondent, and person *C* is the recorder. The roles rotate after each round so everyone will have an opportunity to fill all of the roles. Each triad will need access to their own markers and chart paper.

- **Round one:** Person *A* asks Person *B* the following questions while Person *C* takes notes. "What does it mean when an assessment is *valid*? What does it mean when an assessment is *reliable*? How do you know whether an assessment is valid and reliable?" (four minutes)

- **Round two:** Rotate roles and repeat the process with the following questions: "What are the advantages and disadvantages of using commercially developed assessments? What are the advantages and disadvantages of teams authoring their own assessments?" (four minutes)

- **Round three:** Rotate roles one last time and ask participants, "On a scale of 1 to 5, how confident are you and your colleagues in their ability to write valid and reliable common assessments? What barriers must teams overcome to develop and use common formative and summative assessments on a regular basis?" (four minutes)

- **Round four:** Have triads post their comments on chart paper and direct everyone to engage in a quick gallery walk to look for patterns. (five minutes)

- **Round five:** This warm-up activity ends with the large group sharing at least three patterns or commonalities they see for each of the three rounds of ABC. (eight minutes)

Step 2: Interactive Strategy, Protocol, or Activity—Scavenger Hunt (Thirty-Five Minutes)

Ask participants to form "search parties" of three people. Share the directions aloud, explaining: "This is a three-part protocol. You will be reading the reproducible titled 'Four Steps to Creating Valid and Reliable Common Assessments.' As you read, look for specific information related to a series of tasks or look-fors (see the list of tasks or look-fors that follows). Once you find supporting evidence, underline or highlight the section and number it so you can refer to it later." You may choose to create a two-column T-chart on chart paper listing tasks in the left-hand column with space for the support "search parties" find in the right-hand column.

1. Read "Four Steps to Creating Valid and Reliable Common Assessments." (six minutes)

2. Search the text for the following. (fifteen minutes)

    a. Look for a working definition of *validity* and *reliability*.

    b. Find at least two examples of how teachers use common assessment data.

    c. Identify the first step of the process of developing valid and reliable common assessments.

    d. How many learning targets should teams include on an assessment?

    e. Find at least two reasons why determining DOK levels is important.

    f. Pinpoint at least two factors that influence the selection of item types.

    g. Find where the author explains why designing a test plan or blueprint is important.

    h. Look for at least one recommendation for teams to consider.

    i. Isolate any tips teams should consider when designing common assessments.

3. Using a round-robin approach, ask different "search parties" to identify a task, share what support they find for the task or look-for, and explain why they chose it. If time allows, other "search parties" may also share a different passage to support the task. (ten minutes)

4. Collect and compile the list of tasks or look-fors and corresponding support as a reference tool for teams. (four minutes)

Step 3: Personal Reflection (Five Minutes)

Ask each participant to take five minutes before the next team meeting to reflect on what he or she learned and answer three questions: "What caused me to rethink my practice? What part confused me? What part concerned me?" Ask each person to record and retain their thoughts until the section III debrief with a coach.

Section III: After the Learning

Next Steps and Follow-Up for Coaching Teams

1. Ask participants if they have attempted to design and deliver a common assessment. For those who have, what was their consensus of the experience? For those who have not, what barriers are preventing them from doing so?

2. Ask each member of the team to bring a common assessment they used in their classroom during the previous few weeks. It can be an assessment they created themselves, one the team created, or one commercially available from an external source. Using "Evaluating the Quality of an Assessment" (page 137), ask teachers to talk about how the assessment aligns with the recommendations on the tool. Would they consider the assessment both valid and reliable? If not, what should they adjust? Encourage teachers to reflect on how any new insights will impact the way they currently use assessments. Record the group's comments, questions, and concerns.

3. Refer to the SIG for prerequisite three (page 240) and the Pathways for Prerequisite Three (3.1–3.5; page 245) to help the team determine its current reality, identify some possible next steps, and agree on a plan for moving forward.

4. Establish a timeline for the team to implement its plan at the next collaborative team meeting where members will analyze student assessment data.

Four Steps to Creating Valid and Reliable Common Assessments

By Thomas W. Many

Adapted from Texas Elementary Principals & Supervisors Association's TEPSA Leader, *Spring 2021, Vol. 34, No. 2, www.tepsa.org*

How many times have you heard colleagues ask in exasperation, "How am I supposed to write assessments that are valid and reliable? I'm not an assessment expert!"

Many teachers feel they lack the time and expertise they need to develop high-quality assessments. Instead, they often rely on publisher-created assessment items that rob them of one of the best job-embedded professional development opportunities available: authoring their own locally developed common assessments.

> "But when our purpose is a quick determination of the extent to which students understands skills and concepts, and the equally important purpose of adjusting teaching strategies to help students who have not yet mastered those skills and concepts, then practical utility takes precedence over psychometric perfection."
>
> —Douglas Reeves

Best practice calls for teacher teams to use common assessments as a tool to understand how students are progressing through the curriculum. This process transforms the classroom from a place where teachers "teach, test, and hope for the best" to one where teams constantly ask the question, "What did our students learn as a result of our teaching?" Working together, teachers use assessment results to improve instruction and help students deepen their understanding—all of which lead to higher levels of student learning.

How do teachers create these common assessments? Following are four intentional steps teams can take to create valid and reliable assessments (Bailey & Jakicic, 2012).

1. Identify the target or targets to assess.

The first step in developing any assessment is to determine what teachers want to measure. If teachers want to learn about students' learning, it is crucial that the assessment aligns with instruction; this is what makes assessments *valid*. Teacher teams identify the priority standards in a particular unit and create common assessments that specifically measure learning targets derived from those priority standards. Assessment experts and educational consultants Kim Bailey and Chris Jakicic (2012) recommend teachers choose no more than three or four learning targets for each common assessment so they can quickly intervene and correct specific student misconceptions.

2. Determine the level of rigor or depth of knowledge (DOK).

When teachers identify priority standards, they come to consensus on the level of rigor or cognitive demand they expect students to obtain for proficiency. This allows teams to guarantee all students will receive the same level of instruction and consistent teacher expectations across a class, course, or grade level. When developing a common assessment, teams intentionally create items at the DOK levels the teams identify.

When deciding on DOK levels for each target, teams should consider including multiple items at differing levels. If teachers expect proficiency at DOK 3, certainly include items at DOK 3. However, including items on the same target at DOK levels 1 or 2 may help teachers diagnose where student misunderstandings exist.

page 1 of 2

3. Decide on item types and number of items.

The specific learning target and the team-identified DOK levels for proficiency are instrumental in deciding on an appropriate assessment-item type. For example, selected-response items (multiple choice, true/false, matching) are well suited for DOK levels 1 and 2 (recall and basic skills). However, to accurately assess learning targets at DOK 3 (strategic thinking and reasoning), it is more appropriate to design short-answer or constructed-response items.

There are occasions when multiple choice is the most logical item type to use on a common assessment. In these cases, it is important for teams to keep in mind the power of incorrect responses. Teacher teams can anticipate common mistakes and intentionally create distractor choices that reveal specific student misunderstandings. These items are not intended to trick students, but to uncover misunderstandings so teachers can intervene and correct those mistakes.

In addition, teams must decide on the number of items for each learning target, which leads to test *reliability*. If teams include one selected-response item for a learning target, a student may guess the correct answer. In that case, teachers would not truly know whether the student has mastered the target. On the other hand, if teams include three selected-response items on the same target, they can more confidently assess the student's proficiency level.

4. Consider logistics.

The last step focuses on logistical considerations, with questions like, How long will it take students to complete the test? How will we score the test, What academic vocabulary will we use? How will we clarity the directions? Teams who are intentional about logistics from the beginning find more reliable results in the end.

> "A team should learn something every time they write an assessment—learn how other teammates teach the target, learn what proficiency looks like, learn misconceptions students might have, learn how to write good questions."
>
> —Kim Bailey and Chris Jakicic

The ultimate purpose of common assessments is for teachers to learn about their students' learning. Teacher teams can achieve this goal by creating valid and reliable common assessments and using results to adjust instruction and correct student misconceptions. By engaging in these practices, teachers improve their instruction, students deepen their learning, and schools increase the likelihood that students will be successful overall.

References

Bailey, K., & Jakicic, C. (2012). *Common formative assessment: A toolkit for Professional Learning Communities at Work*. Bloomington, IN: Solution Tree Press.

Bailey, K., & Jakicic, C. (2018). *Make it happen: Coaching with the four critical questions of PLCs at Work*. Bloomington, IN: Solution Tree Press.

Reeves, D. (Ed.). (2007). *Ahead of the curve: The power of assessment to transform teaching and learning*. Bloomington IN: Solution Tree Press.

Evaluating the Quality of an Assessment

	Assessment Planning	Item Planning
Is it valid?	1. We identified specific learning targets. 2. We determined the level of rigor for each target. 3. We matched the assessment to the identified level of thinking.	1. The assessment items match the cognitive demand of the learning target. 2. Students know which items match each learning target.
Is it reliable?	1. We used a sufficient number of questions to ensure reliability (four multiple choice, one well-written constructed-response or performance assessment). 2. The team agrees with the way proficiency has been determined and how the items will be scored.	1. The reading level of the questions won't interfere with the assessment. 2. There are no giveaways in selected-response items. 3. There are no ambiguous answers in selected-response items. 4. There is a context, when appropriate, for constructed-response items.

Source for tool: Bailey, K., & Jakicic, C. (2012). Common formative assessment: A toolkit for Professional Learning Communities at Work *(p. 106). Bloomington, IN: Solution Tree Press.*

Sources: Gareis, C. R., & Grant, L. W. (2008). *Teacher-made assessments: How to connect curriculum, instruction, and student learning.* Larchmont, NY: Eye on Education; Stiggins, R. J., Arter, J. A., Chappuis, J., & Chappuis, S. (2004). *Classroom assessment* for *student learning: Doing it right—Using it well.* Portland, OR: Assessment Training Institute.

How Do We Use the Power of Distractors to Improve Student Learning?

Section I: Before the Learning

Rationale—Why It Matters

Many teacher teams analyze common assessment data in a cursory, superficial, or general way, which often provides only basic information, not the many details about students' learning. However, when teachers design distractors in ways that intentionally reveal student mistakes and misunderstandings, teams can better use the results to improve teaching and learning.

Outcomes

The purpose of this module is to help teachers understand the importance of distractors in selected-response items. By providing teams with specific steps for item creation and time to practice these skills, teachers can use this information to create better common assessments.

SIG and Pathways

SIG prerequisite three (page 240) and the Pathways for Prerequisite Three (3.2, page 245)

Key Coaching Points

1. Emphasize that team-created common assessments are a powerful tool for identifying students who need more time and support, students who are ready for extension, issues with curriculum, and the effectiveness of instructional strategies.

2. Selected response is only one of many ways to assess student learning. When teams use selected response, it is important to ensure each item aligns with a learning target.

3. Teams gain valuable information about their students' thinking when they analyze assessment results by item and use the data to improve instructional practice and student learning.

4. Developing valid and reliable assessments is a skill that takes time and practice. Teams collaboratively building common assessments will continue to improve with coaching.

Important Vocabulary and Terms

Assessment: "Methods or tools educators use to evaluate, measure, and document the academic readiness, learning progress, skill acquisition, or educational needs of students" (Contemporary Educational Psychology, 2014)

Selected response: "Students choose a response provided by the teacher or test developer, rather than construct one in their own words or by their own actions" (Glossary of Education Reform, 2014).

Distractor: "The incorrect answers . . . [that] typically represent common errors that are equally plausible only to students who have not attained the level of knowledge or understanding necessary to recognize . . . the correct answer" (King, Gardner, Zucker, & Jorgensen, 2004, p. 3)

Section II: During the Learning

Preparation—Time and Materials

Complete this module in one sixty-minute session or split into two separate professional development opportunities. The ideal group size is four to six participants per group seated at tables with their grade level- or content-area colleagues. Each group should select a facilitator, timekeeper, recorder, and reporter. Place an easel with chart paper and markers at the front of the room. Each participant will need a piece of chart paper, markers, and a copy of the following handout.

- "The Power of Distractors" (page 141)

Step 1: Getting Ready to Learn—Assessment Training Poll (Ten Minutes)

Using a round-robin approach, ask each teacher to tell the group how many university classes focused on assessment design he or she has taken. As teachers give their number, write it down on the chart paper at the front of the room. When everyone has given an answer, add up the number and divide it by the number of participants to arrive at the average. Most likely, this will be a very low number, illustrating that most teachers do not receive training on how to create common assessments. Teams need to keep a growth mindset as they learn together.

Step 2: Interactive Strategy, Protocol, or Activity: Practice Distractors (Fifty Minutes)

1. **Read the article:** Ask participants to read the article "The Power of Distractors" (page 141) and highlight three to five key points that resonate as they read. (six minutes)

2. **Discuss:** When teachers finish reading, allow them five minutes to discuss the key points each highlighted in the article with their colleagues. (five minutes)

3. **Practice:** Let teachers know that they will be practicing a process for creating a multiple-choice assessment item similar to those the article describes. Provide each team with chart paper and markers to record their question, the correct answer, and possible distractors. (two minutes)

4. **Study:** Provide teams with a standard, a multiple-choice question that aligns with the standard, and the correct answer. We suggest all staff use the same standard and question at the beginning so teams can compare their distractors with those of other groups. (two minutes)

5. **Create distractors:** Direct teams to write the question at the top of their paper, then create a two-column chart underneath. In the left-hand column, teams identify the misunderstandings or mistakes students typically make in answering the question.

In the right-hand column, the team creates distractors that reveal mistakes or misunderstanding. (fifteen minutes)

6. **Gallery walk:** Ask teams to post their charts around the room and conduct a brief gallery walk when teams can compare their colleagues' work to their own. (ten minutes)

7. **Share:** Ask volunteers to share what they learned from the experience and how it might impact their team's creation of common assessments. (five minutes)

Step 3: Personal Reflection (Five Minutes)

Before the next team meeting, participants should answer the following questions and record their thoughts about creating distractors that reveal information about student learning: "Did anything in this module make you reconsider how your school or team approaches this topic? What questions are you still wrestling with, and what do you want to learn more about?" Teachers should retain their personal reflections until the section III debrief with a coach.

Section III: After the Learning

Next Steps and Follow-Up for Coaching Teams

The goal is to help teams identify their current reality regarding the development of high-quality distractors for any selected-response items they might use on common assessments. Possible questions or tasks for the team to consider might include the following.

1. Start by asking teams to review a past assessment they created. Go through the test item by item. What does each distractor reveal about students' thinking? How could teams revise the distractors or assessment as a whole to give them better information?

2. Assist teams as they create a new assessment that includes selected-response items. Ensure each item aligns with a learning target, is at the appropriate DOK level, and includes distractors to reveal typical student misunderstandings or mistakes.

3. Ask the team to set a goal for revising or creating an assessment with selected-response items and intentional distractors. Establish a timeline for the team to implement their plan and check on progress at the beginning of the next team meeting.

The Power of Distractors

By Tesha Ferriby Thomas

Adapted from Texas Elementary Principals & Supervisors Association's TEPSA News, *May/June 2016, Vol. 78, No. 3, www.tepsa.org*

"Assessment is, indeed, the bridge between teaching and learning."

—Dylan Wiliam

Consider for a moment how many of your university classes focused on developing student assessments. In most cases, the answer is *none* or *one* at most. Yet accurately assessing student learning is one of your most important responsibilities as a teacher. When teachers design them intentionally, assessments not only give an accurate measure of student proficiency but also provide teachers with important information on how to adjust instruction and provide students with much-needed intervention.

Coauthors Rick Stiggins and Richard DuFour (2009) make the case that common assessments are an extremely powerful method of promoting student achievement because "teachers can pool their collective wisdom in making sound instructional decisions based on results" (p. 643). However, the results Stiggins and DuFour (2009) are referring to involve more than the percentage of students scoring proficient. Through detailed analysis of correct and incorrect answers (distractors), teams can learn a tremendous amount about students' learning.

Distractors allow teachers to "follow up with additional instruction based on the most common sorts of errors made by an individual student or group of students" (Popham, 2000, p. 244).

Ensure Reliability

Before teachers can analyze the assessment results, they must develop a valid and reliable assessment. While teachers typically spend most of their time and energy crafting rigorous questions and identifying correct answers, developing the wrong answers (distractors) is just as important. Reflecting on distractors allows teachers to think deeply about their expectations of the learning targets within the standard, the possible misunderstandings students might have about the target, and the typical mistakes students could make when applying the concept. When creating multiple-choice items or matching assessment items, effective teacher teams engage in the following steps for each item. To ensure reliability, three to four items should represent each learning target.

1. Identify the specific learning target the item will assess.

2. Craft a question that aligns with the target at the appropriate level of rigor (DOK). This contributes to more valid and reliable assessments.

3. Compose the correct answer.

4. List common mistakes students typically make when answering the question.

5. Brainstorm plausible misunderstandings students might have about the target.

6. Based on what the team decides, create separate distractors to represent the possible mistakes and misunderstandings students may have about the target.

When teams anticipate student mistakes and misunderstandings, teachers can design assessment items that help their teams learn about their students' learning. "Based on the results from distractor analysis, instructors can identify the content areas that need instructional improvement and provide students with remedial instruction in those content areas"

(Gierl, Bulut, Guo, & Zhang , 2017, p. 1086). Teacher teams that analyze results of thoughtfully created assessments are rewarded with powerful information about student needs.

Analyze Trends

Effective teams access this information by analyzing results by item, paying special attention to how many students chose each distractor. They look for patterns and trends that indicate group misunderstandings, which sometimes indicate problems with curriculum or instructional strategies. In other cases, they simply reflect a miscommunication. Either way, teachers can use the patterns distractors identify to make impactful instructional choices for the class as a whole.

Diagnose Specific Student Needs

In addition to studying overall patterns and trends in the distractors students chose, highly effective collaborative teams analyze data by target, teacher, and individual student need. Distractors can be instrumental in diagnosing specific student misunderstandings and creating intervention groups based on those data. "Distractor analysis can help test developers and instructors understand why students produce errors and thereby guide our diagnostic inferences about test performance" (Gierl et al., 2017, p. 1085). Let's take a look at a real-world example.

If a team wants to measure whether students can identify the central idea of a text, members might create an item that directs students to read a short piece of text, and then choose the answer that best depicts its central idea, which educators label *distractor A*. When creating distractors, the team recognizes students often confuse supporting details with the main idea. To help the team understand which students are making this mistake (supporting details versus main idea), members create an answer that focuses on specific details rather than the overall central idea—*distractor B*. The team also realizes some students may need assistance in general comprehension. To help identify those students, the team develops *distractor C*, which provides a central idea opposite of the correct answer. Of course, one answered question does not reliably tell teams whether a student has mastered a target; teams should ideally create three or four items on the same target to accurately obtain that information.

To carry this example further, the team may then identify all students who chose *distractor B* and provide additional time and support on the differences between a main idea and supporting details. The team may also group together students who chose *distractor C* so they can spend more time closely reading text, using strategies that help them identify the author's purpose, and uncover the main idea. In both cases, the team analyzes the data by individual student and responds by providing students with additional time and support to meet their specific learning needs. Educators often refer to this process as *analyzing data by name and need*. Again, this example depicts the analysis of just one question. Teams will ideally analyze all three or four items on the same target to determine if students are routinely confusing supporting details with the main idea or consistently struggling with comprehension.

"The patterns in a student's incorrect responses to items can provide powerful, valuable information to guide instruction."

—Kelly V. King, Doug A. Gardner, Sasha Zucker, and Margaret A. Jorgensen

---

Although creating valid and reliable assessments can be intimidating, teacher teams really need to take a *just do it* approach. The first step is to avoid overfocusing on question stems and correct answers and begin paying close attention to the power of distractors. By designing specific distractor items that reveal information about students' learning, teachers can provide students with additional time and support on the learning targets where they need it most. Even though university classes may not have adequately trained educators to create assessments that provide valuable information about students' learning, it is never too late to learn!

page 2 of 3

References

Gierl, M. J., Bulut, O., Guo, Q., & Zhang, X. (2017). Developing, analyzing, and using distractors for multiple-choice tests in education: A comprehensive review. *Review of Educational Research, 87*(6), 1082–1116.

King, K. V., Gardner, D. A., Zucker, S., & Jorgensen, M. A. (2004). *The distractor rationale taxonomy: Enhancing multiple-choice items in reading and mathematics.* San Antonio, TX: Pearson.

Popham, W. J. (2000). *Modern educational measurement: Practical guidelines for educational leaders* (3rd ed.). Boston: Pearson.

Stiggins, R., & DuFour, R. (2009). Maximizing the power of formative assessments. *Phi Delta Kappan, 90*(9), 640–644.

Wiliam, D. (2018). *Embedded formative assessment* (2nd ed.). Bloomington, IN: Solution Tree Press.

What Is the Purpose of Preassessments?

Section I: Before the Learning

Rationale—Why It Matters

It's not surprising that the majority of teachers feel preassessments are a waste of time; since they have provided no instruction, teachers are fairly confident most students will fail the preassessment. Traditionally, students take a preassessment prior to the beginning of a lesson or unit and the results provide teachers with a list of topics students already know; however, that simply is not enough.

To meet the needs of students, teachers also need to understand students' levels of prior knowledge, prerequisite skills, and academic language.

Outcomes

Teachers will understand the information typical preassessment provides is inadequate. By shifting the scope and purpose of preassessments, teachers obtain information they can use to maximize the effectiveness of their instruction.

SIG and Pathways

SIG prerequisite three (page 240) and the Pathways for Prerequisite Three (3.3; page 245)

Key Coaching Points

1. A preassessment can be a valuable tool to inform teachers' instructional practice, but most teachers are reluctant to use preassessments because they provide little useful information about a student's readiness to learn.

2. To maximize the effectiveness of instruction, preassessments should inform teachers about the level of a student's prior knowledge, mastery of prerequisite skills, and understanding of relevant academic language and terminology.

Important Vocabulary and Terms

Academic language: This is the general or course-specific language (words, phrases, and terminology) students must understand to fully access a teacher's lesson or instructional strategy.

Preassessment: Typically taken prior to the start of instruction, teachers use a preassessment to ascertain the knowledge, skills, and dispositions students already know about a particular lesson or unit of study.

Prerequisite skills: These are the skills students have already learned that teachers can leverage to promote the learning of new information. Educators also refer to these skills as *readiness to learn skills* or *readiness for the next level of learning skills*.

Prior knowledge: This is the knowledge students have already learned that teachers can leverage to promote the learning of new information.

Section II: During the Learning

Preparation—Time and Materials

Complete this module in an hour. The ideal group size is four participants seated at tables. Participants will also need room to mingle and move around. Each group should choose a facilitator, timekeeper, recorder, and reporter, who will need access to chart paper and markers. Each teacher will need a copy of the following handout.

- "Shifting the Purpose of Preassessments: Providing Evidence to Inform Instructional Practice" (page 147)

Step 1: Getting Ready to Learn—Round the Room and Back Activity (15 Minutes)

1. Ask each participant to take out a sheet of paper and write at least one important characteristic of a preassessment; what he or she writes can be either positive, negative, or neutral. (two minutes)

2. Next, direct the participants to set aside their written materials, stand up, and quickly move around the room, verbally sharing the characteristic of preassessments they thought was important with as many colleagues as possible. It is important that the person in charge of the training keep everyone moving and maintain a high level of energy. (three minutes)

3. Now, ask participants to return to their seats and write down as many characteristics or examples as they can remember. (four minutes)

4. Finally, ask each small group to pool their lists of characteristics, capture them on chart paper, and post their lists. If time allows, have the reporters report out a summary of their lists. (six minutes)

Step 2: Interactive Strategy, Protocol, or Activity—Outside In Activity (Forty Minutes)

Begin this activity by placing a sheet of chart paper on each table. Request participants form triads or quads. Each member of the small group must be within easy reach of one corner of the chart paper. Give each participant a different colored marker and have the recorder draw a circle the size of a large pizza on the paper, leaving plenty of blank space around the outside of the circle. (three minutes)

1. **Write and comment:** Direct everyone to work silently and independently and write as much as possible about preassessments. Teachers can write their thoughts, ideas, or feelings about preassessment anywhere on the chart paper as long as it is *outside* the circle. There are no rules limiting what participants can write; it can be what they know, what they feel, what they have seen or personally experienced, or even what they might aspire for themselves or their students. Participants may also comment on what others write. The key is that everyone must keep writing about preassessments without talking to others in the group. (five minutes)

2. **Read the article:** Ask participants to read the article, "Shifting the Purpose of Preassessments" (page 147) and highlight any parts (positive or negative) that resonate. While reading, participants may add information to what they already wrote on the chart paper as long as they write any new ideas, insights, or information *outside* the circle. (seven minutes)

3. **Reach consensus:** Ask each group to reach consensus on five things about preassessments everyone supports. The recorder should write the five agreements *inside* the circle. (five minutes)

4. **Share:** Have the reporter share the five group agreements and explain why. After answering questions, the reporter should post the chart on the wall. (ten minutes)

5. **Summarize:** Summarize the activity and determine if there are any patterns in the answers. (five minutes)

Step 3: Personal Reflection (Five Minutes)

Ask each participant to take five minutes before the next team meeting to think about any ideas, insights, or information that affirms his or her thinking, challenges his or her thinking, or motivates him or her to consider a change in practice. Have participants record and retain their thoughts until the section III debrief with a coach.

Section III: After the Learning

Next Steps and Follow-Up for Coaching Teams

1. The goal is for teams to create a preassessment that aligns with the criteria the article describes. Begin by identifying the learning targets for an upcoming unit; then reach consensus on what teams expect students to know and be able to do. The team also identifies the prior knowledge, prerequisite skills, and academic language students will need to be successful. Next, the team decides how to assess the information and designs a preassessment that aligns with the criteria the article describes.

2. Refer to the SIG for prerequisite three (page 240) and the pathways tool (page 245) to help the team determine its current reality, identify some possible next steps, and agree on a plan for moving forward.

3. Establish a timeline to administer the preassessment and agree on a date when the team will discuss what they learned and whether it changed anything about the criteria from the training.

4. Establish a timeline for the team to implement its plan at the next collaborative team meeting where members will analyze student assessment data.

Shifting the Purpose of Preassessments: Providing Evidence to Inform Instructional Practice

By Thomas W. Many

Adapted from Texas Elementary Principals & Supervisors Association's TEPSA News, *March/April 2016, Vol. 73, No. 2, www.tepsa.org*

"A pre-assessment is not a wide-spread practice among teachers even though the benefits it allows to the students, as well as teachers, are phenomenal."

—English Teaching 101

Ask any group of teachers what they think about preassessments, and you will likely get a variety of responses. Thomas Guskey (2018) does an excellent job of articulating both sides of the argument; he reports that "advocates claim preassessments provide essential data about the knowledge, skills, and dispositions students bring to the learning tasks. Critics contend, however, that most preassessments only confirm what teachers already know: Students don't know what they haven't yet been taught" (p. 52). A traditional preassessment consists of a handful of tasks—usually problems, prompts, or activities similar to those students will engage in during the unit—students respond to before instruction begins. The purpose of a preassessment is to determine what students know before the teacher teaches a unit, but according to Byrd (n.d.), a teacher's preassessment should do more than separate the class into two groups: mastery and nonmastery. It should also inform your lessons.

Instead of calling them preassessments, teacher teams should think of them as a way to check how ready students are to learn. Looking at preassessments as readiness checks shifts the purpose of preassessments from the narrow goal of identifying what students know and don't know to the broader goal of informing instructional practice, assessing a student's readiness to learn, and identifying which aspects of the new material students have already mastered.

Reveal Gaps in Learning

Done well, preassessments will certainly identify what students already know about the upcoming unit of instruction, but they can also detect any gaps in a student's prior knowledge, guide the creation of flexible groups, and provide insight into the most effective teaching strategies, methods, and materials to help the student learn. Preassessments can be a terrific way for teachers to gather more information about the learners in the classroom.

Guide Students

Preassessments can also be beneficial to students. A well-designed preassessment can give students a preview of the content the teacher will cover in the upcoming unit. It can also help students understand what they need to learn, where they currently are in the learning progression, and what they need to do to close the gap between where they are and where they need to be.

Show Prerequisite Learning

A preassessment teachers design to inform their instructional practice would check on students' prerequisite skills acquisition; teachers need to know their students are ready to learn. For students, perhaps the only thing more frustrating than sitting through lessons based on content they have already mastered would be sitting through lessons where teachers expect them to learn new material when the students lack the prerequisite knowledge, skills, and dispositions to be successful.

Students' readiness to learn is compromised when they have gaps or holes in their prior knowledge, misconceptions around important concepts, or simply lack the prerequisite skills necessary to master new material. Preassessments give teachers important information about students' readiness to learn while providing opportunities to reteach the missing skills before beginning to teach.

Assess Knowledge of Academic Language

A preassessment with a more comprehensive purpose would also verify students have a solid grasp of important vocabulary and key terminology. Teachers need to know whether students are able to access the academic language necessary to be successful in the upcoming unit.

For example, the fourth-grade curriculum requires students to identify, add, and subtract equivalent fractions, thus to be successful, fourth-grade students must understand the meaning of *equivalent*. It's rare, however, to hear students ask for an "equivalent turn" in a four square game during recess! Likewise, asking middle or high school students to demonstrate voice in their writing requires students to understand the nuanced definition of *voice* as a literary term. If a solid grasp of the academic language necessary for success in the upcoming unit is lacking, students will struggle with new material.

Inform Teacher Practice

Finally, if the goal of a preassessment shifts from identifying a student's level of mastery to one of informing teachers' practice, teachers need to know more than just who is and isn't proficient. Teachers also must know who is proficient on which aspects of the new material. Using preassessments for this purpose requires teachers to go beyond averages and look at each student's performance on each individual learning target. Once teachers identify the most essential learning targets for a unit, they can use preassessment results to understand what aspects of the upcoming unit they need to emphasize when teaching.

Rather than announcing that only two students are proficient, teams using preassessments to inform their practice might engage in a conversation that goes something like this: "Even though two students demonstrated proficiency on the preassessment, no one got all the questions right and everyone missed questions one and three. Were there any patterns in the students' mistakes? Why did the students struggle with these particular concepts?" Having this kind of conversation about preassessment results provides valuable insight into how to teach the upcoming unit.

"The usefulness of pre-assessments depends on their purpose, form, and utility. They can guide teachers to more effective instruction, but they can also be a waste of valuable instructional time."

—Thomas Guskey and Jay McTighe

Guskey (2018) confirms that, "Among educational experts, the value of pre-assessments is a matter of some debate." While preassessments will certainly identify those students who have and have not already mastered the content, if the goal of a preassessment is to inform a teacher's instructional practice, there should be other priorities as well. Teams would design their preassessments to check a student's readiness to learn, verify a student's understanding of important academic language, and identify which aspects of the unit the student needs more time and attention to learn.

References

Byrd, I. (n.d.). *Six traits of quality pre-assessments*. Accessed at www.byrdseed.com/six-traits -of-quality-pre-assessments on January 26, 2021.

English Teaching 101. (n.d.). *3 reasons why pre-assessment is important.* Accessed at https:// englishteaching101.com/3-reasons-why-pre-assessment-is-important on May 21, 2021.

Guskey, T. (2018). Does pre-assessment work? *Educational Leadership, 75*(5), 52–57.

Guskey, T., & McTighe, J. (2016). Pre-assessment: Promises and cautions. *Educational Leadership, 73*(7), 38–43.

CHAPTER 7

Productive Data Conversations

> **Prerequisite four:** *Educators use the results of common assessments to improve individual practice, build the team's capacity to achieve its goals, and intervene and enrich on behalf of students (DuFour & Reeves, 2016).*

Data conversations occur when "one or more teammates [work] together to unpack what data means and decide what to do about it" (Bialis-White, 2016). These meetings are where teachers turn data into information they can use to improve teaching and learning. This chapter provides teacher teams with the rationale for *why* data conversations are important, describes *what* conditions leaders must consider to ensure data conversations are productive, and suggests *how* coaches can engage teams in effective and efficient data conversations.

There are two reasons why collaborative teams engage in data conversations. The first is to identify which students are and are not proficient—it's like looking through a window at student achievement. The second is to improve teachers' instructional methods; this is analogous to a teacher looking in a mirror to observe his or her professional practice. These meetings are the building blocks of a process to identify which students will require additional time and support to be successful. Using data to determine which students are and are not proficient on essential outcomes is fairly common. Using data to reflect on which instructional strategies teams should retain, refine, or replace is far less common but no less important.

Coaches can build the capacity of teams to use data by developing systems that make data conversations effective (generating useful information) and efficient (completed in a reasonable amount of time). Educators are more likely to engage in data conversations if the data are easily accessible, purposefully arranged, and publicly discussed. If any of these conditions is absent, it becomes very difficult for teams to maximize the impact of data conversations. Experienced school psychologist, teacher, and research consultant Leo Bialis-White (2016) reminds teams that "It's not about the data, it's about what you decide to do with it," so understanding how to move beyond polite conversations about data to intentional actions the data drive is at the heart of effective data conversations.

Teams have discovered an infinite number of ways to organize data; it is not unusual for teams to spend an inordinate amount of time organizing data, leaving members little time for planning or taking action to improve student learning. The process of using data is out of balance; too much time is spent collecting, compiling, arranging—even admiring the data—and too little time is spent doing anything with them. The most effective way teams can respond to this problem is to adopt a standardized approach to how to organize assessment results at the team, school, and district levels. Teams should organize data by target, by teacher, and by student using simple and straightforward strategies to dramatically improve the productivity of data conversations.

Data conversations require conscious, intentional, and purposeful facilitation to ensure a safe and supportive environment where teachers have a voice and take ownership of the outcomes. The most successful teams understand that assessments, and the data they generate, are most beneficial when they inform teachers' professional practice. While there are many different protocols, the authors are not aware of any definitive evidence that one protocol is more effective than another. Our experience shows using protocols is how teachers best promote efficient and effective data use on their team.

Synopsis of Chapter 7 Modules

The modules in this chapter support the fourth prerequisite condition of a PLC which states, *Educators use the results of common assessments to improve individual practice, build the team's capacity to achieve its goals, and intervene and enrich on behalf of students* (DuFour & Reeves, 2016). This chapter explains why teams should engage in data conversations, what conditions are important to have in place to support data conversations, and how collaborative teams operationalize data conversations in their school.

Module 7.1: Why Should Teams Engage in Data Conversations?

There are two reasons why it is important for teams to regularly engage in productive data conversations. According to Bialis-White (2016), "Analyzing data and effectively using it to make informed decisions takes teamwork, consistent and open communication with teachers and students, and a deep understanding of how to use data, when, and why." Teams will investigate the best thinking around the use of data and assess whether the way they use data aligns with best practice.

Module 7.2: What Are the Rules for Managing Data in a PLC?

There are three rules for managing data in a PLC. All are important and work in concert to create a system that promotes productive data conversations. Social science researcher Rachel Rouda (2018) confirms, "There is a growing need to ensure schools and districts have the capacity and systems to effectively work with data." This module provides opportunities to reflect on what impact each rule has on teachers' data use to improve teaching and learning in their school.

Module 7.3: How Do Teams Organize Data to Promote Actionable Data Conversations?

How well teams use data results determines their value or positive outcomes for teachers and students. One of the most common questions teams ask is, "How should we collect, compile, and consider data?" If done poorly, the way teams organize data can actually create confusion and *informational clutter* for teams. Kathy Dyer (2016), who designs and facilitates learning opportunities for educators at the Northwest Evaluation Association, reminds teams, "When you make data actionable, you make assessment matter." This module provides ways to organize data to ensure productive data conversations.

Module 7.4: How Do Teams Ensure Efficient and Effective Data Conversations?

Analyzing and using assessment data can be a time-consuming and cumbersome task for teachers. As Bialis-White (2016) explains, "Numbers and scores provide little insight unless there's a strategy for analyzing the data, a means for sharing it among the right colleagues, and a system for making informed decisions for change." Many teams find using protocols a practical way to create more effective and efficient data conversations. This module introduces the characteristics of protocols and offers teachers some insights into how and when to use them.

Module 7.5: How Do Teams Facilitate Successful Data Conversations?

The most important reason to commit to productive data conversations is to improve student learning and professional practice. Having the right structures in place is a good start, but it is not enough; teams must also pay attention to the process. Bialis-White (2016) encourages coaches to attend to how teams conduct data conversations, saying, "By facilitating conversations about data, you're fostering an environment where educators are exploring the data, gaining deeper understanding about what it means and why it's important." Coaches can help teams understand how to facilitate effective data conversations.

These modules are best thought of either as an opportunity for teachers to learn together or as a starting point for further exploration and investigation. We intentionally designed the professional development activities in this chapter to be flexible; they can be delivered to individual teams or the entire faculty. The modules can be delivered in order within a chapter or through the entire book or, they can be delivered in a way that provides just-in-time job-embedded professional development for teams. The authors' goal is to provide the right information to the right people in the right settings at the right time.

Most importantly, teams need differentiated support, so those coaching teams should match the learning (as reflected in the modules) with what the team needs to work on. Asking teams, "What would you like to work on?" or "What would you like feedback on?" will make teams *feel* better, but these are the wrong questions. It's better to ask teams, "What do the data indicate that you need to work on?" or "What do the data indicate that you need feedback on?" These questions will make teams *do* better and are the right questions those who coach teams should be asking.

Those coaching collaborative teams need to decide whether they want their teams to *feel* better or to *do* better. We believe that the decision of what teams should work on or receive feedback on must reflect what the data indicate is the teams' greatest area of need (GAN), not their greatest area of comfort (GAC). Knowing what teams need to improve their professional practice should guide the choice of module.

Why Should Teams Engage in Data Conversations?

Section I: Before the Learning

Rationale—Why It Matters

Many educators believe the reason to review assessment data and samples of student work is to identify which students need more time and support to master a particular standard or learning target. Although this is certainly part of the reason teachers look at data, it's not the only reason. For teams to maximize the impact data conversations have on teaching and learning, members must also use data to reflect on the effectiveness of their own instructional practice.

Outcomes

Teacher teams will understand the importance of using assessment data for different purposes. They will recognize the most effective teams use data to identify students who need intervention and extension *and* to reflect on the effectiveness of their instructional practice.

SIG and Pathways

SIG prerequisite four (page 240) and the Pathways for Prerequisite Four (4.1–4.5; page 246)

Key Coaching Points

1. Emphasize that using data for more than one purpose is important. Acknowledge that many teams analyze and use data to improve student performance, but it is equally important to analyze and use data to improve teachers' instructional practice. Teams accomplish this goal by engaging in the *three Rs* (retain, refine, and replace) when looking at their instructional practice through the lens of student learning results.

2. Share with teachers that, without looking at data to improve their instructional practice, they are unlikely to change and will likely repeat the unit over and over again and wonder why they don't get better results.

3. Explain to teachers that using data to improve student learning is a lot like looking out the window at someone else, while using data to improve instruction requires educators to look in the mirror at themselves to assess the effectiveness of their professional practice.

Important Vocabulary and Terms

Data: These are formative or summative assessment results, samples of student work, or any other information teams gather to help them understand whether or not students are learning.

Data conversation: This occurs when two or more educators analyze data for developing an action plan to improve student learning.

DRIP (data rich and information poor) syndrome: This is a condition when a school or team has too much data and not enough information to make decisions about improving teaching and learning.

Instructional practice: This is the compilation of individual strategies, techniques, approaches, and materials a teacher may use to ensure students learn what teachers expect them to learn.

Section II: During the Learning

Preparation—Time and Materials

Complete this module in fifty-five minutes. The person responsible for delivering the PD may choose to deliver this module in two separate sessions. The ideal group size is four participants per group, seated at tables, but the activity will work equally well with three to six participants per group. Each group should begin by choosing a facilitator, a timekeeper, a recorder, and a reporter. Each group will need markers and chart paper, and participants need a copy of the following handout.

- "Double Duty Data: Understanding the Dual Roles of Using Data in a PLC" (page 157)

Step 1: Getting Ready to Learn—Sharing Experience (Ten Minutes)

Begin by asking each participant to make a list of things he or she learned from analyzing assessment data, samples of student work, or other student learning information. Items on the list may include information from workshops, reading research on best practice, or personal experience with the process of analyzing data. (three minutes)

Next, ask participants to work with a partner to compare and contrast their lists, highlight similarities and differences, and, if time allows, ask for volunteers to share their list with the whole group. (seven minutes)

Step 2: Interactive Strategy, Protocol, or Activity— Say Something Protocol (Forty-Five Minutes)

This protocol ensures everyone engages in a dialogue about data conversations. Ask participants to count off by four (groups of four is ideal, but this activity works with from three to five participants).

1. **Read the article:** Direct everyone to read the reproducible "Double Duty Data: Understanding the Dual Roles of Using Data in a PLC" (page 157). While reading, participants should highlight at least five key concepts or ideas from the text. (seven minutes)

2. **Describe key concepts:** Once participants have finished reading the article, describe the Say Something protocol as follows.

    a. Person one *succinctly* describes a key concept from the article. (two minutes)

b. Taking turns, person two, person three, and person four *briefly* comment on person one's concept without changing the topic (for example, people might say they agree or that they had a different understanding). (three minutes)

c. Finally, person one *quickly* explains why he or she chose the concept. (two minutes)

To keep the level of engagement high, each round of the protocol moves rapidly from speaker to speaker. Respecting the time designated for each step helps make the process more effective. The timekeeper is responsible for keeping the group aware of the time, and facilitators should guard against any one group member monopolizing the time.

3. **Repeat the process:** Repeat the process in step 2 with person two, three, and four, with each person sharing a new concept. Each round of the Say Something protocol will take a maximum of seven minutes per person or twenty-eight minutes total for a group of four. The protocol will take more or less time depending on the number of participants per group.

4. **Group sharing:** Reconvene as the large group and ask volunteers to share their thoughts on the article. Guide the large-group discussion to correct any misunderstandings. As participants share what they learned, record their comments on chart paper for all to see. (five minutes)

Step 3: Personal Reflection (Five Minutes)

Ask participants to make a list of three to five questions or comments they are still uncertain about that may need further study and research. Ask them to record and retain their thinking until the section III debrief with a coach.

Section III: After the Learning

Next Steps and Follow-Up for Coaching Teams

The coach's goal for this part of the process should be to focus the team on taking action by developing a plan for how they will use what they learned the next time they analyze data in a team meeting. Possible questions or tasks for the team to consider might include the following.

1. Ask each team member to share his or her best thinking about how to ensure both individuals and the team as a whole use student assessment data not only to plan for intervention and extension but also to reflect on their own instructional practices. Record and post the team's comments and commitments.

2. Ask participants to determine how they might address any of the questions they wrote down during their personal reflection in step 3 at the end of the training.

3. Establish a timeline for the team or teams to implement their plan at the next collaborative team meeting where members will analyze student assessment data.

Double Duty Data: Understanding the Dual Roles of Using Data in a PLC

By Thomas W. Many

Adapted from Texas Elementary Principals & Supervisors Association's TEPSA News, *January/February 2015, Vol. 72, No. 1, www.tepsa.org*

"Teachers learn to draw connections between their instructional practice and student learning through the deliberate analysis of data."

—Richard Elmore

Data from common assessments have two roles in a PLC. One educators widely recognize is using these kinds of data to identify students who are and are not proficient. When teachers use common assessment data to identify students who have not mastered a particular standard, they can provide more timely and targeted feedback during interventions. Using data in this way is a critical component of the PLC process as teams work to operationalize the belief that all students can learn when given enough time and the right kind of support.

A second legitimate use of common assessment data is to provide teachers with a way to examine their professional practice. When teams use data to analyze the effectiveness of instructional strategies, they ensure maximum positive impact of effective strategies, while minimizing or altogether eliminating the negative impacts of ineffective strategies. Using common assessment data for this second purpose serves as a powerful way to promote collaboration and continuous improvement in a PLC.

Of the two, educators most widely accept the use of common assessment data as a way to identify students who are and are not proficient. Once teams identify students who have not mastered a particular learning target, teachers focus on efficiently and effectively providing those students with more time and support without the students missing direct instruction in another subject.

This usually is a fairly simple and straightforward task; however, some teams find the process cumbersome and time-consuming. Teams can spend too much time gathering, collecting, and organizing the data. In fact, too much emphasis on the mechanics of compiling data can actually prevent teams from using the data to improve student learning.

Data Rich, Information Poor

At times, the sheer volume of data can overwhelm educators; some teams report there is so much data they don't have time to sort them and even less time to use them all. Teachers in these schools are suffering from *DRIP syndrome*—they are "data rich, but information poor" (Goodwin, 1995)—because they have not translated the results from their common assessment data into information they can use.

If a team is spending too much time collecting and compiling data, it may be because the assessment covers too many learning targets. The fewer the number of targets, the more clarity teachers have about the academic needs of individual students. Spending too much time collecting and compiling data may also indicate a need for training around the use of protocols. Or it may even mean the team is using the task of compiling data as a way of avoiding the more difficult conversations around using the data to improve teaching and learning.

Paralysis by Analysis

Whatever the reason, these teams are victims of what superintendent and consultant Heather Friziellie calls "paralysis by analysis" (H. Friziellie, personal communication, Month Day, 2016). To avoid this frustrating condition, teams should devote 25 percent of their time to the analysis and interpretation of data and the remaining 75 percent of their time on collaboratively planning how to improve student learning. Remember, the goal is to use data, not collect them.

"The best classroom assessments serve as meaningful sources of information for teachers, helping them identify what they taught well and what they need to work on."

—Thomas Guskey

Instructional Practice and Student Learning

To maximize the impact of data on professional practice, researcher Michelle L. Forman (2005) believes "teachers must investigate the manner in which they currently teach the skill and recast the learner-centered problem as a problem of practice." Forman (2005) continues, "In order to reframe the learner-centered problem as a problem of instruction, teachers must reflect on the link between their instructional practice and student learning."

One of the best ways to approach the task Forman (2005) advocates is to separate the effective instructional strategies from the less-effective or totally ineffective strategies. Through careful data analysis, collaborative teacher teams can readily identify those practices that they should retain, refine, or replace.

Using the unit of study as the basis of comparison, teachers identify which lessons, activities, or approaches to a particular skill or concept were most effective in helping students learn. They then retain the highly effective instructional strategies as part of the unit moving forward. In this way, teachers begin to create their own understanding of what best practice looks like in their classrooms.

Teachers also understand that from time to time, instructional strategies will only be partially successful in helping students learn and will fall short of teachers' expectations as ways to promote mastery of specific learning targets. These are the instructional strategies teams identify and then commit to refine. Teachers tweak, clarify, adjust, and look for better ways to implement these strategies in future lessons.

Finally, some instructional strategies just do not work, so teachers must replace them. There are times when the majority of students answer a question incorrectly, fail to master a learning target, or consistently misunderstand a concept. Guskey (2003) points out "If a teacher is reaching fewer than half of the students in the class, the teacher's method of instruction needs to improve. And teachers need this kind of evidence to help target their instructional improvement efforts" (p. 8). When this happens, teams should eliminate and replace the failed instructional strategy with a different one.

Many teams have become quite competent in using data to identify which students are proficient, which students are not, and which need more time and support to learn. Fewer teams have been as successful using assessment data to reflect on their professional practice and retain, refine, or replace instructional strategies as necessary to improve teaching and learning. "When teachers' classroom assessments become an integral part of the instructional process and a central ingredient in their efforts to help students learn, the benefits of instruction for both students and teachers will be boundless" (Guskey, 2003, p. 11).

Relentless Follow-Up

According to former teacher, central office administrator, and principal Kim Marshall (2006), the challenge teacher teams face is not generating data, or even collecting data, but using data to "foster [the] quality of relentless follow-up in every classroom, every grade-level team, and every department" (p. 4) to improve teaching and learning. Using common assessment data to (1) identify the students who are and are not proficient and (2) as a way to examine teachers' professional practice can help teams achieve that goal.

References

Forman, M. L. (2005, July 15). *The use of assessment to improve instruction: The Data Wise Project helps schools turn student assessment data into a tool to enhance organizational performance* [Blog post]. Accessed at https://gse.harvard.edu/news /uk/05/07/use-assessment-improve-instruction on March 16, 2021.

Goodwin, S. (1995). Data rich, information poor (DRIP) syndrome: Is there a treatment? *QRC Advisor*, *12*(2), 1–5.

Guskey, T. R. (2003). How classroom assessments improve learning. *Educational Leadership*, *60*(5), 6–11.

Marshall, K. (2006, April). *Interim assessments: Keys to successful implementation*. New York: New Leaders. Accessed at https://marshallmemo.com/articles/Interim%20Assmt%20 Report%20Apr.%2012,%2006.pdf on March 16, 2021.

What Are the Rules for Managing Data in a PLC?

Section I: Before the Learning

Rationale—Why It Matters

The goal of any data conversation is to help teacher teams become more knowledgeable and conversant about data from common assessments and samples of student work. One of the most common barriers to accomplishing this goal is the lack of a systematic approach for managing the data. Three rules work together to create a system for managing data in a PLC. If teams are struggling with having productive data conversations, it is likely that one of the rules of the data-management system is inadequate or absent.

Outcomes

After completing this module, participants will be able to assess how effectively their data management system supports a teams' efforts to analyze data and identify any *potential improvement points* (PIPs) in the data-management system at the district, school, and team levels.

SIG and Pathways

SIG prerequisite three (page 240) and the Pathways for Prerequisite Three (3.5; page 245)

Key Coaching Points

1. In a PLC, there are three rules for managing data. Districts, schools, and teams must work together to ensure data are (1) easily accessible, (2) purposefully arranged, and (3) publicly discussed.

2. The first rule, data are *easily accessible*, requires teams be able to access their data in a timely fashion. Responsibility for implementation of this rule lies primarily at the district level.

3. The second rule, data are *purposefully arranged*, necessitates that the principal and teacher leaders, with support of district-level administrators, create a system at the school site that will return assessment results to teachers organized in a way that allows for easy analysis and interpretation. Responsibility for implementing the second rule is primarily at the school level.

4. The third rule, data are *publicly discussed*, means teams engage in data conversations to detect any trends or patterns, identify which students need additional time and support, and pinpoint which instructional strategies or practices they should retain, refine, or replace. Responsibility for executing this third rule falls on collaborative teams.

5. For maximum efficiency and effectiveness, educators must follow all three rules; if any rule is disregarded, the effectiveness of a teams' use of data is likely compromised.

Important Vocabulary and Terms

Quantitative data: These data consist of numerical scores or ratings resulting from assessments or samples of student work. The primary advantage is that educators can easily calculate, organize, analyze, and display quantitative data.

Qualitative data: These data involve the use of verbal descriptions or narrative observations, portfolios, interviews, and other ways of gathering data. Qualitative data are most useful when exploring answers of *how* and *why* related to student performance.

Section II: During the Learning

Preparation—Time and Materials

Complete this module in fifty to sixty minutes. The ideal group size is four participants per group, seated at tables. Each group will need to choose a facilitator, timekeeper, recorder, and reporter. Groups will need chart paper and markers, and each participant needs a copy of the following handout.

- "Three Rules to Help Manage Assessment Data" (page 163)

Step 1: Getting Ready to Learn—5-3-1 Activity (Fifteen Minutes)

1. Ask participants to write the first **five** words they think of when someone asks, "How do you feel about data, data conversations, or data management *at the district level?*" These words can describe tasks, feelings, benefits, or barriers related to using data *in their district.* (two minutes)

2. Ask participants to work in pairs to combine lists and reach agreement on the **three** words they use to describe how educators use data *in their school.* (three minutes)

3. Working in small groups, ask the participants to reach consensus on the **one** word that best communicates the current reality of data use *on their teams.* (four minutes)

4. Post the group's work on the wall. Ask each small group to cite evidence or examples that support why they chose their word. (six minutes)

Step 2: Interactive Strategy, Protocol, or Activity—Pair Reading Activity (Thirty-Five to Forty Minutes)

1. **Read the article:** Ask participants to pair up with someone not from their table and decide who will be person one and person two. Explain that instead of reading the article silently to themselves, they will take turns reading it aloud, switching the reader after each paragraph. After each section, the pairs should stop and answer these three questions: (1) "How would you summarize this section of the article?" (2) "What is the most important idea from this section?" and (3) "How do you feel about this section?" Teachers should return to their tables after finishing this part of the protocol. (twenty minutes)

2. **Respond to the text:** As a small team, participants should agree on three ideas to share with the whole group. Ask participants to prepare to explain why these three ideas are important. (five minutes)

3. **Report out:** Have the reporter for each table team share the three *most* important ideas the group identifies. If another group has already mentioned one of the top three, groups should move on to another idea they chose. (ten minutes)

Step 3: Personal Reflection (Five Minutes)

Ask participants to take a moment and reflect on the implications this training has for the way the district, school, and teams manage data. Ask, "Did anything in the module make you reconsider how your team and school manage data? What questions are you still wrestling with, and what do you want to learn more about?" Ask them to record and retain their answers until the section III debrief session with a coach.

Section III: After the Learning

Next Steps and Follow-Up for Coaching Teams

Once teachers understand the three rules for managing data and what level of the system is primarily responsible for operationalizing each, it is fairly common to start the *blame game*. While it is important to talk about what is and is not within the teams' sphere of influence or control, teams should talk about what they need to fully implement data conversations.

The coach's goal for this part of the module is to help teams assess how effectively their data management system supports their efforts to analyze data—What are the strengths and vulnerabilities? Coaches should try to move teams from naming the problem to solving the problem (or at least identifying how they might solve the problem).

Possible questions or tasks for the team to consider might include the following.

1. What are the strongest (and weakest) aspects of the way the team manages data? What are some things the teams could do to improve their own practice? What are some specific things the teams need to advocate for at the school and district levels?

2. Ask members to determine how they might address the questions each team member wrote down during the personal reflection at the end of section II of this module.

3. Establish a timeline for the team to implement its plan at the next collaborative team meeting where members will analyze student assessment data.

Three Rules to Help Manage Assessment Data

By Thomas W. Many

Adapted from Texas Elementary Principals & Supervisors Association's TEPSA News, *March/April 2009, Vol. 66, No. 2, www.tepsa.org*

"It was the best of times, it was the worst of times, it was the age of wisdom, it was the age of foolishness . . ."

—Charles Dickens, *A Tale of Two Cities*

Living in the information age, educators have never before had so much data on student learning so readily available. It is, indeed, the best of times and yet, to harried educators struggling to make sense of the mountains of assessment data, the information age may feel like the worst of times.

Mining those data mountains for information to improve student learning is a daily challenge. The problem is not a lack of data, but rather managing all the data in a meaningful way. Damen Lopez, former principal of Los Peñasquitos Elementary School in San Diego, California, provides three rules or guidelines to consider when collecting and organizing data (D. Lopez, personal communication, August 4–5, 2007).

Lopez believes that in order for teachers to maximize the impact assessments have on teaching and learning, data must be (1) easily accessible, (2) purposefully arranged, and (3) publicly discussed (D. Lopez, personal communication, August 4–5, 2007). In those schools where *making meaning* of assessment data is a powerful experience, school and district-level leaders take primary responsibility for creating the necessary structures associated with the first two rules and insist teacher teams commit to the last. Rather than working individually to make meaning of assessment data, the most successful principals, coaches, and teacher leaders have discovered it is far more productive to create the conditions for *teams of teachers* to make meaning of the data.

Easy Access

For data to add value to efforts to improve student learning, teachers' access to the data must be timely. In addition to figuring out who needs to know what and when, the key question to ask is, "What is the most efficient way to get assessment data back to teachers?"

As Kim Marshall (2008), publisher of the highly regarded *Marshall Memo*, suggests, "When turnaround time after interim assessments is long, the results are stale and outdated by the time teachers sit down and discuss them" (p. 65). Data lose their impact whenever it takes more than forty-eight hours to return the results of a common assessment to teachers.

Outdated information makes it more difficult for teachers to be effective in adjusting instruction, identifying students who need more time and support, or coordinating remedial or extension programs among teachers on the team. To improve the accessibility of data, there needs to be a real commitment to shorten the turnaround time for reporting data.

Purposeful Arrangement

The second rule for maximizing the impact of data calls for assessment data to be purposefully arranged, that is, for the assessment data delivered to teacher teams to be presented in a format that is complete, accurate, and straightforward.

Data should be organized in simple—not simplistic—ways. Fancy graphics and snazzy displays are not the goal; what is important is that teacher teams have data in a format that will foster further discussion. As Kim Marshall (2008) points out, "Succinct spreadsheets and wall charts should make students' current status and progress graphically clear to teachers, administrators, students, and parents" (p. 67).

Teams invest far too much time gathering, organizing, arranging, compiling—and even admiring the data—while too little time is spent doing anything with the data. There are many software packages that quickly, almost instantaneously, provide assessment results in tables, charts, or graphs and make it easy for teachers to digest the results of interim assessments.

From time to time, teachers may create their own tables or graphs or request additional formats for organizing assessment results, but they should receive the initial data in an arrangement that allows teachers to focus on the results—not the presentation format.

Public Discussion

Teachers are uniquely equipped to engage in the meaningful public discussion of assessment data. Coaches can help teams embrace the benefits of publicly discussing the assessment results. Each time they discuss an assessment together, teachers benefit from the collective wisdom of their team. By reviewing results as a team, not only do teachers gain deeper insight into how their students are learning but also the added benefits of deepening their content knowledge and sharpening their pedagogy.

Assessment data and information on student achievement are relevant and necessary—only if educators use them to make decisions and act. Nothing justifies giving an assessment—and with it the associated loss of valuable instructional time—unless teachers discuss the assessment results and adjust their instruction accordingly.

The Age of Wisdom or Foolishness?

The ready availability and discerning management of assessment data can go a long way in contributing to making this the Age of Wisdom for educators seeking to improve students' learning. Principals, coaches, and teams of teachers who are successful in focusing their energies on ensuring that the data are (1) easily accessible, (2) purposefully arranged, and (3) publicly discussed ensure that all students learn.

References

Marshall, K. (2008). Interim assessments: A user's guide. *Phi Delta Kappan, 90*(1), 64–68. Accessed at https://marshallmemo.com/articles/IA%20User%20Guide.pdf on March 16, 2021.

How Do Teams Organize Data to Promote Productive Data Conversations?

Section I: Before the Learning

Rationale—Why It Matters

When poorly organized, data confuse teachers and make it harder to hold productive data conversations. Teams often spend too much time collecting, compiling, and comparing data and not enough time analyzing and taking action on the data. Many teams lack a clear understanding of how to organize data; this module explains how teams can accomplish this task in ways that support productive data conversations.

Outcomes

Teachers will effectively organize and use data during their team meetings. Participants will understand the TAADA framework and generate some insights into how teams can make their data conversations more productive.

SIG and Pathways

SIG for prerequisite three and the Pathways for Prerequisite Three (3.5; page 245)

Key Coaching Points

1. How well teachers analyze data and whether or not it leads to teachers taking action determine the value of common formative and summative assessment data.

2. Organize data in ways that allow teams to spend less time analyzing data and more time using data to plan and take action to improve teaching and learning.

3. There are many ways to organize the data from common assessments, but the most effective and efficient approach is to organize the data by target, by teacher, and by student.

4. The use of technology can facilitate the decluttering of data for teams. There are many software packages and technology solutions that do an excellent job of organizing data.

Important Vocabulary and Terms

Data clutter: These are confusing, convoluted, or overly complicated data that contribute to informational clutter that overwhelms teachers and leads to frustration on the part of collaborative teams.

TAADA: This is a way of organizing information that promotes productive data conversations.

Section II: During the Learning

Preparation—Time and Materials

Complete this module in an hour. The ideal group size is four participants per group seated at tables, but the activity will work with three to five teachers per group. Each group will need to choose roles (facilitator, timekeeper, recorder, and reporter) and have access to chart paper and markers. Direct participants to fold a piece of chart paper into thirds and draw three shapes (a triangle, a square, and a circle), one in each section of the chart paper, leaving room to write responses to a series of questions. Each participant will also need a copy of the following handouts.

- "Types of Data Conversations" (page 168)

- "Unclutter Your Team's Data Conversations" (page 169)

Step 1: Getting Ready to Learn—Shaping the Conversation Activity (Fifteen Minutes)

1. Give participants an opportunity to familiarize themselves with the "Types of Data Conversations" handout (page 168) and review the contents of each row. (three minutes)

2. Begin with the section of the chart paper that has the triangle, asking the small group to answer the following questions, writing the answer to each question on a different point of the triangle on the chart paper. (four minutes)

   a. Which type of data (formative or summative) is the focus of each row?

   b. What type of data conversation takes place most and least frequently?

   c. Which data conversation has the greatest impact on teaching and learning?

3. Moving on to the section of the chart paper where the square is drawn, each small group should reach consensus on which row represents or "squares" with the kind of data conversations that occur in your school. Write the group's responses in, on, or beside the square. (four minutes)

4. Finally, small groups focus on the section of the chart paper where the circle is drawn. Participants should share any questions about data conversations "circling" around in their mind. Write these questions in or around the section of the chart paper where a circle is drawn. (four minutes)

Step 2: Interactive Strategy, Protocol, or Activity—Three Levels of Text (Forty-Five Minutes)

1. **Read the article:** Each participant should read "Unclutter Your Team's Data Conversations" (page 169) and identify two or three passages he or she feels have implications for the team's work. (six minutes)

2. **Respond to the text:** Have the members of each small group number off by four; ask person one to read a passage aloud (literal), succinctly explain what he or she thinks about the passage (interpretive), and describe the effect it might have on his or her work (implications). (three minutes)

The group then briefly responds by identifying the implications what they just heard might have on their team. (two minutes)

3. **Repeat:** Repeat the response process until each person (persons two, three, and four) has an opportunity to talk. (five minutes per round or twenty minutes total for this step of the protocol)

4. **Debrief:** After everyone has an opportunity to speak, ask the table groups to summarize what they learned and identify the most important implications for their work. The group should record what they feel are the most important implications on their chart paper. (five minutes)

5. **Report:** The reporter for each group (without comment from others) briefly shares the important implications their group identifies. (five minutes)

Step 3: Personal Reflection (Five Minutes)

Have the participants take a moment and reflect on their biggest takeaway from the article. Ask, "What implications does the use of a framework like TAADA have for your team? Which aspects of the way the team uses data are strongest and weakest? Did anything in this module make you reconsider how your team approaches data conversations? What questions are you still wrestling with? What do you want to learn more about?" Have participants record and retain their reflections for use during the section III debrief with a coach.

Section III: After the Learning

Next Steps and Follow-Up for Coaching Teams

The coach's goal for this part of the module is to help the team (1) identify the relative strengths and weaknesses of how they organize data and (2) apply what they learned to improve the productivity of their data conversations. Possible questions or tasks for the team to consider might include the following.

1. What are the strongest (and weakest) aspects of the way the team organizes data?

2. Can the team identify any aspect of the way members organize data they could streamline to reduce clutter during data conversations? What can be done about it?

3. Has the team explored utilizing technology? New solutions are constantly created and offer some excellent options for increasing the efficiency of organizing data.

4. Ask members to determine how they might address the questions they recorded and retained from the reflection at the end of section II of this module.

5. Establish a timeline for the team to implement its plan at the next collaborative team meeting where members will analyze student assessment data.

Types of Data Conversations

Type of Data Dialogue	Data Used	Who Is Involved?	Conversation Topics	Frequency
School-improvement team conversations	• State assessments • District benchmarks	• School-improvement team • Entire staff	• Patterns of student achievement • Needs for schoolwide programs (instructional, curricular, professional development) • Needs for additional knowledge and skills for staff	Two times per year
Teacher-supervisor conversations	• State assessments • Benchmark exams • End-of-course assessments • Classroom assessments • Common assessments	• Teacher • Administrator or coach	• Student growth • Overall proficiency of students • Instructional strategies to meet student-learning needs	Two to three times per year
Department or grade-level teams with focus on individual student interventions	• Student performance on classroom and common assessments • Discipline records • Student work	• Core teams • Grade-level teams	• Diagnosis of individual knowledge and skills • Next steps for students • Grouping of students for instruction and intervention • Pyramid of interventions	Once a month or more often
Department or grade-level teams with focus on instructional strategies	• State assessments • Benchmark assessments • Common assessments • Unit assessments	• Grade-level or content-area groups	• Student growth • Patterns of proficiency • Instructional strategies • Assessment strategies	Once a week to once every six to eight weeks
Student goal-setting conversations	• Grades • State assessments • Common assessments • Benchmark assessments	• Teacher • Individual students	• Goal setting • Strategies for success • Celebrations of learning	Once a week to once a month

Source: Harrison & Bryan (2008). Used with permission. For more information, contact authors at harrison.cindy@gmail.com and lcrsbryan@msn.com.

Energize Your Teams © 2022 Solution Tree Press • SolutionTree.com

Visit **go.SolutionTree.com/PLCbooks** to download this free reproducible.

168

Unclutter Your Team's Data Conversations

By Thomas W. Many

Adapted from Texas Elementary Principals & Supervisors Association's *TEPSA News, September/ October 2020, Vol. 77, No. 5, www.tepsa.org*

> "Whatever method you choose to organize your data, it needs to be done with intent and purpose."
>
> —Owen Willis

Analyzing data is an important responsibility of teams in a PLC. Consultants Laura Lipton and Bruce Wellman (2012) note, "High performing teams systematically collect and use data to drive cycles of problem solving, planning, action, and reflection to both improve their own collaborative practices and improve instruction that makes a difference in student learning" (p. 3).

To collect and use data well, teachers often seek out advice regarding the best ways to organize data from common assessments or samples of student work. It is important to get this right because data that are confusing, convoluted, or overly complicated contribute to the kind of informational clutter that can overwhelm teachers and lead to frustration on the part of collaborative teams.

According to former special education teacher and data analysis expert Owen Willis (2016), "Data clutter can prevent teams, schools and districts from fully accessing the student data they have spent countless hours and dollars collecting." More important, Willis (2016) notes, "It [data clutter] can also waste a significant amount of teacher time that could be better spent planning or delivering instruction." Instead of distributing complicated spreadsheets and cluttered printouts that erode a team's commitment to using data, Lipton and Wellman (2012) advocate for "well-crafted data displays" that help "clarify and communicate often complex or abstract information" (p. 65). They point out that a thoughtful and well-designed approach to organizing data can "make different data types more accessible to group work" (p. 66).

> "Good assessments provide a tremendous amount of raw data, but great analysis is impossible unless that data is recorded in a readily useable form."
>
> —Paul Bambrick-Santoyo

Data conversations are structured group conversations that help teachers understand, develop, and work with data through a thoughtful, reflective process. The easiest way to eliminate the possibility that clutter will negatively impact the effectiveness of data conversations is to adopt a standardized approach to organize and display results.

TAADA Process

Kim Bailey developed a practical way of organizing data that helps unclutter data conversations: the TAADA framework. TAADA (turn it around, arrange it, analyze it, discuss it, and act on it) can be a useful tool to teacher teams (K. Bailey, personal communication, 2016). The steps of Bailey's TAADA framework are described in the following paragraphs.

T: Turn It Around

Timeliness is critical to productive data conversations. Old data are stale data, and nothing is worse than working with data past their expiration date. There are many resources, both human and technological, that allow teams to access their data less than forty-eight hours after administering an assessment. It's clear that to be a resource teachers use to drive instructional decisions, assessment data must be current and reflective of ongoing instruction. This requires the principal and teacher leaders, with the support of central office administrators, to make a commitment to return data to teams in a timely manner.

A: Arrange It

Schools and districts can promote the regular use of data by creating systems that reduce or eliminate clutter. Data are most beneficial when arranged in ways that allow teams to look at individual student performance at the target level. While teams may approach this important task in different ways, the most effective way to arrange data is by target, by teacher, and by student.

A: Analyze It

Teams engage in a two-step process to analyze data. The first step begins at the macro level with teams taking a big-picture overview of the data and looking for trends and patterns. Teachers probe for answers to questions like, "Which were the highest- and lowest-performing targets?" and "Were there any common misconceptions between classes of students or different groups of students?"

In the second step of the analysis process, teachers dig deeper and examine the data at the micro level and seek to understand how to improve teaching and learning. The team works to identify which individual students require additional time and support and which specific learning targets will need more attention. Teachers also reflect on their instructional practice and identify which instructional strategies or parts of the unit they need to retain, refine, or replace.

D: Discuss It

This step is the heart of productive data conversations; it is where teachers make meaning of their practice. By this point in the data conversation, the discussion has transitioned from problem finding to problem solving, and the team has converted the raw data into information that becomes the knowledge and wisdom teachers use to develop their action plans.

This step is also when teams benefit most from the use of protocols. The regular use of protocols creates a safe, judgment-free environment where teachers can publicly discuss the data, reflect on the results, and make collective decisions about what needs to happen next to ensure high levels of learning for all.

A: Act on It

The final step is to take action on what the team has learned during the data conversation. Teams focus on responding to PLC critical questions three and four—"How will we respond when students do not learn?" and "How will we extend the learning of those students who are already proficient?" (DuFour, DuFour, Eaker, Many, & Mattos, 2016, p. 36) by intentionally leveraging their schoolwide pyramid of interventions. Teachers reach consensus on what needs to be done to ensure students master the essential outcomes for each unit, and then take action.

Data conversations provide teams with opportunities to make meaning of their practice and inform instructional decision making. The key to making the best use of data is to treat assessments as opportunities to learn. It is also important to reduce clutter because well-organized data increase the chances teachers will engage in productive data conversations and learn more about their students, their teaching, and potential areas for improvement.

"Data provides hints, not answers. But when brought together with context and conversation, data can become actionable insights that translate into powerful changes for students."

—Leo Bialis-White, 2016

The term *data conversation* suggests some level of dialogue or discussion occurs among colleagues to turn the results of common assessments or samples of student work into actions that improve student learning. As Bialis-White (2016) writes, "It's not about the data, it's what you decide to do with it."

References

Bambrick-Santoyo, P. (2010). *Driven by data: A practical guide to improve instruction*. San Francisco: Jossey-Bass.

Bialis-White, L. (2016, January 18). *Using data conversations to accelerate impact and improve outcomes* [Blog post]. Accessed at https://gettingsmart.com/2016/01/using-data-conversations on September 3, 2020.

DuFour, R., DuFour, R., Eaker, R., Many, T. W., & Mattos, M. (2016). *Learning by doing: A handbook for Professional Learning Communities at Work* (3rd ed.). Bloomington, IN: Solution Tree Press.

Lipton, L., & Wellman, B. (2012). *Got data? Now what? Creating and leading cultures of inquiry*. Bloomington, IN: Solution Tree Press.

Willis, O. (2016, October 11). *Three steps to organize student data—and find joy* [Blog post]. Accessed at www.edsurge.com/news/2016–10–11–3-steps-to-organize-student-data on July 3, 2020.

171

How Do Teams Ensure Efficient and Effective Data Conversations?

Section I: Before the Learning

Rationale—Why It Matters

Experience shows us that teams can get stuck when discussing data. When that happens, teams benefit from coaching on how to use protocols to create nonjudgmental environments where teachers feel safe to share assessment results. Module 7.3 (page 165) introduced the TAADA format for organizing data (K. Bailey, personal communication, April 17, 2015). This module places a special emphasis on the *D*—discuss it.

Outcomes

After completing this module, teachers will be able to (1) identify the key characteristics of protocols, (2) recognize there are a number of protocols they can use during a data conversation, and (3) participate in a simulated data conversation using a protocol.

SIG and Pathways

SIG prerequisite four and Pathways for Prerequisite Four (4.1 and 4.4; page 246)

Key Coaching Points

1. All protocols are interactive activities, but not all interactive activities are protocols. Every protocol consists of steps, roles, and time frames for completion.

2. Protocols are powerful tools to help facilitate productive data conversations. Protocols create structures that make it safe for teachers to ask one another challenging questions.

3. Protocols create a culture of continuous improvement, promote higher levels of equity and relational trust, improve personal and professional relationships, and build a sense of community on the team.

4. Protocols require patience and persistence. Initially, protocol use may feel formal and awkward, but with practice, teachers become more comfortable and realize they are making better use of their time (more efficient) and getting better results (more effective).

5. The goal is to use protocols to help teams engage in deep, rich, and insightful data conversations about teaching and learning.

Important Vocabulary and Terms

Norm: These are the standards of behavior by which people agree to operate while in a specific group.

Protocol: This is a set of guidelines that promote productive conversations about teaching and learning.

Characteristics: These are the explicit steps, precise timelines, and specific roles that protocols outline.

Section II: During the Learning

Preparation—Time and Materials

Complete this module in fifty minutes. The person responsible for delivering the training may also choose to deliver this module in two separate sessions. The ideal small group size is four participants per group, seated at tables, but the activity will work with three to five participants per group. Each table group will choose a facilitator and a timekeeper.

Ask the whole group to number off as either person one or person two. The person responsible for delivering the training session should list all the vocabulary from the various modules in chapter 7 on chart paper and post it where all participants can see it. Provide each table group with chart paper and markers. Provide each participant with copies of the following handouts.

- "It's Not Pixie Dust, It's Protocol" (page 175)
- "Protocols: A Powerful Prescription for Professional Learning" (page 178)

Step 1: Getting Ready to Learn—Possible Sentences (Fifteen Minutes)

The rules for this activity are simple: no comment is too irrelevant, no discussion or dialogue is allowed, and no judgment is tolerated. As the coach, you may adjust the time frames if needed.

1. Ask participants, working individually, to choose two words from the chapter 7 vocabulary list on the chart and write a sentence for each word. (three minutes)

2. Participants should find a partner from their own table or any other table group and share their sentences. The goal of this conversation is to get some feedback and decide if any adjustments to the sentences are necessary. (four minutes)

3. Finally, participants return to their original table, and, working as a small group, reach consensus on one sentence for the table. (five minutes)

4. Ask each table group to quickly share—without comment from other groups—and post their sentences. (three minutes)

Step 2: Interactive Strategy, Protocol, or Activity—Challenging Assumptions (Thirty Minutes)

The purpose of this protocol is to surface assumptions and build shared knowledge regarding the use of protocols during data conversations. The training combines the Challenging Assumptions protocol with a Think-Pair-Square strategy to build shared knowledge among participants. Ask each participant to fold a standard sheet of copy paper in half lengthwise. Label the left-hand side of the paper *A protocol is _____*. Label the right-hand side *A protocol is not _____*.

1. **Note prior knowledge:** Each participant works individually to write down what he or she knows from experience or has heard from others about what a protocol is and is not. As an alternative, if the group has experience with protocols, ask participants to answer the question, What happens in a data conversation when a protocol is or is not used effectively? (five minutes)

2. **Read the article:** Assign "It's Not Pixie Dust, It's Protocol" (page 175) to the person one participants and "Protocols: A Powerful Prescription for Professional Learning" (page 178) to the person two participants. Ask participants to read their article (individually) and add their insights to either column or move ideas from one column to the other (Think). (five minutes)

3. **Discuss with a partner:** Ask each participant to find a partner (Pair) who read the other article, compare each other's lists, and discuss what they wrote and why. Participants are free to add ideas or move them from one column to the other. (five minutes)

4. **Expand the discussion:** Have each pair join another set of partners (Square) to discuss their worksheets. Whenever possible, the groups should include two people who read "It's Not Pixie Dust, It's Protocol" (page 175) and two who read "Protocols: A Powerful Prescription for Professional Learning" (page 178). (five minutes)

5. **Share thinking:** Create a larger version of the protocol list on chart paper and summarize the group's thinking. Ask two or three groups of four to share any patterns or common insights their "square" came up with. Post the summary chart. (ten minutes)

Step 3: Personal Reflection (Five Minutes)

Ask participants to record and retain their responses to the following questions before the next team meeting (teachers will refer to their reflections during the section III debrief): "What have I learned about the use of protocols? What difference would the regular use of protocols make for me? What would I like to do next?"

Section III: After the Learning

Next Steps and Follow-Up for Coaching Teams

At the first opportunity, facilitate a simulated data conversation using a protocol to analyze samples of student work or assessment results.

1. To understand which protocol works best for them, teams should be encouraged to explore different protocols. Useful sites for this are the National School Reform Faculty (https://nsrfharmony.org/protocols) and the School Reform Initiative (www.schoolreforminitiative.org).

2. Explain that participants will be using a protocol to engage in a simulated data conversation using results from a fictitious common assessment. Explain how the protocol works, select roles, provide the sample data, and use the protocol to engage in a data conversation.

3. Debrief the simulation and list any questions participants may still have about using protocols to analyze student work. This is also a great opportunity for some action research. Have the team research different protocols, test them with real data, and catalog the strengths and weaknesses of different protocols until the team reaches consensus on a protocol to use as the team's primary method for discussing student work.

It's Not Pixie Dust, It's Protocol

By Thomas W. Many

Adapted from Texas Elementary Principals & Supervisors Association's TEPSA News, *January/February 2010, Vol. 67, No. 1, www.tepsa.org*

Improving schools requires a high level of collaboration among and between teachers. Making time for collaboration during the regular school day is a critical first step in creating the conditions for high-performing collaborative teams. As Diane Weaver Dunne (2012) argues, "Time with colleagues spent in focused inquiry about teaching and learning is a necessity, not a luxury" (p. 7).

Unfortunately, *time* is one of those necessary (but insufficient) conditions for the successful development of collaborative teams. Without designated and protected time for teams to meet during the school day, school leaders cannot expect teachers to have the kinds of conversations necessary to change practice. However, time alone is not enough. Ensuring teachers use time productively is just as important.

Educators often ask, "Why is it that some teams use time so much more productively than others?" Some may think it is magic or luck—or even a sprinkling of pixie dust—that enables some teams to use time more efficiently and effectively. However, it is not pixie dust at all but the thoughtful—even artful—use of well-thought-out, carefully implemented, and skillfully facilitated protocols that make a difference.

Dozens of Protocols—Many Variations on a Theme

The effective use of protocols ensures conversations between and among team members are productive. Stevie Quate, codirector of the Colorado Critical Friends Group, defines a protocol simply as a set of "agreed upon guidelines for a conversation" (S. Quate, personal communication, June 2, 2021), but acknowledges that a protocol is more than that.

Most protocols have a structured format that includes a tentative time frame and specific guidelines for communication among team members. Descriptions of protocols typically identify the purpose, number of participants, length of time required, roles of team members, and expected outcomes.

Quate differentiates a protocol from a *norm*, which consists of agreed-on guidelines for behavior within a team, and suggests a *protocol* is "a structure which everyone understands and has agreed to that permits a certain kind of conversation to occur" (S. Quate, personal communication, June 2, 2021). The kinds of conversations Quate refers to are necessary if principals expect teachers to successfully engage in the analysis of assessment data or the improvement of a lesson.

The design of these protocols promotes examining student work and reflecting on a teacher's pedagogy. Some protocols facilitate the analysis of data while others focus on the examination of a lesson. There are protocols that generate suggestions for setting goals with groups or individual students. Other protocols analyze the relationship between lessons, standards, and rubrics or enable teachers to collect data, make comparisons, and track student progress. Still others delve deeply into the quality of a teacher's pedagogy and identify strategies for improving an assignment, project, or specific aspect of a lesson.

There are literally dozens of protocols—many are variations on the same theme—but Quate emphasizes that in its purest form "a protocol creates the structure that makes it safe for teachers to ask challenging questions of each other" (S. Quate, personal communication, June 2, 2021).

MODULE

7.4

Benefits of Using Protocols

Coauthors Joseph P. McDonald, Nancy Mohr, Alan Dichter, and Elizabeth C. McDonald (2013) study the use of protocols in schools in *The Power of Protocols: An Educator's Guide to Better Practice*. McDonald and his colleagues (2013) agree with Quate and argue that using protocols promotes development of a culture where teachers are "able, willing, and even eager—in consultation with others—to make changes as needed in order to improve the work" (p. 8).

When teacher teams meet to talk about student learning, they sharpen their pedagogy and deepen their content knowledge. According to the National Turning Points Center (NTPC; 2001), teachers who use protocols have a more complete and comprehensive understanding of what students know and are able to do. The regular use of protocols also helps teachers develop a shared language for assessing student work and a common understanding of what quality student work looks like.

The use of protocols creates a culture of continuous learning. As Jennifer Morrison (2008/ 2009) notes, in the process of collecting, analyzing, and reflecting on information about their classes, teachers are able to step outside their assumptions and understand students more clearly. The NTPC (2001) believes protocols promote "collegial feedback and the critical analysis of student and teacher work in a safe and structured format" (p. 5) and recommends using protocols because they foster a culture that "collaboratively assesses the quality and rigor of teacher work" (p. 5). McDonald and his colleagues (2013) write, "When teachers are looking at student work—particularly looking together at student work—it can be threatening. This is why protocols are useful" (p. 4).

Using protocols also builds a sense of community among and between teachers. The NTPC (2001) argues that looking collaboratively at student work and participating in collective problem solving through the use of protocols move teachers away from the isolating concept of *my students* and toward the community concept of *our students*.

Finally, protocols allow teachers to be more efficient in their work. Quate reminds educators that in most schools, time is of the essence and the one resource that no one seems to have enough of (S. Quate, personal communication, June 2, 2021). Once mastered, protocols become valuable, utilitarian tools teachers use to focus conversations on what matters and, thereby, make the most of the time they do have.

"It's scary work, though, and respectful protocols can help."

—Diane Weaver Dunne

As teams begin to use protocols, teachers will undoubtedly have questions. The NTPC (2001) warns, "When teachers first begin using protocols as a way of looking at their students' work, assignments, and instructional practices, the process may feel formal or stiff" (p. 4). The NTPC (2001) continues, "[and] because teachers are not accustomed to sharing work publicly with peers, the process can also feel intimidating at first" (p. 4).

Initially, many teachers feel protocols are a waste of time; but coaches encourage teachers to try them anyway. McDonald and his colleagues (2013) observe, "schools or colleges mired in norms of private practice, and used to ignoring the actual impact of the practice on students' learning, may not take easily to learning with protocols" (p. 3). However, McDonald and his colleagues (2013) find when pressed to see them all the way through "even reluctant participants find something refreshing about protocols" (p. 3).

Like most changes, as teachers gain experience with the use of protocols, their confidence and comfort levels increase, as do the benefits of using protocols. Principals, coaches, and teacher leaders must have confidence that the use of protocols will make teacher teams more productive.

A Means to an End—Not an End in Itself

Quate cautions that it is important to remember, "the point is not to do the protocol well, but to have an in-depth, insightful conversation about teaching and learning" (S. Quate, personal communication, June 2, 2021). It is wise to remember that a protocol is a means to an end, not an end in itself. McDonald (2013) agrees and reminds us that "protocols are no panacea for these or any other kinds of collegial problems, but they are valuable in highlighting . . . problems" (p. 11).

In the end, it is the regular and intentional use of protocols—not pixie dust—that holds the key to helping teacher teams use their time more productively.

References

Dunne, D. W. (2012, August 15). *Teachers learn from looking together at student work together*. Accessed at https://education-world.com/a_curr/curr246.shtml on March 17, 2021.

McDonald, J. P., Mohr, N., Dichter, A., & McDonald, E. C. (2013). *The power of protocols: An educator's guide to better practice* (3rd ed.). New York: Teacher's College Press.

Morrison, J. (2008/2009). Why teachers must be data experts. *Educational Leadership*, 66(4). Accessed at www.ascd.org/publications/educational-leadership/dec08/vol66/num04/Why-Teachers-Must-Be-Data-Experts.aspx on May 21, 2021.

National Turning Points Center. (2001). *Turning Points: Transforming middle schools—Looking collaboratively at student and teacher work*. Boston: Author. Accessed at www.mbaea.org/media/documents/MCREL_Collaborative_Protocols_87D0BB2693E4A.pdf on March 16, 2021.

MODULE
7.4

Protocols: A Powerful Prescription for Professional Learning

By Thomas W. Many and Susan K. Sparks

Adapted from Texas Elementary Principals & Supervisors Association's TEPSA News, *January/ February 2013, Vol. 70, No. 1, www.tepsa.org*

The growing consensus around the importance of high-performing collaborative teams parallels the growing support for the use of protocols. Many principals find the regular use of protocols increases the effectiveness of team meetings. Likewise, many teachers recognize the positive impact protocols have on their practice. Both principals and teachers embrace protocols because ultimately, the effective use of protocols promotes higher levels of professional productivity.

"While protocols vary in significant ways, they all do two things: provide a structure for conversation—a series of steps that a group follows in a fixed order—and specify the roles different people in the group will play."

—Marjorie Larner

In their simplest form, protocols are a set of agreed-on guidelines for a conversation. A protocol typically describes a specific—almost prescriptive—process that structures the work of teams. The description of a protocol outlines such details as the purpose, expected outcomes, step-by-step directions, number of participants, roles of team members, and time requirements. According to consultant, coach, and author Lois Brown Easton (2009), there are four categories of protocols: (1) looking at student work, (2) looking at professional practice, (3) looking at issues and concerns, and (4) looking at professional reading. All can positively impact the productivity of collaborative teams.

Looking at Student Work

As teams grow more skilled at using protocols, they become better students of their own students. This category of protocols places an appropriate emphasis on *using* data rather than *collecting* data. Teams that use these protocols to examine student work become faster and more accurate in their student-data analysis. Teachers using protocols are far more likely to look at student work collaboratively for the purpose of determining student needs than look at student work in isolation for the purpose of assigning grades.

Looking at Professional Practice

As more educators accept the use of protocols, teachers begin to see the value of protocols as a tool to examine their professional practice. Instead of focusing on individual interests in team meetings, this category of protocols helps members focus their conversations on the complex task of improving teaching and learning. The structure of these protocols engages teachers, keeps them on task, and establishes a precedent for collectively questioning current practice.

Looking at Issues and Concerns

Teams also rely on this protocol category to help solve problems. Often teams get stuck and spend hours naming, renaming, or even nicknaming problems. They identify and overidentify issues, but lack the necessary skills to solve them and end up grinding away at their concerns with little success. This cycle of *find and grind* impacts a team's sense of collective efficacy in significant ways. Teachers quickly learn these protocols provide teams with new and effective problem-solving tools.

Looking at Professional Reading

Finally, the regular use of these protocols fosters the development of more reflective practitioners. Sharing professional reading promotes a culture where teachers freely share ideas, openly exploring the strengths and weaknesses. Using these protocols to facilitate discussion of articles allows teachers to thoroughly inspect challenging issues and think about the intended and unintended consequences of their actions.

"Without an explicit structure, conversations about teaching and learning tend to drift, go in many directions at once, or become so abstract that they are unlikely to lead to any useful learning."

—Alexandra Weinbaum and colleagues

The support for using protocols as a way to improve team meetings is compelling, but when principals first introduce the idea, they are often met with resistance. This was certainly the case in Kildeer Countryside School District 96 in Buffalo Grove, Illinois, where the author (Tom Many) was superintendent. Principals found that a combination of *top-down pressure* (insisting teams use protocols) and *bottom-up support* (providing additional training, effective facilitation, and modeling of protocols during faculty meetings) was necessary to incorporate the regular use of protocols into team meetings.

Initially, some Buffalo Grove teachers felt protocols made conversations slow and superficial; they described their discussions as contrived and unnatural. Other teachers felt requiring teams to use protocols somehow limited their academic freedom or diminished their professional autonomy. In general, there was a belief that using a formal process to engage in structured conversations was nothing more than "process for the sake of process."

Some of these concerns are valid; using protocols does disrupt the typical communication patterns in traditional team meetings. This is because using protocols does not allow teams to engage in the kind of random, unfocused conversations they are accustomed to having. For some teachers, this shift to a more transparent, focused, and structured meeting format can be uncomfortable and make them feel vulnerable. What everyone in the system must come to understand is that the regular use of protocols promotes development of trust between and among team members. When teachers feel safe, they listen to one another more intensely and, when combined with effective norms, protocols help teams navigate difficult conversations.

Other teachers find protocols challenging because of isolation cultures in their school and the privatization of their professional practice. Early on in Buffalo Grove, it became clear that the regular use of protocols challenged the mindless precedent of past practice. However, protocols confronted the precedent in more productive ways. Instead of getting comfortable with the old, familiar way of doing things, protocols pushed teams to generate new alternatives. What had previously seemed impossible suddenly became possible. Principals and teachers had to acknowledge no single individual had all the answers and with more knowledge and experience at the table, teachers were able to see possibilities and opportunities they may not have seen before.

Promoting dialogue over discussion or debate makes protocols improve communication between and among teachers as well. Rather than allow individuals to be verbally trampled by an overzealous teammate, protocols structure conversations in ways that ensure every voice is heard. Principals find conversations shift in meetings and see when teams use protocols, teachers engage in focused dialogue to promote the sharing of new ideas and strategies. In

page 2 of 3

contrast, teams that did not incorporate protocols continue to tolerate random discussions that sanction the *hiding and hoarding* of best practice. Protocols encourage exploration and alternative thinking, and by slowing down, teams generate better alternatives.

Principals also see regular use of protocols promotes developing a culture of inquiry which allows teachers, working with others confronting similar problems, to engage in continuous and substantial learning about their practice in the settings where they spend their professional lives. These teachers are more likely to seek out honest, growth-oriented feedback to promote high levels of student learning. In contrast, on teams where teachers resist using protocols, relationships tend to favor the kind of polite, superficial feedback that protects adult relationships.

> "Protocols are one of the most powerful processes that people in PLCs can use for learning."
>
> —Lois Brown Easton

The effort to incorporate protocols as tools to improve the effectiveness of team meetings takes time, but it is worth the effort. The change requires patience and persistence, but principals and teachers find the benefits of using protocols far exceed the challenges of implementing them. As Easton (2009) says, protocols are the "ideal vehicle for holding the professional conversations that need to occur in PLCs—conversations that will lead to increased student achievement and motivation" (p. 1).

References

Easton, L. B. (2009). *Protocols for professional learning*. Alexandria, VA: Association for Supervision and Curriculum Development.

Larner, M. (2007). *Tools for leaders: Indispensable graphic organizers, protocols, and planning guidelines for working and learning together*. New York: Scholastic.

Weinbaum, A., Allen, D., Blythe, T., Simon, K., Seidel, S., & Rubin, C. (2004). *Teaching as inquiry: Asking hard questions to improve practice and student achievement*. New York: Teachers College Press.

Facilitating Productive Data Conversations

Section I: Before the Learning

Rationale—Why It Matters

When considered in tandem with module 7.4 (page 172), this module provides principals, coaches, and teacher leaders with a guide to help teams hold productive data conversations. Data conversations are one of the most important components of the PLC process, and the opportunity to learn from data is one of the most critical tasks teams tackle. When teacher teams analyze data and develop action plans designed to improve teaching and learning, they are engaging in the work described in the fourth prerequisite of the PLC process.

Outcomes

After this module, teachers will understand how to (1) promote productive data conversations and (2) respond to dysfunctional comments and behaviors that negatively impact the team's ability to hold productive data conversations.

Key Coaching Points

1. Productive data conversations are critically important to high-performing teams.

2. Effective facilitation plays an important role in the success of a data conversation.

3. Teams must meet regularly to analyze data and identify what needs to happen to raise student achievement and enhance the effectiveness of teachers' instructional practice.

4. The most effective data conversations are the product of careful planning. To maximize the effectiveness of data conversations, facilitators should pay careful attention to the tone, design, structure, and focus of these meetings.

SIG and Pathways

SIG for prerequisite four and Pathways for Prerequisite Four (4.1–4.5; page 246)

Important Vocabulary and Terms

Facilitation: The act of intentionally engaging teams in a process to create, discover, and apply new learnings so that members more efficiently and effectively accomplish their goals

Tone: The way teams interact, communicate, and behave in order to efficiently and effectively promote productive data conversations

Design: The conscious, purposeful, and intentional way that resources (time, tools, and support) are organized to support the ability of teams to hold productive data conversations

Structure: The tools, interactive activities, and protocols facilitators choose in order to ensure team members are able to fully participate and contribute to successful data conversations

MODULE

7.5

Focus: Specific facilitation skills that help teams use assessment data and samples of student work to improve the level of student achievement and enhance the effectiveness of teachers' instructional practice

Section II: During the Learning

Preparation—Time and Materials

This module can be completed in an hour. The ideal group size is four participants, and seating at tables is preferred. Each small group will need to select roles (facilitator, timekeeper, recorder, and reporter), and participants will need the following handout.

- "Facilitating Productive Data Conversations" reproducible (page 184)

Step 1: Getting Ready to Learn—Window Notes, Part I (Fifteen Minutes)

1. Prepare for the activity by asking each participant to fold a blank 8.5-inch × 11-inch piece of copy paper in half (horizontally), and in half again (vertically), to create four "window panes." Starting with the upper left quadrant and moving in a clockwise direction, label each quadrant as follows. (two minutes)

   a. *Facts*—What are the important facts and details?

   b. *Questions*—What comes to mind, and what am I curious about?

   c. *Connections*—How does this relate to my experiences or other things I have learned?

   d. *Feelings*—How do I react to or feel about what I am learning?

2. **Share purpose:** Once the windowpanes are labeled, share the purpose of each quadrant before starting the activity. (three minutes)

   - *Facts*—Help the reader remember important information from the article.

   - *Questions*—Enable the reader to clarify uncertainties and exercise their curiosity.

   - *Connections*—Encourage the reader to tap into prior knowledge.

   - *Feelings*—Expressing feelings and recording reactions make the learning personal.

3. **Read the article:** Have participants read the article, "Facilitating Productive Data Conversations" (page 184). While reading, participants should record their notes in each section of the window pane. Encourage participants to include notes, comments, or insights for each quadrant. (ten minutes)

Step 2: Interactive Strategy, Protocol, or Activity—Window Notes, Part II (Forty-Five Minutes)

1. **Share:** The recorder for each table group should create a "window pane" on a large piece of chart paper. Then, using a round-robin approach to ensure that everyone has an opportunity to speak, ask participants to share two important **facts** from the article. If a fact has already been shared, the next person can share a different fact or expand on a previous comment, insight, or observation. Record the **facts** on

chart paper. Repeat the same process for the other quadrants and record the group's **questions**, **connections**, and **feelings**. (Five minutes per quadrant or a total of twenty minutes)

2. **Reflect, look for patterns, and reach consensus:** Allow participants two minutes to reflect before looking for patterns. Reach consensus and circle the most important facts, best questions, clearest connections, and strongest feelings. (ten minutes)

3. **Report:** Ask the reporter to share and post each group's window pane on the wall. (ten minutes)

Step 3: Personal Reflection (Five Minutes)

Before the next team meeting, participants should record and retain responses to the following questions: What did I learn about this topic? What questions do I have about this topic? What connections did I make to the topic and my work? and What am I feeling about this topic?

Section III: After the Learning

Next Steps and Follow-Up for Coaching Teams

1. Debrief the recent professional development session and list any questions the team may still have about facilitating data conversations. Participants can refer to the questions they wrote during the personal reflection at the end of section II of the module.

2. Locate a video of a team meeting that closely aligns with the grade level or departmental team you are coaching. As the team watches the video, ask them to look for examples of tone, design, structure, and focus. Debrief the team's observations and clarify any confusion or misconceptions.

3. Ask the team to identify what could be done to maximize the strengths and minimize the vulnerabilities of their team's data conversations.

Facilitating Productive Data Conversations

By Tesha Ferriby Thomas and Susan K. Sparks

Adapted from Texas Elementary Principals & Supervisors Association's TEPSA News, *August 2021, Vol. 78, No. 4, www.tepsa.org*

> "In my experience working directly with scores of PLCs, those that flourish and achieve high results for themselves and for their students are almost without exception led by well-trained coaches. . . . Without guidance from a skilled teacher to facilitate this important work, even the best-intentioned teams often flounder."
>
> —Daniel R. Venables

If you think back to the most successful teams you have been a part of, you might realize that effective facilitation played a major role in the team's success. A team leader, coach, or facilitator probably followed a purposeful agenda, elicited balanced participation, and intervened when the group energy was low, the team was off task, or a norm was violated. On successful teams, teacher leaders bring a set of facilitation skills into meetings to support teams that might otherwise struggle.

When teams convene to review samples of student work or analyze data from common assessments, they are participating in one of the most essential discussions associated with the PLC process. To get the most out of these crucial data conversations, principals, coaches, and teacher leaders intentionally use their facilitation skills (structure, process, and expertise) to proactively navigate unexpected challenges and barriers. The following elements enable coaches to effectively facilitate data conversations.

Set the Tone

Effective facilitators set the tone for productive data conversations. Talking about results regularly uncovers vulnerabilities and weaknesses in instructional practice. To hold constructive and honest conversations about their practice, teachers need to feel safe, so it is important to set norms that address trust and safety. Norms parallel our values and set the tone for how team members interact with each other.

A facilitator can also emphasize norms that are pertinent to the task at hand. For example, a team might commit to suspending judgment or assuming positive intentions when discussing the results of common assessments. When reviewing or bringing new norms into team meetings, effective facilitators describe why they may be helpful to the conversation.

Design for Success

When planning for a data conversation, effective facilitators utilize an agenda to anticipate the team's needs and identify a protocol to help achieve the desired outcomes. The key is "to develop teachers' capacities to use data to inform decision making, to act on their decisions, and to use data as evidence in their work" (Killion & Harrison, 2017, p. 41). Facilitators select protocols that will ensure each person contributes and helps the team learn about their students and their teaching.

Provide Structure

To help the team successfully implement a process or protocol, effective facilitators provide structure by introducing the protocol, describing the format, explaining the steps, and assigning key roles. When teams are working to create a product (such as a chart, graph, or list), facilitators may consider utilizing the Third Point strategy introduced by Michael Grinder (1997). This strategy combines the data from the entire team into a single, shared product in order to shift the conversation from individual teachers focused on "my students" to teams focused on "our students." The focus on how our students performed on the assessment promotes a sense of collective responsibility and cooperation among team members.

Focus Conversations

The most effective facilitators are intentional about how teachers discuss, debate, and deliberate about data. They encourage data conversations focused on the right work and discussed in the right way. Lipton and Wellman (2012) believe, "When working with data, how groups talk is as important as what they talk about" (p. 80). In order to ensure data conversations are productive, facilitators pay particular attention to several important verbal and nonverbal skills.

Listen Without Judgment

Sometimes teachers feel anxious or threatened by data conversations because they worry they will be judged or view student performance as a reflection of their own self-worth. To help teachers move past these feelings of vulnerability, facilitators create the conditions where participants listen to learn while withholding judgement. Listening to learn builds understanding, develops empathy, and strengthens relationships.

Pause to Create Space for Reflection

Pausing during conversation allows participants to slow down, reflect, and think critically. Pausing also creates more time to process new information, be creative, and generate potential solutions. "Experienced and aware groups and experienced and aware facilitators come to realize that complex thinking takes and requires time" (Wellman & Lipton, 2004, p. 21). Pausing the conversation allows the necessary time and space teams need to promote learning and creativity.

Paraphrase to Support Relationships and Increase Thinking and Understanding

Paraphrasing demonstrates that we are seeking to understand and learn from others. In addition to paraphrasing to support relationships, we also paraphrase to help summarize main points, communicate respect, acknowledge emotion, and shift the team's thinking to higher conceptual levels.

Inquire to Focus and Open Thinking

Open-ended questions promote inquiry and learning. Wellman and Lipton (2004) offer examples of open-ended questions that might be asked in a data conversation, such as, "As you interpret these test scores, what are some of the things you are noticing? Compare the results to the goals for your students; what are some possible factors that influence these outcomes?" (p. 32). Open questions support more elaboration and reflection and generate ideas and broaden perspectives.

In addition, effective facilitators use questions that elicit detail and lead to deeper understanding, and using words such as *some*, *might*, *notice*, and *seems* serves to expand rather than limit the participants' thinking. For example, a facilitator might ask, "What are some things that surprise you? What are some possible options we might consider? Are there other perspectives we might be missing?"

Effective facilitators anticipate and respond to challenges. They expect, and accept, that barriers to effective collaboration will pop up and require skillful and strategic facilitation to move the team forward. By being proactive and deliberate in their planning of data conversations, facilitators prevent teams from becoming sidetracked by disputes and dysfunction.

MODULE
7.5

"A facilitator helps the team free itself from internal obstacles or difficulties so members more efficiently and effectively accomplish their goals."

—Joellen Killion

Facilitating data conversations can be a tricky business that requires intentionality, purposeful planning, and lots of practice. When facilitators set the tone, design for success, provide structure, and focus conversations on the right work, teams are far more likely to have the kind of data conversations that result in improved student learning.

References

Grinder, M. (1997). *The science of nonverbal communication*. Battleground, WA: Michael Grinder and Associates.

Killion, J. (2013). *School-based professional learning for implementing the Common Core: Unit 2–Facilitating learning teams*. Oxford, OH: Learning Forward.

Killion, J., & Harrison, C. (2017). *Taking the lead: New roles for teachers and school-based coaches* (2nd ed.). Oxford, OH: Learning Forward.

Lipton, L., & Wellman, B. (2012). *Got data? Now what? Creating and leading cultures of inquiry*. Bloomington, IN: Solution Tree Press.

Many, T., Maffoni, M., Sparks, S., & Thomas, T. (2018). *Amplify your impact: Coaching collaborative teams in a PLC at Work*. Bloomington, IN: Solution Tree Press.

Venables, D. R. (2014). *How teachers can turn data into action*. Alexandria, VA: Association for Supervision and Curriculum Development.

Wellman, B., & Lipton, L. (2004). *Data-driven dialogue: A facilitator's guide to collaborative inquiry*. Sherman, CT: MiraVia.

CHAPTER 8

The Pyramid of Interventions

Prerequisite five: *The School (or Each Team) Provides a Systematic Process for Intervention and Extension (DuFour & Reeves, 2016).*

The fifth and final prerequisite condition of becoming a PLC underscores the importance of schoolwide and systematic pyramids of interventions. In our experience, most educators associate a pyramid of interventions with providing support for students who are not yet performing at grade level; however, this final prerequisite has broader implications for teams.

RTI experts and coauthors Austin Buffum, Mike Mattos, and Janet Malone (2018) define an *intervention* as "anything a school does above and beyond what all students receive to help certain students succeed academically" (p. 27). Their definition does not distinguish between students performing above or below grade level, and while students who are not yet proficient must receive extra time and support, it is equally true that students who are "above level or advanced in their academics, also need support to thrive in school" (Coleman, 2010, p. 9).

In their book *Raising the Bar and Closing the Gap*, coauthors Richard DuFour, Rebecca DuFour, Robert Eaker, and Gayle Karhanek (2010) explain what the fifth prerequisite condition of a PLC looks like in practice:

> The PLC model is based on the premise that *all* students benefit when placed in a challenging and supportive environment. The staff of a PLC attempts to create a culture that stretches all students beyond their comfort zone and then provides the support to help them be successful in meeting the challenge. Students who have become comfortable in self-contained special education classes or remedial classes are called upon to meet the challenge of the standard curriculum. Students comfortable in the standard curriculum are called upon to stretch to meet the challenges of an accelerated curriculum. Students in the most rigorous curriculum are challenged to see how far they can go in extending their learning. In a PLC *every* student is urged to pursue more challenging levels of learning, but at the same time, the school assures those students that they will receive the additional time and support they need to be successful to meet that challenge. (p. 174)

DuFour and his colleagues (2010) envision a well-rounded and holistic approach to interventions. Planning for an effective schoolwide and systematic pyramid of interventions is not an either/or proposition. It is not answering PLC critical question three *or* critical question four; it is addressing *both*. In a PLC, the belief is *all means all*. Thus, if collaborative teams commit to meeting the needs of *all* students, they must respond just as consciously, purposefully, and intentionally to critical question four as they do to question three.

The modules in this chapter provide teachers opportunities to explore their beliefs about interventions and create a clearer understanding of why providing students with more time and support is so important. Two modules introduce teams to what an effective pyramid of interventions might look like by describing the critical conditions and specific criteria teams should keep in mind as they design and implement their responses to critical question three ("How will we respond when students do not learn?"; DuFour et al., 2016, p. 36) and question four ("How will we extend the learning for students who are already proficient?; DuFour et al., 2016, p. 36). Finally, using concrete examples that will immediately translate to their professional practice, teams will discover how they can overcome some of the more common obstacles to operationalizing a pyramid of interventions.

Synopsis of Chapter 8 Modules

The fifth prerequisite of a PLC highlights the important role a systematic and schoolwide pyramid of interventions plays in an effective PLC. The modules in this chapter explain why schools should implement a pyramid of interventions, what characteristics are in an effective pyramid of interventions, and how collaborative teams operationalize a pyramid of interventions on their team.

Module 8.1: Why Should Schools Implement Systematic Interventions?

This module focuses on understanding *the why* and provides teams with an overview of the necessary support for a systematic and schoolwide pyramid of interventions. The faculty's will and the school's culture around teaching and learning will heavily influence the success of any system of support. In this module, teams will have opportunities to explore the values, beliefs, and other conditions necessary to implement a systematic and schoolwide pyramid of interventions.

Module 8.2: What Are the Characteristics of an Effective Pyramid of Interventions?

In a landmark study of what constitutes best practice, researchers (Balu et al., 2015) identify four conditions essential to any system of support. When these conditions are present, the likelihood increases that a school's, as well as an individual team's, pyramid of interventions will positively impact student learning. After completing this module, teams will be able to identify what those conditions are and determine if they are present and in place on their team. Teachers will close this module by assessing whether the pyramid of interventions on their team aligns with best practice.

Module 8.3: What Are the Criteria for Operationalizing an Effective Pyramid of Interventions?

This module provides teams with guidance regarding what they will do to operationalize their response to critical question three ("How will we respond when students do not learn?";

DuFour et al., 2016, p. 36). The module will introduce teachers to the SPEED (systematic, practical, effective, essential, and directive) criteria (DuFour, DuFour, Eaker, & Many, 2010) and examine ways they can use it to assess whether the critical components of an effective pyramid of interventions are present. The module concludes with teachers discussing what, if any, aspect of their school's pyramid of interventions they should modify.

Module 8.4: How Do Teacher Teams Operationalize a Pyramid of Interventions?

This module offers teachers an opportunity to talk about how to deliver Tier 2 interventions, which are defined as supplemental interventions by Buffum and colleagues (2018), to their students by comparing and contrasting two different approaches. Teams will have an opportunity to study both approaches and decide which strategy is the best match for their situation. The module uses a modified version of the Philosophers' Chairs protocol as the context for a structured conversation about the advantages and disadvantages of different ways to deliver Tier 2 interventions.

Module 8.5: How Do Teacher Teams Operationalize a Pyramid of Interventions?

One of the challenging aspects of a PLC is finding ways within the school's system of support to provide opportunities to extend the learning for students who have performed at proficient levels and beyond. This module will provide teams with a way of looking at how critical questions three and four are alike and different. Once teachers understand the relationship between intervention and extension, they are in a better position to design systems to simultaneously support students who have and have not learned.

Why Should We Implement Systematic Interventions?

Section I: Before the Learning

Rationale—Why It Matters

One of the most challenging, and most rewarding, elements of the PLC process is the successful implementation of a schoolwide and systematic pyramid of interventions. Whether called *response to intervention* (RTI), a *multitiered system of supports* (MTSS), or simply a *system of support*, providing additional time and support for students who have and have not learned is one of the things that separates schools that get results from those that do not.

Outcomes

Completion of this module will accomplish three things. First, teachers will understand the research regarding the important and positive impact interventions have on learning. Second, the module will provide an opportunity for teams to talk about some of the barriers that may prevent them from creating the kind of robust systems of support they want for their students. Finally, teachers will explore commonly held beliefs that can either enhance or inhibit efforts to successfully implement a systematic and schoolwide pyramid of interventions.

SIG and Pathways

SIG for prerequisite five (page 241) and Pathways for Prerequisite Five (5.1–5.3; page 248)

Key Coaching Points

1. Even though research shows systemic and schoolwide systems of support have a positive impact on student learning and provide principals and teacher leaders with one of the most impactful leverage points of the PLC process, schools often underutilize pyramids of interventions.

2. Most of the obstacles to creating an effective pyramid of interventions fall into one of three categories: (1) school structures (such as the master schedule), (2) past practice ("This is the way we have always done it around here"), and (3) the misalignment of fundamental beliefs about teaching and learning (the faculty does not support the idea that when given enough time and support, all students can learn to high levels).

3. All schools have the resources to provide extra time and support for students. The absence of effective systems of support is more often due to a staff's lack of will, not lack of skill.

4. School culture impacts the success of any initiative to establish a pyramid of interventions.

Important Vocabulary and Terms

Beliefs: These are the values, often based on previous experiences, which help shape how teachers view their roles and responsibilities to ensure all students learn to high levels.

Interventions: This is any support a school provides above and beyond what all students receive to help certain students succeed academically (Buffum et al., 2018).

Systematic and schoolwide: This refers to a process that provides all students, regardless of their teacher, consistent access to universally available interventions.

Section II: During the Learning

Preparation—Time and Materials

Complete this module in forty-five minutes. The ideal group size is four participants per group, seated at tables, but the activity will work equally well with three to six participants per group. Each table group will need one set of standard dice and access to markers and chart paper. Each participant needs a copy of the following handouts.

- "Why Should We Implement Systematic Interventions?" (page 193)

- "Dialogue Dice" (page 195)

Step 1: Getting Ready to Learn—Reciprocal Interviews (Twenty Minutes)

1. Ask participants to review "Why Should We Implement Systematic Interventions?" (page 193) and choose three statements they agree with. (six minutes)

2. When the group is ready, have everyone find a partner from outside of their small group. Each participant briefly shares one statement from the handout with his or her partner that resonates, explaining why he or she chose it. These are quick conversations (ninety seconds per person). (three minutes)

3. Repeat the reciprocal interview two more times, each time with a different partner, again from outside of their table group. When finished, ask participants to return to their tables. (six minutes)

4. Using a round-robin approach, give each member of the small group an opportunity to talk about what he or she learned during the reciprocal interviews. (five minutes)

Step 2: Interactive Strategy, Protocol, or Activity—Dialogue Dice Activity (Twenty Minutes)

Provide each small group with dice and each participant with a copy of the "Dialogue Dice" (page 195). Explain that each small group will respond to a number of questions on the handout. All of the questions represent values, beliefs, or logistical questions that teams should consider when designing a schoolwide and systematic pyramid of interventions. (twenty minutes)

1. **Roll the dice and discuss the question:** Ask participants to choose a facilitator and a timekeeper. The participant with the longest tenure in education rolls the dice and reads the corresponding question aloud. Once the facilitator confirms there is no confusion with terminology, the table group initiates a discussion of the question. (five minutes)

2. **Repeat rolling and discussing:** After five minutes (or less if there are no additional comments), close the discussion and move on to the next person who rolls the dice and repeats the process. Groups should continue discussing different topics until the coach reconvenes the larger group. Typically, there is enough time to discuss two or three more questions. (ten minutes)

3. **Reflection:** Use a 3:2:1 reflection strategy as the participants' exit ticket. Participants write down three things from the activity that confirmed their thinking, two things they learned, and one thing that surprised them. Based on the time available, provide as many participants as possible an opportunity to comment on any aspect of this activity. (five minutes)

Step 3: Personal Reflection (Five Minutes)

Ask participants to record and retain their thoughts about why schools should implement interventions: "Did anything make you want to reconsider how the school or team is currently providing extra time and support for students? What questions do you want to learn more about?" Personal reflections will be discussed as part of the section III debrief with a coach.

Section III: After the Learning

Next Steps and Follow-Up for Coaching Teams

The first goal of this module is to understand why a particular element of the PLC process is important. The coach's goal for this part of the debrief should be to focus the teams' attention on reaching consensus on why it is important that schools and teams implement a systematic pyramid of interventions. Possible questions or tasks for the team to consider might include the following.

1. Give each person a chance to share what he or she wrote during the 3:2:1 activity. Listen for patterns or common ideas among group members. Are there any consistent insights that could create areas of agreement? Likewise, are there any areas of disagreement? Based on the discussion, write a belief statement (Begin the statement with, "We believe . . ." and make sure that it is something that everyone agrees to) about providing more time and support to students who do or do not learn.

2. Ask members to determine how they might address the reflection questions recorded during the personal reflection step at the end of section II of this module.

Why Should We Implement Systematic Interventions?

Characteristics of high-performing schools include setting high expectations for all students, using assessment data to support student success, and employing systems for identifying intervention (Ragland, Clubine, Constable, & Smith, 2002).

"Reforms must move the system toward early identification and swift intervention, using scientifically based instruction and teaching methods" (President's Commission on Excellence in Special Education, 2002, p. 8).

"A criterion for schools that have made great strides in achievement and equity is immediate and decisive intervention. . . . Successful schools do not give a second thought to providing preventive assistance for students in need" (Reeves, 2006, p. 87).

"The most significant factor in providing appropriate interventions for students was the development of layers of support. Systems of support specifically addressed the needs of students who were 'stretching' to take more rigorous coursework" (Dolejs, 2006, p. 3).

"High-performing schools and school systems set high expectations for what each and every child should achieve, and then monitor performance against the expectations, intervening whenever they are not met. . . . The very best systems intervene at the level of the individual student, developing processes and structures within schools that are able to identify whenever a student is starting to fall behind, and then intervening to improve that child's performance" (Barber & Mourshed, 2009, p. 34).

In order to raise student achievement, schools must use diagnostic assessments to measure students' knowledge and skills at the beginning of each curriculum unit, on-the-spot assessments to check for understanding during instruction, and end-of-unit assessments and interim assessments to see how well students learned. "All of these enable teachers to make mid-course corrections and to get students into intervention earlier" (Odden & Archibald, 2009, p. 23).

In higher performing school systems, "teachers identify struggling students as early as possible, and direct them towards a variety of proven intervention strategies, developed at both the school and district level, that assist all students in mastering grade-level academic objectives" (National Center for Educational Achievement, 2009, p. 34).

"One of the most productive ways for districts to facilitate continual improvement is to develop teachers' capacity to use formative assessments of student progress aligned with district expectations for student learning, and to use formative data in devising and implementing interventions during the school year" (Louis, Kruse, & Marks, 1996, p. 214).

"If a school can make both teaching and time variables . . . and target them to meet each student's individual learning and developmental needs, the school is more likely to achieve high levels of learning for every student" (Mattos & Buffum, 2015, p. 2).

page 1 of 2

References

Barber, M., & Mourshed, M. (2009, July). *Shaping the future: How good education systems can become great in the decade ahead* (Report on the International Education Roundtable). New York: McKinsey & Company. Accessed at www.mckinsey.com /locations/southeastasia/knowledge/Education_Roundtable.pdf on January 1, 2010.

Dolejs, C. (2006). *Report on key practices and policies of consistently higher performing high schools*. Washington, DC: National High School Center. Accessed at www .betterhighschools.org/docs/ReportOfKeyPracticesandPolicies_10-31-06.pdf on January 10, 2010.

Louis, K. S., Kruse, S. D., & Marks, H. M. (1996). Schoolwide professional community. In F. M. Newmann & Associates (Eds.), *Authentic achievement: Restructuring schools for intellectual quality* (pp. 179–204). San Francisco: Jossey-Bass.

Mattos, M., & Buffum, A. (Eds.). (2015). *It's about time: Planning interventions and extensions in secondary school*. Bloomington, IN: Solution Tree Press.

National Center for Educational Achievement. (2009, January). *Core practices in math and science: An investigation of consistently higher performing school systems in five states*. Austin, TX: Author. Accessed at www.act.org/content/dam/act/unsecured /documents/Core-Practices-in-Math-and-Science.pdf on December 1, 2015.

Odden, A. R., & Archibald, S. J. (2009). *Doubling student performance . . . and finding the resources to do it*. Thousand Oaks, CA: Corwin Press.

President's Commission on Excellence in Special Education. (2002, July). *A new era: Revitalizing special education for children and their families*. Washington, DC: U.S. Department of Education Office of Special Education and Rehabilitative Services. Accessed at http://ectacenter.org/~pdfs/calls/2010/earlypartc/revitalizing_special _education.pdf on December 17, 2015.

Ragland, M. A., Clubine, B., Constable, D., & Smith, P. A. (2002, April). *Expecting success: A study of five high performing, high poverty schools*. Washington, DC: Council of Chief State School Officers.

Reeves, D. B. (2006). *The learning leader: How to focus school improvement for better results*. Alexandria, VA: Association for Supervision and Curriculum Development.

Dialogue Dice

Directions: Each person in your group takes a turn rolling the dice and then briefly shares his or her response to the corresponding questions. Discuss the question and response with all group members. Take a maximum of three minutes per question.

Roll	Respond to the Following Questions
2	How can we encourage the belief that all students can learn while we acknowledge that all students don't learn in the same way or at the same time?
3	What can we do if a student's needs are not academic, but instead the student simply lacks the organizational skills or motivation to try?
4	How do we provide support to students who lack basic, foundational skills and still give them access to the grade-level curriculum?
5	How do we determine what interventions to offer, and what do we do if a student requires help in multiple subject areas?
6	How do we transition students to the correct interventions, and, once they get there, how do we hold students accountable to attend?
7	How can we provide more time and support using our current resources without asking teachers to work beyond their contractual obligations?
8	Who is going to organize all this, and how do we prevent the intervention process from becoming a paperwork nightmare for teachers?
9	Who is going to provide the extra instruction, and how are we going to assign staff? Is this voluntary, or will we assign it as an extra duty for teachers?
10	How do we move beyond a traditional study-hall approach and actually provide specific, targeted, direct instruction student by student and skill by skill?
11	What are the teachers' beliefs around the importance of ensuring all students have access to additional time and support for learning?
12	How does the current schedule support opportunities for all students to get extra time and support without missing direct instruction in other essential skills?

What Are the Characteristics of an Effective Pyramid of Interventions?

Section I: Before the Learning

Rationale—Why It Matters

Researchers (Balu et al., 2015) have identified four characteristics or conditions of an effective response to intervention (RTI). To make the best decisions possible about the allocation of resources (time, materials, and personnel), faculty and staff must become familiar with these characteristics and how they impact student learning.

Outcomes

Teachers will understand and can articulate what characteristics or conditions are essential to the proper implementation of the RTI process. Teams will also be able to assess their school's RTI process in light of best practice and use that information to improve their RTI programming across the district, in their school, and on their teams.

SIG and Pathways

SIG for prerequisite five (page 241) and Pathways for Prerequisite Five (5.1–5.3; page 248)

Key Coaching Points

1. Researchers find schools must ensure (1) leaders assign the most effective staff members to work with the most vulnerable students, (2) students have access to interventions without missing direct instruction in the core subjects, (3) interventions must be of sufficient frequency and duration to positively impact learning, and (4) actionable data are the basis of identification, assignment, and movement of students within intervention programs (Balu et al., 2015).

2. Guide the faculty in determining the degree to which the school's current RTI aligns with the four conditions research identifies as critical to success.

Important Vocabulary and Terms

RTI: This is a multitiered and systematic process to ensure every student receives the additional time and support he or she needs to learn to high levels. The support is timely, targeted, and systematic (Buffum et al., 2018).

Section II: During the Learning

Preparation—Time and Materials

Complete this module in an hour. The ideal small group size is four participants (one person for each section of the article) per group, seated at tables. Each small group should count off by four and choose roles; the group will need a facilitator, timekeeper, a recorder, and a reporter. Each small group will need access to markers and chart paper. Participants will need copies of the following handout.

- "Ensure the Successful Implementation of Interventions in a PLC" (page 199)

Step 1: Getting Ready to Learn—KWL (Fifteen Minutes)

1. Begin by asking each participant to reflect for a moment about the most effective pyramid of interventions he or she has ever seen, heard about, or been involved with and jot down three or four characteristics that made it effective. (five minutes)

2. Next, the recorder for each table should draw a three-column KWL (know, want to know, and learned) chart (lengthwise) on a piece of chart paper. Label column one with a *K*, column two with a *W*, and column 3 with an *L*. Working together, teachers should identify the things they already know about effective intervention and write them under the *K* in the first column. (five minutes)

3. Ask participants to continue by recording what they would like to learn more about in relation to an effective pyramid of interventions under the *W* in the second column. The group should leave the third column (*L*) empty for now. (five minutes)

4. If time allows, ask for volunteers to share what they wrote; once the first two columns of the KWL chart are complete, the group is ready to read the article.

Step 2: Interactive Strategy, Protocol, or Activity—Each Teach Protocol (Forty-Five Minutes)

Provide participants with a copy of "Ensure the Successful Implementation of RTI in a PLC" (page 199). Explain that using the Each Teach protocol, each member of the group will read a segment of an article and teach the information to the other members of the group. Each participant will have ten minutes to read the article and prepare a micro-lesson on their section of the article. Each micro-lesson should include a summary statement, key points, and a concrete example of how the idea might apply to the group's school or team.

1. **Read the article:** Ask participants to read the beginning and end of the article *and* their section. Person one reads "Condition 1: Ensure leaders assign the most effective staff members to work with our most vulnerable students." Person two reads "Condition 2: Ensure students have access to interventions without missing direct instruction in core subjects." Person three reads "Condition 3: Ensure interventions are of sufficient frequency and duration to positively impact student learning." Person four reads "Condition 4: Ensure actionable data are the basis of identification, assignment, and movement of students within intervention programs." Each person should reflect on their section and decide what is important for other teachers to know. They will be expected to communicate this to others during the next step of the protocol. (ten minutes)

2. **Teach micro-lessons:** After ten minutes of reading, person one has four minutes to teach his or her micro-lesson. Continue until each participant has the opportunity to teach his or her micro-lesson. (sixteen minutes)

3. **Identify learning:** Ask participants to take turns identifying what they learned about the conditions necessary for effective intervention. Ask participants to share what they learned; the recorder for each group should complete the last column of their group's KWL chart (What did we learn?). The recorder also captures any consensus the group reaches on a separate sheet of chart paper. As the final step in the protocol, participants list any questions, issues, or concerns that need further study or research. (fifteen minutes)

Step 3: Personal Reflection (Five Minutes)

Before the next team meeting, participants should reflect on and familiarize themselves with the "How Do Our School's Current Practices Align With the Essential Elements of RTI?" (page 202) handout. Each team will use the handout later to assess the relative strengths and weaknesses of the school or team's current intervention offerings. Teachers should save their worksheet; their reflections will be the starting point for discussions at a future team meeting.

Section III: After the Learning

Next Steps for Coaching Collaborative Teams

The coach's goal should be to help the team reach a consensus regarding the existing interventions, specifically in relation to the conditions the article in the activity outlines. The focus of the teams' attention should be on taking action and developing a plan for how they will use what they learned when responding to PLC critical question three. Possible questions or tasks for the team to consider might include the following.

1. Ask each team member to share his or her best thinking about the strengths and weaknesses of the team's current interventions. Seek a consensus on any potential improvement points (PIPs). Record and post the team's comments.

2. Refer to the "How Do Our School's Current Practices Align With the Essential Elements of RTI?" (page 202) handout and determine if there are any gaps in their school's or team's system of interventions. Ask members to determine how they might address these gaps.

3. Establish a timeline for the team to implement its plan at the next collaborative team meeting where members will analyze student assessment data.

Ensure the Successful Implementation of Interventions in a PLC

By Thomas W. Many

Adapted from Texas Elementary Principals & Supervisors Association's TEPSA News, *January/ February 2018, Vol. 75, No. 3, www.tepsa.org*

> "When it comes to how educators should respond when students struggle in school, the research and evidence in our field have never been more conclusive—response to intervention (RTI) is the right way to intervene."
>
> —Austin Buffum, Mike Mattos, & Janet Malone

There is agreement that RTI is the most effective way to respond to students who are not learning, and an RTI framework is commonplace in schools, yet implementing the RTI process is one of the most confounding challenges principals and teachers face.

To shed some light on this conundrum, the U.S. Department of Education commissioned a study of the intervention practices of schools across the United States (Balu et al., 2015). Results of the study suggest that to successfully implement RTI, principals should ensure four conditions exist in their schools. First, leaders must assign the most effective members of the faculty and staff to work with the most vulnerable learners. Second, students must have access to additional time and support without missing direct instruction in core subjects. Third, intervention programs must be of sufficient frequency and duration to positively impact learning. Finally, teams must use data from multiple sources to make decisions about student participation in intervention programs.

Condition 1: Ensure Leaders Assign the Most Effective Staff Members to Work With Our Most Vulnerable Students

It seems obvious that the most effective staff members should be responsible for working with students who are not yet proficient, but this is not always the case. In schools with limited interventions for students performing below expectations, researchers Rekha Balu and her colleagues (2015) find a combination of specialists, classroom teachers, and paraprofessionals delivers interventions. Paraprofessionals represent the most common alternative at 37 percent, with classroom teachers at 26 percent, and specialists at 18 percent.

The question principals must consider is not who would deliver but who would *best* deliver the additional time and support. The choice of who is best suited to provide students with support is based on factors like background and experience, specialized training and expertise, or instructional effectiveness (that is, the performance of a group of students on a recent common assessment). Principals must ensure that whoever delivers interventions has the necessary tools and strategies to help students succeed.

Students deserve the most qualified—not the most available—adult to deliver interventions. If the goal is to create interventions that work, principals must commit to assigning the most effective and qualified staff members to work with the most vulnerable and struggling students.

Condition 2: Ensure Students Have Access to Interventions Without Missing Direct Instruction in Core Subjects

Any effective intervention program is built on the belief that all students can learn. While it's true that not all students learn at the same time or in the same way, schools functioning as PLCs believe that given enough time and support, all students will learn (DuFour, DuFour, Eaker, Many, & Mattos, 2016). An effective intervention program provides extra support in addition to core instruction. This would seem logical but, once again, Balu and her colleagues (2015) report this condition is not always present.

Balu and her colleagues (2015) find that students received additional time and support both inside (during) and outside (in addition to) the core instructional block. In some schools, more than half of all intervention groups met during core (Tier 1) instruction. As a result, not all students received intervention services in addition to their core instructional time. The implication of this practice is "intervention may have *replaced* rather than supplemented some instruction services during the core" (Balu et al., 2015, p. 60). Too often, educators pull students from classroom instruction when they struggle. This practice means the most vulnerable students miss important initial instruction, which causes them to fall further and further behind. Whenever intervention supplants rather than supplements classroom instruction, underperforming students—those with the greatest needs—may actually receive less direct instruction.

In schools functioning as a PLC, principals ensure students have access to additional time and support without missing direct instruction in another core subject. Struggling students need more time to learn, not less.

Condition 3: Ensure Interventions Are of Sufficient Frequency and Duration to Positively Impact Learning

Our experience tells us the frequency and duration of intervention programs fall short of what we recommend. Best practice calls for ninety minutes of reading instruction during core instruction (Balu et al., 2015). For students not learning as teachers expect in Tier 1 instruction, they must provide additional Tier 2 and Tier 3 interventions to their core instruction.

Balu and her colleagues (2015) find the length of daily intervention sessions falls within a range of twenty to forty minutes. The research team recommends teachers deliver Tier 2 interventions three times a week and Tier 3 interventions four to five times a week. Using thirty minutes (the midpoint of the range) as the standard, students in Tier 2 would receive ninety minutes of additional intervention programming and as much as 150 minutes in Tier 3. This simply is not what is typically available to students in most schools.

Commitment 4: Ensure Actionable Data Are the Basis of Identification, Assignment, and Movement of Students Within Intervention Programs

Without an assessment system that generates a variety of formative and summative measures for classroom teachers, students' movement from one tier to another is determined by relatively few points of data from a single source (Pierce & Jackson, 2017). This practice is problematic because it assumes all assessments provide actionable data, all students have the same needs, and a standard set of interventions will be equally effective for all students. Unfortunately, none of these assumptions is true. "Regular data collection allows staff to critically gauge the effectiveness of their instruction and interventions" (Pierce & Jackson, 2017, p. 6).

"Because RTI is proven to be the best way to intervene when students need additional time and support, schools that function as a PLC should not view RTI as a new initiative but instead, as deepening their current intervention practices."

—Austin Buffum, Mike Mattos, & Janet Malone

Balu and her colleagues (2015) focus on reading interventions at the elementary level, but their findings are applicable in other settings. What is clear is that if schools want to increase the likelihood that interventions will help students learn, they must ensure that (1) the most effective staff members work with the most vulnerable students, (2) students have access to interventions without missing direct instruction in core subjects, (3) interventions are of sufficient frequency and duration to positively impact learning, and (4) data from multiple sources are the basis of identification, assignment, and movement of students within intervention programs.

References

Balu, R., Zhu, P., Doolittle, F., Schiller, E., Jenkins, J., & Gersten, R. (2015, November). *Evaluation of response to intervention practices for elementary school reading.* Washington, DC: U.S. Department of Education, Institute of Education Sciences, National Center for Education Evaluation and Regional Assistance. Accessed at https://files.eric.ed.gov/fulltext/ED560820.pdf on March 1, 2021.

Buffum, A., Mattos, M., & Malone, J. (2018). *Taking action: A handbook for RTI at Work.* Bloomington, IN: Solution Tree Press.

DuFour, R., DuFour, R., Eaker, R., Many, T. W., & Mattos, M. (2016). *Learning by doing: A handbook for Professional Learning Communities at Work* (3rd ed.). Bloomington, IN: Solution Tree Press.

Pierce, J., & Jackson, D. (2017). *Ten steps to make RTI work in your schools.* Washington, DC: American Institutes for Research. Accessed at https://air.org/resource/ten-steps-make-rti-work-schools on January 26, 2021.

Sparks, S. (2015). Study: RTI practice falls short of promise. *Education Week.* Accessed at www.edweek.org/ew/articles/2015/11/11/study-rti-practice-falls-short-of-promise.html on January 26, 2021.

MODULE
8.2

How Do Our School's Current Practices Align With the Essential Elements of RTI?

Essential Element of RTI	Our Current Reality	Our Desired Outcome (Long-Term Goal)	Our First Steps (Short-Term Goal)
Have we embraced that RTI is not a special education or regular education program, but rather a schoolwide process that requires collective responsibility to ensure that all students learn?			
Is our instructional program standards-based and research-based?			
Is our instructional program delivered with fidelity by highly qualified teachers?			
Do we universally screen all students with comprehensive literacy and mathematics assessments several times a year?			
Do we frequently progress monitor students at risk in all tiers?			
Do we know when to provide students more intensive support?			
Do we communicate regularly with parents and other stakeholders?			

What Are the Criteria for Designing an Effective Pyramid of Interventions? The Need for SPEED

Section I: Before the Learning

Rationale—Why It Matters

This module provides guidance regarding what criteria teams should use to assess the effectiveness of their team's RTI. Whether teams are just beginning to implement RTI or have years of experience and are revisiting existing interventions, the SPEED criteria help deconstruct the complex process of designing an effective RTI into smaller and more manageable tasks.

Outcomes

Teachers will become familiar with and can apply the SPEED criteria to the interventions in their school. After working through this module, teams can identify which aspects of their intervention offerings are and are not working, and why.

SIG and Pathways

SIG for prerequisite five (page 241) and Pathways for Prerequisite Five (5.1–5.3; page 248)

Key Coaching Points

1. Coaches should focus on building common vocabulary. Teachers should know, define, and be able to give an example for each element of the SPEED criteria.

2. Once teachers establish a common vocabulary, attention shifts to helping teams complete an analysis of the alignment between the SPEED criteria and existing interventions.

3. Teams use the SPEED criteria to maintain and improve an effective RTI or redesign existing structures.

Important Vocabulary and Terms

Systematic: This a schoolwide intervention, independent of individual teachers, and publicly communicated by the school in writing.

Practical: The intervention is affordable given the school's resources in terms of time, space, staff, and materials.

Effective: The intervention is accessible, available, and operational early enough in the year to make a difference.

Essential: The intervention focuses on essential standards and targets to support the students' specific needs.

Directive: Participation in the intervention must be mandatory (not invitational) and part of the regular school day.

Section II: During the Learning

Preparation—Time and Materials

Complete this module in fifty minutes. The ideal group size is four participants per group, seated at tables. Each small group should choose roles (facilitator, timekeeper, recorder, and reporter) and have access to markers and chart paper. Participants need copies of the following handout.

- "The Need for SPEED: Criteria for Designing an Effective Pyramid of Interventions" (page 206)

Step 1: Getting Ready to Learn—Pairs Squared (Ten Minutes)

1. Ask participants to imagine they are invited to visit a neighboring school to conduct an external audit of that school's RTI programming.

2. Have participants find a partner from another small group and create a list based on what they know about effective RTI programming. Explain that they are developing a tool teachers could use to assess the effectiveness of an intervention in the district, at the school, and on the team. (If participants completed module 8.2, refer them to their previous work.) Think about what an effective pyramid of interventions would look like, sound like, and feel like. (five minutes)

3. After five minutes, ask each pair to join another pair (Pairs Squared), combine their lists, and create a final set of criteria for the upcoming audit. When finished, ask the teachers to return to their seats. (five minutes)

Step 2: Interactive Strategy, Protocol, or Activity—Last Word Protocol (Forty Minutes)

The facilitator should go around and have the large group count off by four for this activity.

1. **Read the article:** Have participants read the article "The Need for SPEED: Criteria for Designing an Effective Pyramid of Interventions" (page 206) and identify three or four of the most significant ideas from the text. (seven minutes)

2. **Share ideas:** Working in their small groups, person one has two minutes to briefly share his or her idea and state why it is significant, but he or she should not elaborate. The rest of the group has three minutes to quickly agree, disagree, question, or expand on person one's idea. Once the group is finished, person one gets the remaining time to build on what others said, thereby getting the "last word" on the idea. Each cycle lasts five minutes. The group repeats the process as persons two, three, and four share a different idea they thought was important or significant, with feedback from the rest of the group. (twenty minutes)

3. **Identify takeaways:** To close the activity, ask teams to identify the biggest takeaways from the article. Have the participants individually review the original list of effective RTI practices they wrote in step 1, Getting Ready to Learn, and decide if they

would change the list of attributes *after* reading the article. If time allows, have the participants share any new ahas, amens, or atta boys. The recorder should capture any comments on chart paper. (eight minutes)

Step 3: Personal Reflection (Five Minutes)

Before the next team meeting, ask each teacher to reflect on the viability of the SPEED criteria. Encourage teachers to use the following space to write down any questions, issues, or concerns that may need further study or research. Record and retain the personal reflections until the section III debrief with a coach has been completed.

Section III: After the Learning

Next Steps for Coaching Collaborative Teams

1. The coach's goal is to help the team reach consensus regarding how well their team's interventions align with the five criteria of SPEED (systematic, practical, effective, essential, and directive).

2. While all the criteria are important, coaches should encourage the team to decide if one is more important than the others; urge participants to write down why the criteria they chose are the most important.

3. Identify some possible next steps, and agree on a plan for moving forward. Establish a timeline for the team to implement the next steps.

MODULE

8.3

The Need for Speed: Criteria for Designing an Effective Pyramid of Interventions

By Thomas W. Many, Barbara W. Cirigliano, Heather Friziellie, and Julie A. Schmidt

Adapted from Texas Elementary Principals & Supervisors Association's TEPSA News, *January/ February 2011, Vol. 68, No. 1, www.tepsa.org*

> "What happens in our school when a student does not learn? We consider this question to be the fork in the road—the one question more than any other that will demonstrate a school's commitment to learning for all students and its progress on the road to becoming a PLC."
>
> —Richard DuFour, Rebecca DuFour, Robert Eaker, & Gayle Karhanek

Many educators are overwhelmed trying to meet the needs of every learner in their school. When students struggle, teams often struggle with how to help. Teachers often ask for help in designing effective ways to provide students with more time and support. The desire to help all students learn necessitates the need for criteria to guide the development of appropriate pyramids of interventions; it creates the need for SPEED.

The SPEED criteria serve as a guide for designing an appropriate pyramid of interventions. The acronym stands for systematic, practical, effective, essential, and directive (DuFour, DuFour, Eaker, & Many, 2010). When schools develop a pyramid of interventions that meets the SPEED criteria, educators create ownership by the faculty, meet the needs of individual learners, and maximize the school's available resources.

The SPEED Criteria

To be *systematic*, a pyramid of interventions must be schoolwide, independent of the individual teacher, and communicated in writing by the school (who, why, how, where, and when) to everyone: staff, parents, and students. When author Tom Many was superintendent of Kildeer Countryside School District 96 in Buffalo Grove, Illinois, every school designed a brochure they revised annually and made available to parents at the start of each year. The brochure described the system of interventions in enough detail that when students needed more time and support to learn, teachers and parents knew exactly what was available, what needed to happen based on data, who could provide the instruction, and when it was offered during the school day.

Systematic and schoolwide pyramids of interventions provide tiered instruction of increasing time and intensity to support struggling students. Effective pyramids begin with differentiated classroom (core) instruction and increase in time and intensity based on each learner's needs. Teacher teams allocate the vast majority of resources to the core curriculum because helping all learners initially will surely limit the number of students who need interventions later.

To be *practical*, a pyramid of interventions must be affordable, given the school's available resources (time, space, staff, and materials). Intervention plans don't need to cost a lot, nor do they have to come in a box. Instead, teams must first think about how to use or reallocate existing resources to fully utilize what is already available.

Time is one of a school's biggest resources, and the daily schedule represents an opportunity to maximize the impact of interventions. DuFour and his colleagues (2004) suggest teachers consider three questions when thinking about their schedules. First, do they believe it is the purpose of their school to ensure all students learn to high levels? Second, do they acknowledge that students learn at different rates with differing levels of support? And finally, have they created a schedule that guarantees students will receive additional opportunities to learn through extra time and support in a systematic way, regardless of who their teacher might be? If the answer to these questions is *yes*, teacher teams can organize the schedule to create time during the day when every available person becomes part of the pyramid of interventions.

For example, teacher teams can build a thirty-minute intervention block into the school day. The intervention block represents dedicated and protected time that guarantees students access to more time and support. Teams decide which students will participate in which interventions at the beginning of each week based on formative assessment data. This embedded time during the school day is a sacred time during which teachers provide interventions to students.

To be *effective*, the pyramid of interventions must be accessible, available, and operational early enough in the school year to make a difference for students. This component of the SPEED criteria rejects the traditional notion that schools wait for a student to fail before intervening. Intervention plans should have flexible entrance and exit criteria responsive to students' needs.

DuFour and his colleagues (2004) define the goal of an effective pyramid of interventions as providing additional time and support as necessary until:

> Students demonstrate they are ready to assume greater responsibility for their learning. The focus is on gradually weaning the student from the extra time and support as the student becomes successful in classes. The interventions then serve as a safety net if the student should falter, but they are not intended to be a permanent crutch. (p. 167)

This goal is only possible when the faculty develops clear criteria that move students from one tier to another until the student demonstrates mastery and eventually exits from the interventions.

To be *essential*, the pyramid of interventions must focus on the essential outcomes of the district's curriculum and target a student's specific learning. Using data, teachers regroup students based on their identified outcomes to provide the appropriate intervention that focuses on the specific area of need for that group of learners. For example, a mathematics lab provides target-aligned support to help students master specific skills using a collaborative team–created prescription sheet.

After discussing the results of formative assessments, teachers can better provide targeted time and support. According to author Thomas R. Guskey (2010), effective interventions possess three essential characteristics: (1) they present concepts differently, (2) they engage students differently, and (3) they provide students with successful experiences. It is critical for teacher teams to collaboratively identify essential standards and analyze assessment data together to purposefully plan and target their instruction.

To be *directive*, a pyramid of interventions must be mandatory—not invitational—and a part of the student's regular school day. For example, teachers in an early childhood center use the very beginning of each school day to deliver specific interventions to specific students while the remainder of the students focus on *welcome work* that extends and reinforces their learning. Students cannot opt out, and parents and teachers cannot waive students' participation in the intervention programs. Learning is not an optional activity, and school leaders must remain resolute in their responsibility to respond when students don't learn.

As DuFour and his colleagues (2016) suggest, "It is disingenuous for any school to claim its purpose is to help all students learn at high levels and then fail to create a system of interventions to give struggling learners additional time and support for learning" (p. 175). In District 96, the staff took that message to heart and embraced the SPEED criteria to ensure our pyramid of interventions answered the question, "How does our school respond when students don't learn?"

References

DuFour, R., DuFour, R., Eaker, R., & Karhanek, G. (2004). *Whatever it takes: How professional learning communities respond when kids don't learn*. Bloomington, IN: Solution Tree Press.

DuFour, R., DuFour, R., Eaker, R., & Many, T. W. (2010). *Learning by doing: A handbook for Professional Learning Communities at Work* (2nd ed.). Bloomington, IN: Solution Tree Press.

DuFour, R., DuFour, R., Eaker, R., Many, T. W., & Mattos, M. (2016). *Learning by doing: A handbook for Professional Learning Communities at Work* (3rd ed.). Bloomington, IN: Solution Tree Press.

Guskey, T. R. (2010). Formative assessment: The contribution of Benjamin S. Bloom. In H. L. Andrade & G. J. Cizek (Eds.), *Handbook of formative assessment* (pp. 106–124). New York: Routledge.

How Do Teacher Teams Operationalize a Pyramid of Interventions? Best Thinking on Ways to Organize and Deliver Tier 2 Interventions

Section I: Before the Learning

Rationale—Why It Matters

This module addresses a common question teams have about implementing schoolwide and systematic pyramids of interventions: "How do we deliver Tier 2 interventions?" In previous modules, teams worked to understand why interventions matter, identified conditions that must be present for interventions to be effective, and explored criteria to measure the quality of their intervention programming. This module adds one more layer and helps teams with designing the most effective and efficient delivery system for Tier 2 interventions for their school.

Outcomes

Teacher teams will become familiar with the strengths and vulnerabilities of two different methodologies—the regrouping and classroom approach—for delivering Tier 2 interventions to students who need more time and support. Teams will be able to explain why the regrouping approach is preferred and also consider ways to implement it on their teams.

SIG and Pathways

SIG for prerequisite five (page 241) and Pathways for Prerequisite Five (5.2; page 248)

Key Coaching Points

1. Participants build a shared understanding of different approaches to delivering Tier 2 interventions. Teachers can articulate the similarities and differences of the approaches.

2. Either approach is better than having no agreed-on way to deliver Tier 2 interventions. Teachers can build a rationale for why one approach is preferred over another.

3. Finally, coaches help teachers identify the next steps for designing and operationalizing a system to deliver Tier 2 interventions on their team.

Important Vocabulary and Terms

Classroom approach: This is when individual teachers pull small groups of students for help during independent work.

Essential grade-level curriculum: The standards teams have agreed all students must know

Common assessment: The same assessment teachers give to all students at the same time, with the team using the results to identify students who have similar needs for more time and support.

Regrouping approach: This is when teams pull students with the same needs from multiple classrooms for intervention.

Section II: During the Learning

Preparation—Time and Materials

Complete this module in fifty-five minutes. The ideal small group size is four participants per group, seated at tables. Each table group will choose roles (facilitator, timekeeper, recorder, and reporter) and have access to markers and chart paper. Each participant needs a copy of the following handout.

- "Regrouping Versus the Classroom Approach: Choosing the Better Way" (page 212)

Step 1: Getting Ready to Learn—Where Do You Stand? (Twenty-Five Minutes)

1. Explain the differences between the *classroom approach* and *regrouping approach* for delivering Tier 2 interventions. It is important to provide teachers with a definition of both approaches; avoid value statements or positions in favor of one approach or the other. (five minutes)

2. Next, ask participants to line up based on their years of teaching experience. Divide the group into two equal parts, and have each group move to opposite sides of the room. Announce that one side will be advocating for the classroom approach and the other for the regrouping approach. Each side builds the case for why they prefer their approach and chooses a spokesperson to deliver their argument to the other half of the room. (five minutes)

3. Starting with the classroom side, allow five minutes for the spokesperson to make the case. After the classroom side is finished presenting its rationale, allow anyone from the regrouping side to switch over to the classroom side. Repeat the same process with the spokesperson from the regrouping side presenting reasons why they prefer their approach. Once the regrouping side finishes its argument, give everyone on the classroom side a chance to switch over to the regrouping side. (ten minutes)

4. Have both sides reconvene, revise their arguments, and try a second time to persuade their colleagues to switch sides. This second time, sharing the rationale should go faster. (five minutes)

5. Once the second round is complete, ask everyone to return to their seats. Optional: If time permits, the small groups should have a few moments to share their reactions and debrief the activity.

Step 2: Interactive Strategy, Protocol, or Activity—Supporting Evidence Activity (30 Minutes)

1. **Read the article:** In preparation for the activity, each table group recorder should draw a two-column chart (lengthwise) on chart paper, labeling the left-hand column *Key Concepts* and the right-hand column *Supporting Evidence*. Ask the participants to

read the article "Regrouping Versus the Classroom Approach: Choosing the Better Way" (page 212) and identify three or four key concepts. (seven minutes)

2. **Identify key concepts:** Participants seated at the same table should number off by four. Ask person one to write one key concept and evidence from the article that supports the idea on the chart paper. After writing the key concept and supporting evidence, person one invites colleagues to ask questions and make comments. (three minutes)

3. **Repeat the process:** Repeat the process, as persons two, three, and four share a different concept. After writing each concept and the supporting evidence on the chart, they also invite questions and comments from the rest of the group. (three minutes per round; nine minutes total)

4. **Identify insights:** Ask participants to identify any insights gained from this activity. Ask if anyone changed his or her position after reading and talking about the article. Seek consensus on how teams should organize the delivery of Tier 2 interventions. Capture any agreements on chart paper. Also, ask the teachers to raise any questions, issues, or concerns that may need further study or research and record each on chart paper for follow-up at a later time. (six minutes)

Step 3: Personal Reflection (Five Minutes)

Ask participants to think about the pros and cons of the two approaches. They should ask themselves, "Did anything make me rethink the way my team is delivering Tier 2 interventions?" Each person should record and retain their individual reflections; they will be used as the starting point for a future team meeting.

Section III: After the Learning

Next Steps for Coaching Collaborative Teams

The coach's goal is to help the team design (or redesign) the way teachers will deliver Tier 2 interventions. Encourage the team to think about the pros and cons of both approaches. Identify any barriers to implementing either method. Ask if those barriers are grounded in beliefs about why interventions matter (module 8.1) or structures (modules 8.2, and 8.3)? The team can use the information they discussed in prior modules as reference points for their conversations.

1. Ask the team to describe how they are currently delivering Tier 2 interventions. Look for common patterns. Seek consensus on any potential improvement points (PIPs) and identify the next steps the team should consider. Record and post the team's comments and commitments.

2. Reach consensus on some possible next steps, and agree on a plan for moving forward. Establish a timeline for the team to implement the next steps.

MODULE
8.4

Regrouping Versus the Classroom Approach: Choosing the Better Way

By Thomas W. Many

Adapted from Texas Elementary Principals & Supervisors Association's TEPSA News, *May/June 2020, Vol. 77, No. 3, www.tepsa.org*

"We know that all students do not learn in the same way or at the same speed."

—Austin Buffum, Mike Mattos, & Chris Weber

There are two schools of thought on how best to deliver Tier 2 interventions during the regular school day—the *classroom approach* and the *regrouping approach*—and supporters of both claim their approach is the preferred method of organizing students for Tier 2 interventions.

The Classroom Approach

A single teacher in a single classroom implements the *classroom approach*. The basic structure of this method requires individual classroom teachers to work with students who need extra time and support during free time or while other students are working independently. While the majority of students engage in extension or enrichment activities, teachers pull together small groups and provide Tier 2 interventions to the students who demonstrate specific skill deficits on recent common assessments.

Advocates of the classroom approach believe it is more effective because students are more comfortable working with a familiar adult and since the students are already in the teacher's class, and this teacher knows them best, he or she better be prepared to differentiate and deliver the kind of support each student needs. Some concede it is difficult to monitor the rest of class while working with small groups, but supporters believe this approach is more efficient because there is less time lost in transitions and working with students in your own classroom creates more flexibility; it is far easier to manage the schedule and grouping of students if there is no need to coordinate with other members of the team.

According to coauthors Austin Buffum, Mike Mattos, and Janet Malone (2018), "Some educators claim their school doesn't need to create Tier 2 time in their master schedule because each individual teacher provides supplemental interventions in his or her own classroom" (p. 186). However, the authors maintain, "That model failed to achieve the goal of high levels of learning for all students because it is unrealistic to expect classroom teachers to simultaneously reteach essential grade-level curriculum to some students, while introducing new essential standards to the entire class" (Buffum et al., 2018, pp. 186–187).

The Regrouping Approach

On the other hand, teams of teachers implement the *regrouping approach*. The basic structure of this approach involves organizing students into tiered intervention groups based on common assessment results. Teachers deliver extra time and support to small groups of students who may be from different classrooms but share the same needs. Regrouping works best when grade-level or departmental teams designate a common block of time and build the time for Tier 2 interventions into the master schedule of their school.

Advocates of this approach claim it is more effective because it places greater emphasis on direct instruction and teams are better suited to deliver more targeted interventions based on specific skills. Supporters also highlight the positive impact teacher collaboration has on developing a commitment to *our students in our school* as opposed to *my students in my classroom*.

page 1 of 2

Supporters reject the notion that regrouping students has to be a lengthy, time-consuming, or sophisticated process. As long as teachers agree on what is essential and identify the highest-leverage learning targets, the logistics of regrouping students are not complicated.

Coauthors Mike Mattos, Richard DuFour, Rebecca Dufour, Robert Eaker, and Thomas W. Many (2016) contend, "there is no way an individual teacher has all the skills, knowledge, and professional time necessary to meet the diverse needs of all the students assigned to his or her classroom" (p. 128). The authors maintain, "Schools can only meet these diverse student needs when the staff leverages their collective knowledge and skills" and works together to deliver Tier 2 interventions (Mattos et al., 2016, p. 128).

Mike Mattos makes two other important points in support of the regrouping approach. He observes correctly that students often benefit from a fresh perspective or different approach to reteaching a specific skill. Mattos poses a hypothetical question when he asks, "If you taught it as well as you could the first time, what makes you think that more of 'you' is the answer? Is it possible that a colleague has a better way?" (M. Mattos, personal communication, February 28, 2020). Giving another teacher an opportunity to reteach the same skill will enhance the chances that students ultimately master the skill. At the very least, exposing students to different teachers makes it more likely the strategies they use to reteach the skill in Tier 2 will be different than those they used when they initially taught the skill during Tier 1 instruction.

Mattos also argues the regrouping approach is more targeted than the classroom approach and suggests, "The more targeted the intervention, the more likely it will work" (M. Mattos, personal communication, February 28, 2020). Consider the situation where an individual teacher is working with five students from his or her own classroom, all of whom need additional time and support but each needing help with a different skill. Mattos points out that in this scenario, each student theoretically receives 20 percent of the teacher's time and attention. In another school, a teacher is also working with a group of five students, all of whom also need extra time and support. These students coming from different classrooms were regrouped around the same skill. In this second scenario, each student theoretically receives 100 percent of the teacher's time and attention (M. Mattos, personal communication, February 28, 2020).

Not an Either/Or Proposition

Organizing Tier 2 interventions isn't an either/or proposition, but the consensus is that regrouping is a more effective approach. In schools where regrouping is the primary vehicle for organizing and delivering Tier 2 interventions, individual teachers can still pull together small groups and provide more instruction to students while the majority of the class works independently. In fact, a combination of both approaches is an excellent way to ensure high levels of learning for all. The classroom approach may seem logical—and is certainly better than the complete absence of Tier 2 interventions—but experts identify a number of benefits to working as a team to regroup students. Educators consider regrouping the most effective and efficient way to organize and deliver the extra time and support students need to succeed.

References

Buffum, A., Mattos, M., & Malone, J. (2018). *Taking action: A handbook for RTI at Work*. Bloomington, IN: Solution Tree Press.

Buffum, A., Mattos, M., & Weber, C. (2012). *Simplifying response to intervention: Four essential guiding principles*. Bloomington, IN: Solution Tree Press.

DuFour, R., DuFour, R., Eaker, R., Many, T., & Mattos, M. (2016). *Learning by doing: A handbook for Professional Learning Communities at Work* (3rd ed.). Bloomington, IN: Solution Tree Press.

Mattos, M., DuFour, R., DuFour, R., Eaker, R., & Many, T. W. (2016). *Concise answers to frequently asked questions about Professional Learning Communities at Work*. Bloomington, IN: Solution Tree Press.

How Do Teacher Teams Operationalize a Pyramid of Interventions?

Section I: Before the Learning

Rationale—Why It Matters

In our experience, most teams spend more time and energy on responding to PLC critical question three—sometimes at the expense of question four. If this is the case in your school, it may be because of a decision to place greater emphasis on helping students who are not yet proficient, or it may reflect the belief that while some students need more help, the others are "doing just fine." In either case, in a PLC the belief is that *all means all*, and if teams are committed to meeting the needs of *all* students, they must respond equally and intentionally to questions three and four.

Outcomes

Responding to critical questions three and four is most effective when teams view them *interdependently*, or as two different aspects of the same process. Teachers will understand the similarities and differences in how the different tiers function to answer questions three and four. After this module, teams will take action to design (or redesign) their pyramid of interventions to ensure it serves students who take longer to learn as well as those who learn quickly with equal effectiveness.

SIG and Pathways

SIG for prerequisite five (page 241) and Pathways for Prerequisite Five (5.3; page 248)

Key Coaching Points

1. Coaches help teams see the relationship between questions three and four by making sure the terminology is clear. There are four terms (*intervention*, *remediation*, *extension*, and *acceleration*) teachers should define and be able to describe how they are related.

2. This is another opportunity for those coaching teams to check values and beliefs. How do teachers feel about students, whether performing above or below grade level, receiving additional time and support?

3. After reading the article, coaches should highlight the complementary nature of the tiers for answering questions three and four and emphasize the importance of viewing both as part of educators' commitment to serving the needs of *all* students.

Important Vocabulary and Terms

Intervention: In general, this is anything a school does to address a student who is not learning, above and beyond what all students receive; specifically, more support on the essential outcomes for a class, course, or grade level.

Remediation: This is the intensive instruction designed to fill gaps in a student's education with special emphasis on prerequisite skills and prior knowledge.

Extension: This is when a student is stretched beyond the essential grade-level curriculum or levels of proficiency (Buffum et al., 2018, p. 28).

Acceleration: This is the strategy of exposing students to higher-level content and more challenging assignments earlier in their education careers (The Glossary of Educational Reform, 2014).

Section II: During the Learning

Preparation—Time and Materials

Complete this module in an hour (the person delivering the training may choose to spread the activities across two separate meetings). The ideal group size is four participants per group, preferably seated at tables. Teams will need to choose roles (facilitator, timekeeper, recorder, and reporter) and have access to markers and chart paper. Provide each participant with the following handout.

- "Responding to That 'Pesky' Question Four in a PLC: How Will We Extend the Learning for Students Who Are Already Proficient?" (page 218)

Step 1: Getting Ready to Learn—Analogies (Ten Minutes)

Working in pairs, ask teachers to complete the following analogy.

Intervention is to _____ (extension), as remediation is to _____ (acceleration).

Explain to the group that today, they are going to talk about how their team responds to critical questions three (intervention and remediation) and four (extension and acceleration). In order to assess the level of the group's understanding of these concepts, coaches should instruct the participants to focus their discussion on one of the following: (1) how are intervention and remediation alike and different, (2) how are extension and acceleration alike and different, or (3) how are intervention and remediation (together) alike and different from extension and enrichment (together)? Teachers should base their response on what they know or think they know without explanation or elaboration from the person delivering the training.

Step 2: Interactive Strategy, Protocol, or Activity—Inter-VENN-tion Protocol (Fifty Minutes)

The Inter-VENN-tion protocol uses tight time frames and a one-to-two-to-four person (Think-Pair-Square) grouping pattern to help the participants focus and stay on task. Participants begin this professional development activity individually, and then move to pairs, and finally form groups of four.

1. **Brainstorm:** Start by asking each participant to write on a piece of paper, working quietly to individually brainstorm how responding to critical questions three and four is alike and different. Identify as many ways as possible; the goal is to generate lots of ideas. (three minutes)

2. **Compare:** Participants should find a partner and compare the two lists. Look for any patterns in what each participant thought about how teams respond to questions three and four in a PLC. (five minutes)

3. **Read the article:** Next, ask participants to read the article "Responding to That 'Pesky' Question Four in a PLC" (page 218). After finishing the article, each person should add to and update his or her individual list. (seven minutes)

4. **Create a Venn diagram:** Once everyone has finished reading, ask participants to work in their small groups and draw a *Venn diagram* (two overlapping circles) on a piece of chart paper. (See the graphic that follows.) Label the left-hand circle *Responding to question three* and the right-hand circle *Responding to question four*. Tell participants to work together to write the similarities in the overlapping section of the Venn diagram and the differences inside the corresponding circle. (fifteen minutes)

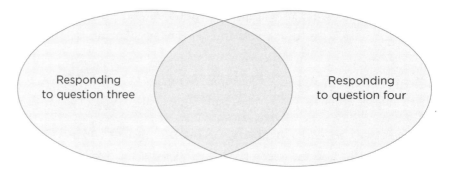

Responding to question three

Responding to question four

5. **Reflection:** For about two minutes, encourage each participant to silently reflect on what he or she initially listed during the brainstorming at the start of the training and what he or she learned today. Use the remaining time in a round-robin approach to give each participant a chance to share any new ideas or insights. (five minutes)

6. **Gallery walk:** Post the Venn diagrams and conduct a brief five-minute gallery walk. Each group should debrief about what they saw on other Venn diagrams, and draft a summary statement of what they have learned today and next steps they are considering. Ask the reporters for each table group to share their collective thinking with the other groups. (ten minutes)

Step 3: Personal Reflection (Five Minutes)

Before the next meeting, participants should think about the importance of responding to *both* questions three and four. Is there a moral imperative that goes with meeting the needs of all students, whether they are above or below grade level? Ask participants to reflect, record, and retain their thoughts on what they would want schools, teams, or individual teachers to be doing to meet the needs of *all* students. The personal reflections will be used during the section III debriefing session with a coach.

Section III: After the Learning

Next Steps for Coaching Collaborative Teams

Your goal as the coach is to help teams understand that to meet the needs of all students, teams must consider how their efforts balance responses to questions three and four. What are the strengths and vulnerabilities of the way teams are currently providing support to students who are performing above *and* below grade-level expectations?

1. Ask each participant to share his or her best thinking about whether the team has a moral obligation to respond to the needs of all students, regardless of the level of their performance.

2. Seek agreement on any potential improvement points (PIPs), record, and post the team's comments and commitments. Ask participants to determine how the questions recorded and retained during the personal reflection time at the end of step 2 might be addressed.

3. Identify some possible next steps, and agree on a plan for moving forward.

MODULE
8.5

Responding to That "Pesky" Question Four in a PLC: How Will We Extend the Learning for Students Who Are Already Proficient?

By Thomas W. Many

Adapted from Texas Elementary Principals & Supervisors Association's TEPSA News, *August 2020, Vol. 77, No. 4, www.tepsa.org*

> "All students, including the most gifted and talented, will need additional time and support in their learning at one time or another."
>
> —Mike Mattos, Richard DuFour, Rebecca DuFour, Robert Eaker, & Thomas W. Many

Collaborative teams focus on answering the four critical questions of learning in a PLC, and most teams are clear about how to approach the first three. It is responding to the fourth and final question, the one education leadership professors Douglas Fisher and Nancy Frey (2017) label "a bit pesky," that is so important if teams are to meet the needs of all students.

Of the four critical questions (DuFour, DuFour, Eaker, Many, & Mattos, 2016), the last two are most similar to each other. In fact, question three ("How will we respond when students do not learn?"; DuFour et al., 2016, p. 36) and question four ("How will we extend the learning for students who are already proficient?"; DuFour et al., 2016, p. 36) share so many of the same characteristics, Mattos and his colleagues (2016) suggest schools view "intervention and extension as two sides of the same coin" (p. 127).

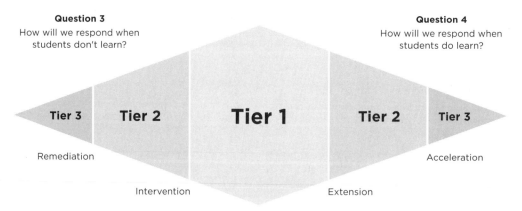

Question 3
How will we respond when students don't learn?

Question 4
How will we respond when students do learn?

Tier 3 — Tier 2 — **Tier 1** — Tier 2 — Tier 3

Remediation

Acceleration

Intervention

Extension

CORE INSTRUCTION

Certainly, there are differences with terminology and whether students are working above or below grade level. For example, question three is designed to provide more time and support for students who are not yet proficient on the essential outcomes. Conversely, question four provides additional time and support for students who have demonstrated mastery on the essential outcomes for a class, course, or grade level. Teachers working with question three will use terms like *intervention* and *remediation* while teachers working on question four will more commonly use words like *extension*, *enrichment*, and *acceleration*.

Striking Similarities

Despite these differences, when teachers take collective action to ensure all students learn to high levels, the number of similarities between how teams respond to questions three and four is striking. Responding to both questions relies on how students are progressing through a standards-based curriculum using a tiered approach. When done well, responding to both questions requires some form of universal screening, progress monitoring, differentiated instruction, and the use of research and evidence-based strategies. A team's response to either question is based on student needs, provides flexible and fluid support, and relies on a team approach to using data. How teams respond to questions three and four is much more alike than different.

With so many similarities in the way teams respond to questions three and four, one might think the term *pyramid of interventions* would refer to both—and perhaps it should—but the majority of educators view the process of responding to these two questions as distinctly separate.

"If a school is going to build flexible time, support, and collaboration into its school week, it can apply these efforts to support students in advanced coursework as well."

—Austin Buffum, Mike Mattos, & Janet Malone

Buffum and his colleagues (2018) define an *intervention* as "anything a school does above and beyond what all students receive to help certain students succeed academically" (p. 27). Their definition does not distinguish between students performing above or below grade level, and while students who are not yet proficient must receive extra time and support, it is equally true that students who are performing above level or advanced in their academics also need support to thrive in school (Coleman, 2010).

Two Sides of the Same Coin

Just as Mattos and his colleagues (2016) argue that intervention and extension are best thought of as two sides of the same coin, remediation and acceleration could be complementary if educators view them in the same way. Some teams find that turning the RTI triangles on their sides to create a diamond shape helps them visualize questions three and four differently. Educators often refer to the *differentiation diamond*; the figure on page 218 shows how the tiers associated with question three (core instruction, intervention, and remediation) on one side mirror the tiers of question four (core instruction, extension, and acceleration) on the other. If teams had this kind of parallel structure in place for question four, Tier 1 would continue to focus on the important (nice to know) and essential (need to know) standards; Tier 1 would provide extension only on the most essential standards; and Tier 3 would accelerate learning by introducing new content and concepts.

When you view the traditionally separate triangles together as a diamond, the image promotes developing a more flexible and fluid perspective. This kind of thinking better accommodates students who might need intervention, perhaps even remediation, in one subject while simultaneously engaging in extension or acceleration in another. Together, the diamond serves the full spectrum of students and makes it clear that responding to critical questions three and four is part of the same process.

"All students deserve to attend a school where their learning needs are met."

—Mary Ruth Coleman

The relationship between questions three and four is neither separate nor linear. Though schools might initially devote more resources or place greater emphasis on question three, question four is just as important as the others. Well-designed intervention systems have a reciprocal quality; they are equally adept at serving students who take longer to learn as well as those who learn quickly.

A Balance

Teachers on the most effective teams recognize that success requires a balance of consideration to questions three and four. They report that looking at the two questions side by side allows them to simultaneously provide services that intervene, extend, remediate, and accelerate their students' learning in more holistic ways. In short, teachers report that when they consider questions three and four together, the team does a better job of responding to the needs of all students.

References

Buffum, A., Mattos, M., & Malone, J. (2018). *Taking action: A handbook for RTI at Work*. Bloomington, IN: Solution Tree Press.

Coleman, M. R. (2010, October 19). *RTI for gifted students* [Interview transcript]. Accessed at www.rtinetwork.org/mpdf_print.php?htc=YToxOntzOjEzOiJyZXBvcnRfaWRaGF0IjtzOjI6IjI0Ijt9 on March 17, 2021.

DuFour, R., DuFour, R., Eaker, R., Many, T. W., & Mattos, M. (2016). *Learning by doing: A handbook for Professional Learning Communities at Work* (3rd ed.). Bloomington, IN: Solution Tree Press.

Fisher, D., & Frey, N. (2017, February 15). *That pesky fourth PLC question*. Accessed www.solutiontree.com/blog/that-pesky-fourth-plc-question on April 14, 2020.

Mattos, M., DuFour, R., DuFour, R., Eaker, R., & Many, T. W. (2016). *Concise answers to frequently asked questions about Professional Learning Communities at Work*. Bloomington, IN: Solution Tree Press.

PART III

ONE TEAM'S TRANSFORMATION

CHAPTER 9

Willis ISD: Practical Implications of Coaching Teams

By Brian Greeney, Assistant Superintendent of Innovation, Teaching, and Learning, Willis Independent School District

> *We see it all the time; coached teams are more effective than uncoached teams and schools go further faster when the primary goal of coaching is to help collaborative teams, rather than individual teachers, improve their professional practice.*
>
> **—THOMAS W. MANY**

Willis Independent School District, north of Houston, Texas, serves more than 8,000 students and has five Title I elementary schools, two middle schools, and one high school. The student population is just over 60 percent economically disadvantaged. In 2018, the state of Texas rated the school a *D* district. Fast forward to 2020, and the district has raised its rating to a *B*.

What caused such a rapid and positive turnaround? The primary improvement strategy Willis used to make such dramatic improvement over the course of two years was the intentional coaching of collaborative teams in a PLC. This is their story.

The Willis leadership team began implementing the PLC process during the 2017–2018 school year based on the belief that collaboration is the key to improving teachers' professional practice. Furthermore, the consensus among district leadership was that developing high-performing collaborative teams within a PLC is the best long-term strategy for improving student achievement in the district.

Initially, the district did all the right things: identified essential standards, created collaborative teams, assessed student learning, and set aside dedicated and protected time during the regular school day for interventions, but after about a year and a half of hard work, it was clear there was a problem.

The district had seen growth; however, the growth was not at the level that leaders expected, and no one could pinpoint the reason why; so the administration began exploring different ways to leverage the power of the PLC process to improve the teachers' professional practice. What resulted is an example of how a school can move from *PLC lite* to *PLC right* to *PLC tight* by becoming more intentional about coaching collaborative teams within a PLC.

To their credit, district leaders did not blame anyone. Instead, leaders focused on being reflective and identifying the next steps. It was clear that everyone in the district was doing the best they could with what they knew how to do; clearly, it was not a question of effort. What was clear: the district needed to provide something more to help clarify the *why, how,* and *what* of a successful PLC.

Assess the Current Reality

The district's first task was to ascertain the current level of collaboration on teams across the district. The good news was that master schedules reflected dedicated and protected time for team meetings during the regular school day; teachers who taught the same class, course, or grade level had been assigned to the meaningful teams; and there was little resistance to the idea of collaborating with others. The initial review of the district's teaming practices was encouraging, but leaders decided to go one step further and observe some teams in action. What they saw surprised them; despite all of their best efforts, the majority of collaborative teams was operating as PLC lite.

For example, during one collaborative team meeting, the entire meeting focused on the behavior of one student. Each teacher explained how he or she had written discipline referrals on the student because he was noncompliant and refused to do his work. They discussed how they could use positive behavior rewards to get him to comply and complete his work. The focus was on what the student needed to change—not what the teachers could do differently to ensure the student would succeed. The team never discussed any of the student's academic assessments or reflected on their own practice and how it could impact the student's performance. Had they held that discussion, they would have realized this student was not being academically challenged and his behavior was likely the result of boredom.

In another meeting, teachers were responding to the question, "How do we know if every student who experiences difficulty in acquiring essential knowledge and skills will receive additional time and support for learning in a timely, directive, and systematic way?" One of the team members responded by saying, "We have dedicated time built into the schedule for additional support. We follow up with detailed documentation that is discussed, reviewed, and reflected upon, but honestly, we don't know." The part of the conversation that struck the observers was the statement, *honestly, we don't know.* The team knew intuitively that it needed to do something more, but the members couldn't clearly articulate what to do next.

While the team meetings were disappointing, what made matters worse was the leaders' realization that these meetings were not an anomaly. Across the district, there was a great deal of inconsistency in how teams went about their business. Some teams were working independently and others interdependently; some assessments were based on curriculum materials, while others reflected the essential standards; some interventions were available on a daily basis while others were voluntary or scheduled as an "intervention class" as part of the student's schedule. Things were done differently from team to team or school to school, but what was disconcerting was no one could explain *why* things were different. More often than not, the response was, "It's just the way we've always done things around here."

It became clear that the most consistent thing about collaborative teams in Willis was their *lack* of consistency. And what was even more maddening was that these inconsistencies were not only between schools, but also *within* the same school. Everyone was working hard and trying to do the right thing, but the gap between what teams were doing and the work they should be doing was widening because the district had not agreed on a standard of best practice for collaborative teams. Everyone was doing his or her best, but something was missing. The bottom line was the district just wasn't getting results.

Revisit PLC Best Practices

So, what did the leaders of Willis do? To build capacity for more effective PLCs, the district's guiding coalition decided to revisit its understanding of the PLC process. The goal was to ensure everyone had the same perception of best PLC practice. Generating a common understanding of *why* would reinforce the district's commitment to high levels of learning for all, promote a stronger sense of ownership around how to accomplish the district's goals, and clarify what next steps teams would need to take to be successful.

The leadership team recognized one of the biggest problems was the lack of agreement on what to do next or even where to begin. The consensus was that highly effective collaborative teams are the key to the successful implementation of the PLC process. So naturally, if teams were not being as productive as the leaders hoped, the teams would need additional time and support (just like students!).

Willis has a strong coaching culture. Over the years, the traditional model of instructional coaching focused on helping individual teachers receive ongoing and sustained support. Each school has access to instructional coaches who work directly with teachers, and there is a commonly held belief that the one-to-one coaching of individual teachers was an effective way to help teachers improve their professional practice.

District leaders quickly realized that if coaching individual teachers is good, coaching collaborative teams is better, and they began to explore ways to leverage the district's coaching culture to improve the productivity of collaborative teams. To do this, the district decided to engage the guiding coalition in the "How do we know?" activity. The team was asked and answered the following eight questions centered on the most important aspects of the PLC process.

1. "How do we know if the district has a widely understood common language?"

2. "How do we know if educators throughout the district understand what is *loose* and *tight*?"

3. "How do we know if leaders organized educators into meaningful collaborative teams, that are working interdependently and focused on the right work?"

4. "How do we know if teachers are monitoring each student's learning on a frequent and timely basis?"

5. "How do we know if we are using assessment results to inform and improve our professional practice?"

6. "How do we know if every student who experiences difficulty in acquiring essential knowledge and skills will receive additional time and support for learning in a timely, directive, and systematic way?"

7. "How do we know what resources and support people need throughout the district to help them succeed at what they are called to do?"

8. "How do we know if we are providing teacher teams with the necessary resources and support?"

Each member of the guiding coalition had to answer these questions first individually and then as a group. The goal was to reflect on the current reality of the district's efforts to operationalize the PLC process. The guiding coalition sought to understand things like, was it communicating *the why* of being a PLC in a coherent way, how common was the vocabulary used across the district, were learning expectations consistent, and was there any consensus on what the district needed to do next? It became painfully obvious during our "How do we know?" activity that the district had two major problems.

First, there was a great deal of knowledge about various aspects of the PLC process spread across the district; the problem wasn't a lack of knowledge but a lack of *shared* knowledge, which resulted in everyone having different interpretations about how collaborative teams should operate. To one degree or another, everyone knew what needed to be done, but as a whole, the faculty and staff were not putting what they knew into practice in any coherent and consistent way.

Second, the district had fallen into what is widely known as the *knowing-doing gap* (Hulme, 2014; Pfeffer & Sutton, 2001). The guiding coalition had lots of thoughts about what the district needed to do, but when the members drilled deeper, they found no agreement on what the *right work* was or how and by whom it should be done. Early on, it became clear that the district was going to have to create some kind of guiding document for the work because teachers and administrators lacked a consensus on what collaborative teams should be doing in a PLC. Creating clarity became the crux for what came next in the district.

From Lite to Right to Tight

By the time the guiding coalition completed the "How do we know?" activity, the members were both exhausted and exhilarated. The discussion among district leaders clearly illustrated that many members held very different views about how collaborative teams should operate. It was also clear that for the last couple years, the district had been shuffling along in PLC lite. Within one day, the district leaders had taken a huge step toward PLC right.

In the most successful school-improvement initiatives, there is direction and support from teacher leaders and administrators. Some leaders are so worried about being labeled *micro-managers* or trying to get unanimous agreement from the entire staff, they fail to provide any direction at all. The result is that the whole initiative becomes paralyzed and nobody decides anything. The feedback generated by the "How do we know?" activity helped shape Willis's journey, as the guiding coalition began building a plan for moving from lite to right and on to tight on the district's PLC journey.

Constructing the SIG

As we discussed in chapter 1, a SIG is an effective way to bring clarity to the PLC process. Not only does creating a SIG help eliminate any ambiguity about the work, it also builds common language and promotes ownership of the PLC process. The guiding coalition at Willis recognized that creating a SIG would be the best way to move the district forward.

A SIG consists of a series of anchor statements and a matching progression of indicators describing different levels of implementation for each of the five prerequisite conditions DuFour and Reeves (2016) argue are essential when establishing a PLC (and the organizing structure for this book).

1. Educators work in collaborative teams, rather than in isolation, and take collective responsibility for student learning.

2. Collaborative teams implement a guaranteed and viable curriculum, unit by unit.

3. Collaborative teams monitor student learning through an ongoing assessment process that includes frequent, team-developed, common formative assessments.

4. Educators use the results of common assessments to improve individual practice, build the team's capacity to achieve its goals, and intervene and enrich on behalf of students.

5. The school (or each team) provides a systematic process for intervention and extension.

Willis chose DuFour and Reeves's (2016) five prerequisite conditions as the anchor statements for their SIG. An *anchor statement* describes the ideal or desired state for each of the five prerequisite conditions of a PLC. These anchor statements represent the constants of PLCs; they do not change over time. Anchor statements should reflect the organization's consensus of what it will look like to fully implement the PLC process.

Indicators or *descriptors* are analogous to a learning progression in that they define what dispositions, knowledge, and skills collaborative teams must master before moving from one level to the next on the SIG.

Natalie DeBrock, a teacher at C.C. Hardy Elementary School, explains the impact the indicators had on her team, saying, "By laying out the descriptors [indicators] for each of the different levels, the SIG encourages us to try new teaching strategies and new ways of planning in order to move to the next category on the rubric [SIG]" (N. Debrock, personal communication, March 12, 2020). The district guiding coalition adjusted the indicators every year to retain the rigor of the SIG, but they are purposely designed to be developmental, each reflecting increasingly higher levels of complexity and sophistication from one category to the next.

Leaders believed having clear indicators would make the teams more efficient and effective. Judy Akin, a teacher at Brabham Middle School, explains how the indicators provided clarity to help her team, saying:

> My partner and I now come into our meetings better prepared to use our time wisely. We do "homework" and share our results. Our meetings are centered on data and planning, and our discussions are geared toward how we can use the data to achieve better results. My team learned faster and more efficient ways

to present our data for ourselves and for others to observe. We also organized
ourselves with backwards planning of the unit tests and retests. (J. Akin, personal
communication, March 13, 2020)

District leadership delegated the task of drafting the first set of indicators to the district's PLC guiding coalition, and through the writing process, the team learned a few things. First, members learned the importance of avoiding the ambiguity that accompanies phrases like *I think*, *I feel*, and *in my opinion*. The goal was to help teams move away from making decisions based on good intentions to ones grounded in research. To support that move, the specific words the guiding coalition used in each indicator really mattered.

Next, the guiding coalition realized after observing teams in action, few if any members were discussing their team goals and reflecting on whether or not their work was getting them any closer to their team goals. Having goals is an important part of the PLC process; goals help educators move from being a group of individuals to a team with a common purpose. Wherever appropriate, the guiding coalition added language regarding goals to individual indicators.

Finally, the addition of the word *consistently* to the indicators in the beyond proficient column helped teams realize it is *how* they conduct business all the time that matters. The goal was to promote developing habits of professional practice. It was important to minimize the idea that if teams demonstrated a particular behavior once, they had "made it" and were ready to move on to the next level of the SIG. (See the process the district used to accomplish this goal on page 234.)

The goal of writing the indicators is to define or describe how teams perform in each of the three categories. The guiding coalition used the same process for developing indicators in each category, but it is most effective and efficient to start by writing the indicator for the proficient category. Once the team agreed on the indicator for proficient, they moved to the next category—beyond proficient—and began writing the next indicator. Once the indicator for beyond proficient was finished, the team repeated the same cycle for the below-proficient indicator.

The only addition to the process of developing the indicators for above and below proficient was that any tasks members identified in the initial brainstorming session, and not included in the description of proficient performance, were considered again as part of developing the indicator for the beyond-proficient level.

After completing the indicator for beyond proficient, teams followed the same steps in the same sequence to develop an indicator for below proficient. By the third time through this cycle, the teams had developed a set of three different indicators for the first anchor statement.

This part of the process typically prompts an intense discussion, and it is not unusual for teams to have difficulty determining the criteria for a collaborative team to move from one level to the next. However, the discussion around the indicators is powerful, and, in Willis's case, it helped build common understanding of the *right work* of a collaborative team more than anything the staff had done in the previous two years of their PLC journey.

Committing to Change

All leaders want to improve teacher performance. Educators know if teachers' professional practice improves, so will student performance. Leaders often make the mistake to assume if they simply assign teachers to a collaborative team, schedule time for the team to meet, and put the four critical questions of a PLC in front of them, improvement in professional practice will organically happen. It just doesn't work that way.

While everyone at Willis celebrated the guiding coalition's successful efforts to create the SIG, their work wasn't finished. It was important for the guiding coalition to figure out how to get the rest of the district committed to changing their PLC practices to align with what the SIG represented as best practice.

Setting the Stage

All great theater directors know they must set the stage before a performance can happen. It is the same with collaborative teams; it is the leader's responsibility to set the stage or make sure team members understand what the leader expects of them. To achieve this, the guiding coalition at Willis set out to design a rollout plan for the SIG.

At Willis, the impact of creating the SIG as a districtwide guiding document changed how the district conducted business. In addition to making team meetings more efficient, leaders shared a deeper understanding of the work and were able to provide more focus and align feedback to help teams grow. With the short time teachers have to plan, teach, and assess student work, operating with greater efficiency and effectiveness was a huge step forward for teams.

The district PLC guiding coalition decided to introduce the document before the start of the new school year. They also decided the rollout would be districtwide rather than as a pilot at one school or on a few collaborative teams. This might not be the right decision in every situation, but the district leaders had already invested two years of time and resources into the PLC journey and there was a sense of urgency. The good news is that through the process of designing the SIG, relationships had been built among members of the guiding coalition. The district leaders were confident there were champions of the process at every school.

Rolling Out the Plan

The goal of the rollout plan was to leverage author and former administrator, teacher, and coach Mike Schmoker's (2004) notion that "clarity precedes competence" (p. 85). The goal was to introduce the concept of a SIG to the faculty in an effort to create a deeper understanding of what would constitute proficient performance for each of the five anchor statements.

The district decided to use the Looks Like, Sounds Like, Feels Like protocol as the vehicle for accomplishing this goal. This protocol is a great way to familiarize teachers with a new document (see page 235).

For the first time, the district had a unified vision of what the work of collaborative teams should look like because of the development of the SIG. With the rollout of the SIG complete and teachers now familiar with the document, the district began to recalibrate the primary focus of coaching from individual teachers to collaborative teams.

From One-to-One Coaching to Coaching Teams

Tim Harkrider, superintendent of Willis ISD, decided the district would continue to provide coaching for individual teachers, but the emphasis shifted from the traditional one-to-one model to the more contemporary one-to-many approach. This was an important adjustment in the way the district went about improving instructional practice. Before, coaches would work with one teacher on improving instruction, now coaches shifted to working with an entire team of teachers. As a result, the district was able to build the *collective* efficacy of all teachers, not just the select few who were struggling or new to the profession.

The district saw evidence that coached teams progressed further faster than uncoached teams. Kim Truett, an instructional coach at C.C. Hardy Elementary, talks about her experience with coaching teams, explaining, "It [the shift from coaching individuals to coaching teams] has amplified our impact! We have conversations together that will advance us together. Instead of that conversation happening with one teacher, it happens with the team." Truett continued, "It is less intimidating for teachers to take on the challenge of growth as a team. They realize they are growing together, and that feels better than thinking they have been singled out for growth" (K. Truett, personal communication, March 13, 2020).

A conscious and deliberate effort to calibrate the SIG facilitated this shift from coaching individual teachers to coaching collaborative teams. Leaders asked coaches to pair up, pick an anchor statement, and observe teams together. The consensus was that calibrating the SIG had a positive impact on the accuracy and precision of the coaches' observations and feedback. The Willis SIG and a description of the process of calibrating feedback follow.

Calibrating Feedback

Two coaches watched the same team and focused on anchor statement two, which deals with creating a guaranteed and viable curriculum. The coaches used a sequence of five questions to engage in some self-reflection about how aligned and actionable their feedback was and whether their feedback was consistent with what the SIG describes as best practice.

1. Take two minutes to identify any areas of commonality in your observations.
2. Have a five-minute or less conversation about any areas where your observations were different.
3. Reach consensus on the proficiency level of this team based on the anchor statement on the SIG.
4. Have a five-minute or less conversation on the next step this team needs to take to improve.
5. Take two minutes to review the advice you gave to the team. Does it align and provide actionable feedback to the team? Is it likely the team will be able to take the next step successfully?

The best thing about coaching teacher teams using this approach is that everyone can coach and receive coaching; even other teams within the same school or district can help coach their colleagues.

The district leaders gathered data based on the SIG that indicated how teams were growing in terms of their PLC practice. Next, the district created a database which generated a list of teams that had demonstrated the characteristics described as beyond proficient on anchor statement two. After reviewing the data, coaches realized that there were other teams in other schools doing extremely well on creating a guaranteed and viable curriculum. Armed with this information, the coaches were able to connect exemplary teams with less-proficient teams and schedule an observation of an upcoming team meeting. The coaches believed that teachers could learn a lot from other teachers, and that is exactly what happened! After observing their colleagues, the team was able to see how they could identify the essential standards and define targeted learning targets.

The coaches agreed the growth in the team in this example (which took place in a little over five months) had a huge impact on student learning and demonstrated that coached teams can significantly improve their practice in just a few short months. In looking back at their notes, the coaches agreed that before being coached, this team did not have a grasp of what students should know and be able to do, much less how to measure student learning. The team went from having little direction in team meetings to being laser focused on what students needed to know and be able to do.

The Pathways Documents

To help further support the team's improvement efforts, the coaches also decided to begin referring to the Pathways documents. As discussed in chapter 1, Pathways are based on the five prerequisite conditions (see the appendix, page 242) and serve several important purposes: they help those coaching teams identify the next logical steps, and promote the development of consistent terminology and a common language, while simultaneously minimizing the likelihood that teams will get different advice from different people on the same improvement target. The Pathways provide guiding questions for coaches to ask and teams to consider in a nonjudgmental format. Based on their observations, the coaches decide which pathway would be most appropriate for the team.

Using the Pathways effectively is an area of growth within the district, but it is clear that combining the SIG and Pathways has provided the clarity and support that everyone needed to succeed. The work, anchored in a specific row of the SIG and the appropriate Pathway supports, set the stage for continuous improvement as the team moved to the next part of the PLC process: using common assessments to improve teaching and learning in their school.

Culture Building

Developing collaborative teams has a direct impact on the overall culture of a school. For Willis, developing a SIG and the Pathways provided the catalyst for collaborative teams to become more successful, thereby increasing collective efficacy of teachers and the performance of students. More important, the district staff are now more confident than ever that they are moving through the continuum of PLC practice; they can track this progress from PLC lite to PLC right to PLC tight.

The SIG and Pathways are an integral part of the team coaching process. However, they are nothing more than guiding documents; it is all the time and energy teacher leaders and administrators invested in creating the documents that are so important. When everyone feels a sense of ownership about the SIG and Pathways, the commitment to the PLC process increases for coaches, teachers, and administrators. The SIG and Pathways belong to everyone, and because teams embrace them as the agreed-on standard of best practice, when teams fall short of what the members expect of themselves, they are willing to accept the challenge that comes with the collective inquiry and continuous improvement of a PLC.

Kim Truett shares the impact the SIG had on her campus when she explains:

> Every team on our campus has improved because of the SIG. Last year, teams would come to meetings and they would be unsure of what data to have, or what conversation needed to happen. There would often be 'off topic' conversation to fill in the gaps. This year, every team comes in with a data-driven agenda. They have clear expectations of each other and know exactly what they are looking to accomplish. (K. Truett, personal communication, March 13, 2020)

Truett is also clear that the Pathways have been an equally valuable tool for coaching teams. She continues:

> We need to polish it [the coaching of collaborative teams] by using the Pathways documents. Once we do that, the expectations will become even clearer. The SIG and Pathways have given anyone who is coaching teams a common language that keeps teams headed in the same direction. It also helps get those uncomfortable conversations started by giving those coaching teams something to begin with; after all, this isn't what I think, this is what the SIG and Pathways tell us is best practice! (K. Truett, personal communication, March 13, 2020)

Lynnly Muncherjee, an instruction coach at Brabham Middle School, talks about the effect that coaching collaborative teams has had on her campus: "I believe that the Amplify coaching model has helped teachers improve not only their own efficacy but has also improved student learning. When teachers feel confident in their own ability to teach the standards, students will receive higher-quality instruction." She adds, "This approach provides coaches with a good framework for coaching collaborative teams in order to improve teacher's knowledge and student performance" (L. Muncherjee, personal communication, March 13, 2020).

There were other benefits as well. According to Mary Puckett, a teacher at Parmley Elementary School,

> We have a deeper shared knowledge of the work. The SIG laid out the four critical questions of a PLC in a very understandable way. We were able to see where we were at the beginning of the year and how we were able to progress in various areas. Because we focus on the four questions and the SIG, we have been able to run our team meetings more efficiently. (M. Pucket, personal communication, March 13, 2020)

The combination of the SIG and Pathways document is a powerful combination, but one of the biggest questions principals have with this coaching framework is, "Where do you start? Is it best to develop the SIG or the Pathways first? Or is it better to develop both tools simultaneously?" Based on experience, the Willis team doesn't believe there is a right or wrong answer; they chose to start with the SIG because it fit the needs of the district.

Willis had a consistency and messaging problem leaders needed to correct before they could begin coaching teams. The district lacked a common vision of what a successful team looked like, but the district leaders believed that if they could define the target, the teams were more likely to hit it. It was important to be clear on what practices an effective collaborative team should engage in; thus, Willis leaders decided to begin by developing the SIG.

Progress, Not Perfection

Was the process perfect? No, in fact, the district leaders admit they still occasionally struggle with how to coach teams effectively and how best to provide them with meaningful feedback. However, teachers will tell you that because coaching collaborative teams has become an accepted practice, they now have a more clearly articulated standard of best practice to operate from and use information from the SIG and Pathways to inform and improve their practice.

A Step-by-Step Process for Developing the Indicators

Once the group agrees on anchor statements, participants form teams (four to six people per team is ideal) and choose roles. At a minimum, we recommend the teams designate different people to be the timekeeper, scribe, and facilitator.

1. Review the Anchor Statement and Identify What Is Essential (Five Minutes)

Teams begin by reviewing each anchor statement and identify its essential tasks. To facilitate this conversation, teams ask and answer two questions: (1) "What are the essential *words or phrases* in the anchor statement?" and (2) "What aspects of the anchor statement must the team address (tight) as part of the PLC process?" By answering these two questions, the team better prepares to define the indicators. As each team reviews the anchor statement, their discussion should focus on the tasks they consider essential to developing a highly effective collaborative team. We recommend the scribe highlight the key words or phrases. Before completing this step, the team reviews its work.

2. Brainstorm Tasks Associated With the Anchor Statement (Five Minutes)

Each team engages in a five-minute brainstorming to identify what a team needs to do to demonstrate proficiency on the anchor statement. The key question to consider at this point is, What work within the anchor statement, if not completed successfully, would lead to the failure of the collaborative team to achieve its goal? At this point, there is no debate or judgement; the goal is to generate as many ideas as possible. The scribe records the results of the brainstorming on chart paper.

3. Identify the Tasks That Would Be Present or Evident if a Team Were Proficient (Fifteen Minutes)

The team takes five minutes and reaches consensus on which practices from the brainstorm list are necessary for the team to be proficient on the anchor statement. The team may not consider all the original tasks essential and leave some off the list. Once the team identifies the initial list, the team takes ten more minutes to review what was and was not included and confirms whether it should add back any of the remaining tasks to the list of practices the team must demonstrate for proficiency. The goal at this point is for the team to agree about what is on the list.

4. Combine With Another Team and Draft the Initial Indicator for Proficient Performance (Fifteen Minutes)

Each team joins with another team and compares their lists of practices that demonstrate proficiency. The combined team spends five minutes identifying areas of overlap (agreement) and then ten more minutes discussing which tasks were not included on the agreed-on list; teams should be given an opportunity to explain why a particular task was or was not included on the list. After doing this, the combined team drafts its first attempt at an indicator for the Proficiency column. The scribes record the draft indicator on chart paper.

5. Share Indicators With Other Teams in the Room (Fifteen Minutes)

Once completing a draft of the indicator, the team reviews its work and reaches agreement that the statement accurately addresses the essential elements of the anchor statement at a proficient level. The teams post indicators around the room, and each team has an opportunity to present their indicator to one other team for five minutes. Allow two minutes for a question-and-answer period. Teams then go back and make any final changes to their continuum before submitting them to a writing team that will work on crafting the final language of each indicator while the other teams move on to the next indicator for that anchor statement.

Looks Like, Sounds Like, Feels Like Protocol

The Looks Like, Sounds Like, Feels Like protocol takes about fifty minutes from start to finish. To prepare, write the anchor statements (in Willis's case, the anchor statements were the five prerequisite conditions of a PLC) on chart paper and post them around the room.

Begin by asking teachers to count off by five and gather at the corresponding anchor statement (ones go to the first anchor statement, twos to the second anchor statement, and so on). Once the faculty gathers at the appropriate anchor statement, ask the group to choose a facilitator, timekeeper, and scribe. Begin the protocol with a quick overview.

Step 1 (Ten Minutes)

Each team takes ten minutes to describe what a team proficient on its anchor statement would look like, sound like, and feel like. The focus of the discussion should be on clarifying what would constitute proficient performance. To accomplish this, teachers ask and answer three questions: (1) "What would the work look like if it was done successfully?" (2) "What would you hear if you were sitting in the team meetings?" and (3) "What would it feel like to be a participant of that team?" Using chart paper, the scribe creates a three-column note catcher and labels one column *Looks Like*, one column *Sounds Like*, and the last column *Feels Like*. The scribe records the group's best thinking on chart paper using a three-column note catcher.

Step 2 (Twenty Minutes)

After ten minutes, the team rotates to the next anchor statement and for five minutes reviews what the initial group thought it would look like, sound like, and feel like, and then uses sticky notes to leave the team any feedback. Teams continue rotating, visiting a new anchor statement every five minutes, and add any feedback to what their colleagues initially created.

Step 3 (Ten Minutes)

Once the team completes providing feedback and rotates through all five anchor statements, it will return to the starting place. For the next ten minutes, each team discusses the feedback or new ideas other teams contributed, and makes any changes to its original three-column chart.

Step 4 (Fifteen Minutes)

To complete this protocol, ask teachers to reconvene in their grade-level or departmental teams. Use the SIG to decide which indicator best describes where the team is on the SIG (*beyond proficient*, *proficient*, or *below proficient*) for each anchor statement.

APPENDIX A
SIG and Pathways Tools

Strategy Implementation Guide

Anchor Statements	Beyond Proficient PLC Tight	Proficient PLC Right	Below Proficient PLC Lite
Prerequisite One: Educators work in collaborative teams, rather than in isolation, and take collective responsibility for student learning.	Teachers meet weekly in collaborative teams for a minimum of sixty minutes during the regular school day. Teams work interdependently to improve their practice and enhance student learning. Teams monitor their collaborative practice and continuously utilize notes, refine SMART goals, and adjust protocols to increase effectiveness and efficiency. They identify practices they want to keep that are working, those they want to drop that are ineffective, and ones they need to create to increase productivity. The strength of each team member is leveraged, and new team members are seamlessly merged into the PLC process. The teachers embrace cognitive dissonance, ultimately reaching consensus. Team members hold each other accountable to the collective decisions made.	Teachers meet weekly in collaborative teams for a minimum of sixty minutes during the regular school day. They write norms and SMART goals and participate in common planning to improve student learning. Teams work together to improve their practice and enhance student learning. They delegate to maximize efficiency. The team encourages all voices and ideas to be heard, and consensus is reached.	Teachers meet in teams for a minimum of forty-five minutes per week during the regular school day. They depend on the outside support to establish norms and goals to make the shift from discussing topics of mutual interest and sharing ideas, materials, and resources to a focus on aligning to common outcomes that impact student learning. The team errs on the side of congenial, surface-level interactions as they try to reach agreement.
Prerequisite Two: Collaborative teams implement a guaranteed and viable curriculum, unit by unit.	Teams reflect on student data and the prioritized standards, learning targets, "I can" statements, and pacing guides they identified for the prior year. This informs the team what needs to be adjusted for the upcoming year or unit. Teacher teams consistently review prior and successive grade- or course-level standards to determine the prerequisite skills students need to access new learning. Teams identify levels of student proficiency and commit to teach to mastery, rather than cover the curriculum.	Teams prioritize and unwrap standards, identify learning targets, write "I can" statements, and create common pacing guides. Proficiency levels are determined for each standard and learning target. Teacher teams occasionally review prior and successive grade- or course-level standards to determine the prerequisite skills students need to access new learning. They commit to teach to mastery rather than cover the curriculum.	Teacher teams prioritize and unwrap standards, identify learning targets, and follow pacing guides created by the district or the publisher. Decisions are influenced by what teachers believe. Lessons are based on what they know the best, like the most, have materials for, or what is included in the textbooks in order to meet the needs of all students. Curriculum decisions are based on perception and past practice.

Energize Your Teams © 2022 Solution Tree Press • SolutionTree.com
Visit **go.SolutionTree.com/PLCbooks** to download this free reproducible.

Anchor Statements	Beyond Proficient PLC Tight	Proficient PLC Right	Below Proficient PLC Lite
Prerequisite Three: Collaborative teams monitor student learning through an ongoing assessment process that includes frequent, team-developed, common formative assessments.	Teams reflect on student data and the valid and reliable common formative and summative assessments they administered during the prior school year. This informs the team what common formative and summative assessments they need to refine for the upcoming year or unit. Assessments are created prior to teaching the unit. Summative assessments align to the standard and common formative assessments to learning targets. Teams ensure alignment between test items, essential standards, learning targets, and proficiency levels. A clear timeline for administering and scoring assessments is established.	Teacher teams share the responsibility for creating the common formative and summative assessments they administer on a regular basis throughout the school year. Assessments are created prior to the team teaching the unit. Assessment items align to the essential standards, learning targets, and proficiency levels. A clear timeline for administering and scoring assessments is established.	Teacher teams rotate the responsibility for creating common summative assessments they administer periodically throughout the school year. Teams lean heavily on district- or publisher-created assessments designed to monitor all standards. Discussions of assessment results focus on general overall scores by group of students so grades can be assigned.
Prerequisite Four: Educators use the results of common assessments to improve individual practice, build the team's capacity to achieve its goals, and intervene and enrich on behalf of students.	Teacher teams reflect and analyze the prior year's state, district, and their own common formative and summative assessment results to determine the impact of their teaching. This informs the team on patterns and effectiveness of their shared practice. Teams combine this analysis with results from common assessments given in each unit to determine which instructional strategies they should retain, refine, or replace. Patterns in answers are investigated to determine students' strengths and common errors. The team identifies specific groups of students for intervention and extension by name and by skill.	Teacher teams analyze the results of common formative and summative assessments to identify which students need more time and support. Teams begin to make the shift from intervention and extension based on overall score to identifying specific groups of students for intervention and extension by name and by skill.	Teacher teams review results from state-, district-, and publisher-created summative assessments to monitor overall student progress or generate grades.

Anchor Statements	Beyond Proficient PLC Tight	Proficient PLC Right	Below Proficient PLC Lite
Prerequisite Five: The school (or each team) provides a systematic process for intervention and extension.	Teacher teams provide students with environment and remedial support as well as targeted and timely interventions that are systematic, practical, effective, essential, and directive, without missing instruction in another core subject. Teams provide students certain access to intervention and extension on essential standards and learning targets in the middle of the unit (Tier 1) and the end of the unit (Tier 2). The school has structures in place to support students needing remediation on foundational skills (Tier 3). The school and team consistently reflect on data to identify the effectiveness of their intervention and environment process. Students are provided feedback, so they are clear on how to improve and extend their learning.	Teacher teams provide students with extension and remedial support as well as targeted and timely interventions that are systematic, practical, effective, essential, and directive, without missing instruction in another core subject. Teams provide students certain access to intervention and extension on essential standards and learning targets in the middle of unit (Tier 1) and the end of the unit (Tier 2). The school has structures in place to support students needing remediation on foundational skills (Tier 3).	Teacher teams provide students with opportunities to receive additional intervention, extension, and remedial support based on an overall score or grade.

Pathways for Coaching Collaborative Teams in a PLC: The Five Prerequisites of a PLC

Prerequisite one: Educators work in collaborative teams, rather than in isolation, and take collective responsibility for student learning.	Prerequisite two: Collaborative teams implement a guaranteed and viable curriculum, unit by unit.	Prerequisite three: Collaborative teams monitor student learning through an ongoing assessment process that includes frequent, team-developed, common formative assessments.	Prerequisite four: Educators use the results of common assessments to improve individual practice, build the team's capacity to achieve its goals, and intervene and enrich on behalf of students.	Prerequisite five: The school (or each team) provides a systematic process for intervention and extension.
What are the keys to promoting the development of highly effective collaborative teams?	What knowledge, skills, and dispositions should every student acquire as a result of this class, course, or grade level?	How will we know when each student has acquired the essential knowledge, skills, and dispositions?	How will we use assessment data or samples of student work to monitor student learning and reflect on our professional practice?	How will we respond when some students do or do not acquire the essential knowledge, skills, and dispositions?
1.1: Determine the focus or purpose of the team meeting.	2.1: Prioritize the most essential standards.	3.1: Identify the appropriate depth of knowledge (DOK) for each target.	4.1: Analyze assessment data.	5.1: Ensure all students have access to the same core curriculum.
1.2: Use structures to promote team productivity.	2.2: Identify the highest-leverage learning targets.	3.2: Choose item types and distractors.	4.2: Analyze samples of student work.	5.2: Ensure all students have access to interventions when they struggle to meet essential standards.
1.3: Clarify roles and responsibilities.	2.3: Create student-friendly / *can* statements.	3.3: Develop a test plan that includes assessment logistics.	4.3: Analyze the impact of instructional strategies on learning.	5.3: Ensure all students have access to extension when they have already mastered essential standards.
1.4: Build relationships between and among members.	2.4: Determine age-appropriate proficiency levels.	3.4: Create valid and reliable common assessments.	4.4: Identify student proficiency levels.	
1.5: Choose processes and protocols to facilitate team decision making.	2.5: Select teaching strategies and pacing for the unit.	3.5: Collect and organize results in ways that align with the three rules of data.	4.5: Reflect on the quality of assessment items and answer choices.	

Pathways for Prerequisite One:
Educators Work in Collaborative Teams,
Rather Than in Isolation, and Take Collective
Responsibility for Student Learning

What are the keys to promoting the development of highly effective collaborative teams?

1.1: Determine the Focus	1.2: Use Structures	1.3: Clarify Roles and Responsibilities	1.4: Build Relationships	1.5: Choose Processes and Protocols
What are the purpose and non-purpose of this team meeting?	What are the long- and short-term SMART goals the team is trying to accomplish?	Will internal or external facilitators lead the team meetings?	How does the team promote respectful and professional dialogue?	What protocols does the team use to reach consensus?
How does the team goal connect to the four critical questions of learning?	How does the team create, share, and revisit norms during meetings? How does the team address violations of norms?	What other roles will team members fill during meetings? Has the team clearly defined those roles? Are they in writing?	How does the team foster a climate that allows for productive levels of professional dissonance?	What protocols does the team use to analyze student work?
How will the team document its progress toward meeting the goal?	When, where, how often, and for how long will the team meet?	How will the team allocate roles among the members? Will the team assign roles, or will members volunteer for roles?	What steps has the team taken to build relational trust among and between team members?	What protocols does the team use to address issues and concerns as they arise?
What materials do team members need to bring to achieve the meeting goal?	How does the team develop agendas, and when does the team share the agendas with team members?	Will the roles rotate? If so, how often? If not, how long will members keep the same roles?	How does the team encourage cognitive conflict, discourage affective conflict, and resolve conflict when it occurs?	What protocols does the team use to reflect on members' instructional practice?
What protocols will the team use to keep the focus on its goal?	How does the team document progress and identify next steps?			What protocols does the team use to encourage professional reading?

Pathways for Prerequisite Two: Collaborative Teams Implement a Guaranteed and Viable Curriculum, Unit by Unit

What knowledge, skills, and dispositions should every student acquire as a result of this class, course, or grade level?

2.1: Prioritize Essential Standards	2.2: Identify Learning Targets	2.3: Create *I Can* Statements	2.4: Determine Proficiency Levels	2.5: Determine Strategies and Pacing
Which standards provide endurance?	What process will the team use to unwrap the essential standards?	How will the team rewrite targets in student-friendly language to create *I can* statements?	What prerequisite skills and vocabulary do students need to demonstrate proficiency on this target?	Which strategies should the team retain from the last time this unit was taught? Explain why.
Which standards provide readiness for the next level of learning?	What learning targets did the unwrapping process reveal?	How will the team ensure students understand each *I can* statement?	To what depth of knowledge (DOK) level should students show proficiency?	Which strategies should the team refine from the last time the unit was taught? Explain why.
Which standards provide leverage?	Are any of the targets more important to student success than other targets?	How will you ensure students understand each *I can* statement?	How will you communicate levels of proficiency to students?	Which strategies did not work the last time the unit was taught that the team should replace? Explain why.
Which standards do standardized tests most often assess?	Which targets does the curriculum not adequately address? How will the team include them in the unit?	How will students set learning goals using *I can* statements?	What exemplars of proficiency does the team have or will it create to share with students?	What additional strategies might help students better understand the learning targets?
If the team could only teach ten standards in this course, which would they be? Why?	How will your team address any targets the curriculum does not adequately address?	How and when will students monitor progress toward the learning goals they established with their *I can* statements?	What exemplars of proficient work do you have—or will you create—to share with students?	How long will it take for students to demonstrate proficiency on each learning target?
				How will you monitor and adjust pacing of instruction for each learning target?

Pathways for Prerequisite Three:
Collaborative Teams Monitor Student Learning Through an Ongoing Assessment Process That Includes Frequent, Team-Developed, Common Formative Assessments

How will we know when each student has acquired the essential knowledge, skills, and dispositions?

3.1: Identify Appropriate Depth of Knowledge (DOK)	3.2: Choose Item Types and Distractors	3.3: Develop a Test Plan That Includes Logistics	3.4: Create Valid and Reliable Common Assessments	3.5: Collect and Organize Assessment Results
At what DOK level does the team expect students to demonstrate proficiency?	Which item types best demonstrate the team's description of proficiency?	How will you ensure that the assessment is scored or graded consistently across all classrooms?	What learning targets from this unit will the team need to address on the assessment?	How frequently does the team assess student progress?
How many test items are there at each DOK level (1–4)? How many items ask students to perform at the proficiency level?	How does the assessment provide a blend of item types to accurately measure student learning?	How long will students have to complete the assessment? How will teachers respond if students do not finish?	What learning targets from previous units will the team need to reassess on the assessment?	Where does the team house assessment data? Are assessment data easily accessible? Can teachers access them in a timely manner?
Do the test items cover a range of DOK levels that will help teachers diagnose student levels of understanding?	If using constructed- or extended-response items, does the prompt fully address the target being assessed?	What resources (notes, calculators, the text, and so on) does the team allow students to use during the assessment?	Which standard or learning target does each test item assess? Do they match the standards and targets the team has taught?	Does the team purposefully arrange the data? Do the data show student performance levels by target, by teacher, and by student?
What opportunities have you given students to practice at the expected DOK level?	If using selected-response items on the assessment, did you include between three and five selected-response items per learning target?	What are the specific test conditions? Will teachers leave visual cues in the classroom?	How many items are on the test for each standard or learning target? Are there enough to tell whether students have mastered the content?	Which formats (charts, graphs, and so on) best display the data to facilitate team discussion?
	Review the test item by item. What mistakes are students likely to make? What will each distractor tell teachers about student learning?	How does the test layout contribute to students' ability to read and respond to items?	Does the number of items per standard or target correspond to the amount of time and emphasis teachers give during instruction?	Does the team publicly discuss the data? When? What process does the team use to discuss the data?

Pathways for Prerequisite Four:
Educators Use the Results of Common Assessments to Improve Individual Practice, Build the Team's Capacity to Achieve Its Goals, and Intervene and Enrich on Behalf of Students

How will we use assessment data or samples of student work to monitor student learning and reflect on our professional practice?

4.1: Analyze Assessment Data	4.2: Analyze Examples of Student Work	4.3: Analyze Strategies	4.4: Identify Student Proficiency Levels	4.5: Reflect on Quality of Items and Answer Choices
What assessment data did members bring to discuss as a team?	What student work samples did members bring to discuss as a team?	What instructional strategies did the team use?	Which students were proficient? What patterns do you notice about these student answers?	Which items did large numbers of students answer incorrectly? Why?
What are the overall team proficiency rates for each assessed target?	What patterns do you see in samples of student work you deem proficient?	Which strategies do the data indicate were successful? Cite evidence.	Which students were close to proficient? What patterns do you notice about these student answers?	To what does the team attribute this large number? Consider academic vocabulary, team phrasing, confusing answer choices, and so on.
What are the proficiency rates of each target by class? Are proficiency levels higher in some classes than others? Why?	What patterns do you see in samples of student work you deem below proficient?	Which strategies do the data indicate were unsuccessful? Cite evidence.	Which students were below proficient? What patterns do you notice about these student answers?	How would rephrasing the item (while maintaining the DOK level) impact student answers?
Which items did students most often answer incorrectly? What patterns do you see among wrong answers?	Which items did students most often answer incorrectly? What patterns do members see among incorrect responses?	How can the team refine these strategies to make them more successful?	Which students were beyond proficient? What patterns do you notice about these student answers?	Which items did large numbers of students answer correctly?
Did some groups outperform others? Why? How can you transfer that success to other groups?	Did some student groups outperform others? Why? How can the team transfer that success to other student groups?	What other strategies might help students better understand the targets?	Which students need intervention or extension and on which targets?	Are these items at an appropriate DOK level? Do they provide the information the team is seeking?

page 1 of 2

4.1: Analyze Assessment Data	4.2: Analyze Examples of Student Work	4.3: Analyze Strategies	4.4: Identify Student Proficiency Levels	4.5: Reflect on Quality of Items and Answer Choices
What connections can the team make between student performance and instructional strategies?	What connections can the team make between student performance and instructional strategies?		How could you group students according to need for the purpose of intervention and extension?	Are there logistical details the team should consider refining to improve the assessment?
How will the team address targets that need additional whole-class instruction?	How will the team address targets that need additional whole-class instruction?			

Energize Your Teams © 2022 Solution Tree Press • SolutionTree.com
Visit **go.SolutionTree.com/PLCbooks** to download this free reproducible.

Pathways for Prerequisite Five:
The School (or Each Team) Provides a Systematic Process for Intervention and Extension

How will we respond when some students do or do not acquire the essential knowledge, skills, and dispositions?

5.1: Ensure Students Have Access to the Same Core Curriculum	5.2: Provide Students With Access to Interventions	5.3: Provide Students With Access to Extensions
How do we ensure all students have access to the essential standards?	How will you regroup students for Tier 2 intervention? On what data will those decisions be based?	How will you regroup students for Tier 2 extension? On what data will you base those decisions?
How does your team monitor delivery of the essential standards?	How will you adjust the strategies you use to deliver content for Tier 2 intervention students?	How will you adjust the strategies you use to deliver content for Tier 2 extension students?
How does your team monitor student mastery of the essential standards?	How will you adjust the strategies you use to help Tier 2 intervention students process the material?	How will you adjust the strategies you use to help Tier 2 extension students process the material?
How do you ensure all students are provided with appropriate intervention and extension?	How will you adjust the products Tier 2 intervention students will create to demonstrate their proficiency?	How will you adjust the products Tier 2 extension students will create to demonstrate their proficiency?
How do you ensure student intervention and extension opportunities do not take place during Tier 1 instruction?	How and when will you reassess Tier 2 intervention students to ensure the intervention was successful?	How and when will you reassess Tier 2 extension students to ensure the extension was successful?
When does regularly scheduled intervention take place during the school day?	How will you provide Tier 3 intervention to students who lack essential prerequisite skills or background knowledge?	How will you provide Tier 3 intervention to students who have mastered the essential standards?
	Are there students who consistently struggle the team should refer to the school intervention leadership team?	Are there students who consistently excel the team should consider for acceleration?

APPENDIX B

Index of Strategies, Activities, and Protocols

Module and Focus: Why, What, or How?	Articles and Handouts	Warm-Up or Protocol?	Title	Source for Activity
Highly Effective Collaborative Teams				
Module 4.1 (p. 45) *Why*	"Why Should We Collaborate"	Warm-up	Repeat Before Response	Muir (2019)
	"Are We A Group or A Team?"	Protocol	Are We a Group or a Team	Buffum et al. (2018)
Module 4.2 (p. 52) *What*	No additional article or handout	Warm-up	You Might Be a Team if . . .	SRI (2014)
	"Conditions to Consider Before Establishing Collaborative Teams"	Protocol	Surfacing Significant Ideas	Glaude (2011)
Module 4.3 (p. 58) *How*	No additional article or handout	Warm-up	Write a Movie Review	Unattributed
	"Focus: A State or Condition Permitting Clear Perception and Understanding"; "Structures: The Building Blocks of Collaboration"; "Clarifying Roles and Responsibilities"; "Investments in High-Trust Relationships Produce Big Dividends for Collaborative Teams"; "Connoisseurs of Ineffective Tools and Strategies: How Teams Use Process"	Protocol	Jigsaw	Glaude (2011)
Guaranteed and Viable Curriculum				
Module 5.1 (p. 80) *Why*	"Why Should We Ensure Access to a GVC?"	Warm-up	Block Party	SRI (2014)
	"Are We Making a List or Delivering on a Promise?"	Protocol	Convert-Stations	Muir (2019)
Module 5.2 (p. 89) *What*	No additional article or handout	Warm-up	T-Chart	Gregory & Kuzmich (2007)
	"Guaranteed and Viable Curriculum is Not a Proper Noun"	Protocol	Making Meaning	SRI (2014)
Module 5.3 (p. 94) *How*	No additional article or handout	Warm-up	Give-and-Go	Gregory & Kuzmich (2007)
	"Prioritizing Standards Using R.E.A.L. Criteria"	Protocol	First Word	Lipton & Wellman (2012)
Module 5.4 (p. 102) *How*	No additional article or handout	Warm-up	M&Ms and Essential Standards	Unattributed
	"Unwrapping the Standards: A Priceless Professional Development Opportunity"	Protocol	Text-Rendering	Glaude (2011)

Module	Article or handout	Type	Name	Attribution
Module 5.5 (p. 108) *How*	No additional article or handout	Warm-up	Promissory Note	Gregory & Kuzmich (2007)
	"Crafting *I Can* Statements: A Practice Worth Pursuing"	Protocol	"Four A"	SRI (2014)
A Balanced and Coherent System of Assessment				
Module 6.1 (p. 119) *Why*	"Why Should We Use Common Assessments?"	Warm-up	Quotation Mingle	Daniels & Steineke (2011)
	"The Secret To Success"	Protocol	Unpacking Luggage	Lipton & Wellman (2011)
Module 6.2 (p. 125) *What*	No additional article or handout	Warm-up	Reflection on a Word	McDonald et al. (2007)
	"A Balanced and Coherent System of Assessment"	Protocol	Text on Text	Daniels & Steineke (2011)
Module 6.3 (p. 131) *How*	No additional article or handout	Warm-up	ABC Conversations	Gregory & Kuzmich (2007)
	"Four Steps to Creating Valuable and Reliable Common Assessments"	Protocol	Scavenger Hunt	McTighe & Silver (2020)
Module 6.4 (p. 138) *How*	No additional article or handout	Warm-up	Assessment Training Poll	Unattributed
	"The Power of Distractors"	Protocol	Practice Distractors	Unattributed
Module 6.5 (p. 144) *How*	No additional article or handout	Warm-up	Round the Room and Back	Wellman & Lipton (2004)
	"Shifting the Purpose of Preassessments"	Protocol	Outside In	Unattributed
Productive Data Conversations				
Module 7.1 (p. 154) *Why*	No additional article or handout	Warm-up	Sharing Experience	Unattributed
	"Double Duty Data"	Protocol	Say Something	Lipton & Wellman (1999)
Module 7.2 (p. 160) *What*	No additional article or handout	Warm-up	5-3-1	Lipton & Wellman (1999)
	"Three Rules Help Manage Assessment Data"	Protocol	Pair Reading	Daniels & Steineke (2011)
Module 7.3 (p. 165) *How*	"Types of Data Conversations"	Warm-up	Shaping the Conversation	Unattributed
	"Unclutter Your Team's Data Conversations"	Protocol	Three Levels of Text	Easton (2009)
Module 7.4 (p. 172) *How*	No additional article or handout	Warm-up	Possible Sentences	Lipton & Wellman (1999)
	"It's Not Pixie Dust, It's Protocol"; "Protocols: A Powerful Prescription for Professional Learning"	Protocol	Challenging Assumptions	Glaude (2011)

Module and Focus: Why, What, or How?	Articles and Handouts	Warm-Up or Protocol?	Title	Source for Activity
Module 7.5 (p. 181) _How_	"Facilitating Data Conversations"	Warm-up	Window Notes, Part I	Lipton & Wellman (2012)
	"Facilitating Data Conversations"	Protocol	Window Notes, Part II	McTighe & Silver (2020)
Pyramids of Interventions				
Module 8.1 (p. 190) _Why_	"Why Should We Implement Systematic Interventions"	Warm-up	Reciprocal Interviews	Lipton & Wellman (1999)
	"Dialogue Dice"	Protocol	Dialogue Dice	Macomb SD 185, Macomb, Michigan
Module 8.2 (p. 196) _What_	No additional article or handout	Warm-up	KWL	Gregory & Kuzmich (2007)
	"Endure the Successful Implementation of Intervention in a PLC"	Protocol	Each Teach	Lipton & Wellman (2012)
Module 8.3 (p. 203) _How_	No additional article or handout	Warm-up	Pairs Squared	Unattributed
	"The Need for SPEED"	Protocol	Last Word	Easton (2009)
Module 8.4 (p. 209) _How_	No additional article or handout	Warm-up	Where Do You Stand?	Daniels & Steineke (2011)
	"Regrouping Versus the Classroom Approach"	Protocol	Supporting Evidence	Glaude (2011)
Module 8.5 (p. 214) _How_	No additional article or handout	Warm-up	Analogies	Unattributed
	"Responding to That Pesky Question Four in a PLC"	Protocol	Inter-VENN-tion	Lipton & Wellman (2012)

REFERENCES AND RESOURCES

Ainsworth, L. (2003). *"Unwrapping" the standards: A simple process to make standards manageable.* Englewood, CO: Advanced Learning Press.

Ainsworth, L. (2004). *Power standards: Identifying the standards that matter the most.* Englewood, CO: Advanced Learning Press.

Ainsworth, L. (2013). *Prioritizing the Common Core: Identifying the specific standards to emphasize the most.* Englewood, CO: Lead + Learn Press.

Ainsworth, L. (2015a). *Common formative assessments 2.0: How teacher teams intentionally align standards, instruction, and assessment.* Thousand Oaks, CA: Corwin Press.

Ainsworth, L. (2015b, March 25). *Unwrapping the standards: A simple way to deconstruct learning outcomes* [Blog post]. Accessed at https://edweek.org/education/opinion-unwrapping-the-standards-a-simple-way-to-deconstruct-learning-outcomes/2015/03 March 1, 2021.

Ainsworth, L., & Viegut, D. (2006). *Common formative assessment: How to connect standards-based instruction and assessment.* Thousand Oaks, CA: Corwin Press.

AllThingsPLC. (2016). *Glossary of key terms and concepts.* Accessed at www.allthingsplc.info/files/uploads/Terms.pdf on August 24, 2020.

Atherton, J. S. (2009). *Cognitive dissonance and learning.* Accessed at www.learningandteaching.info/learning/dissonance.htm on August 8, 2021.

AZquotes. (n.d.) *Maya Angelou quotes.* Accessed at https://azquotes.com/quote/346302 on August 29, 2020.

Bailey, K., & Jakicic, C. (2012). *Common formative assessment: A toolkit for Professional Learning Communities at Work.* Bloomington, IN: Solution Tree Press.

Bailey, K., Jakicic, C., & Spiller, J. (2014). *Collaborating for success with the Common Core: A toolkit for Professional Learning Communities at Work.* Bloomington, IN: Solution Tree Press.

Balu, R., Zhu, P., Doolittle, F., Schiller, E., Jenkins, J., & Gersten, R. (2015, November). *Evaluation of response to intervention practices for elementary school reading.* Washington, DC: U.S. Department of Education, Institute of Education Sciences, National Center for Education Evaluation and Regional Assistance. Accessed at https://files.eric.ed.gov/fulltext/ED560820.pdf on March 1, 2021.

Bambrick-Santoyo, P. (2010). *Driven by data: A practical guide to improve instruction.* San Francisco: Jossey-Bass.

Bangert-Drowns, R. L., Kulik, J. A., & Kulik, C. H. (1991). Effects of frequent classroom testing. *The Journal of Educational Research, 85*(2), 89–99.

Barber, M., Chijioke, C., & Mourshed, M. (2010). *How the world's most improved school systems keep getting better.* London: McKinsey.

Bialis-White, L. (2016, January 18). *Using data conversations to accelerate impact and improve outcomes* [Blog post]. Accessed at https://gettingsmart.com/2016/01/using-data-conversations on September 3, 2020.

Black, M. (2017). *Helping students track their own progress.* Accessed at https://studentfutures.org/college-planning/helping-students-track-their-own-progress on September 16, 2019.

Bradley, A. (1993, July 14). *N.Y.C.'s District 2 gives top priority to educators' learning* [Blog post]. Accessed at https://edweek.org/education/n-y-c-s-district-2-gives-top-priority-to-educators-learning/1993/07 on January 25, 2021.

BrainyQuote. (n.d.) *Vince Lombardi quotes.* Accessed at https://brainyquote.com/quotes/vince_lombardi_138158 on August 29, 2020.

Brewster, C., & Railsback, J. (2003, September). *Building trusting relationships for school improvement: Implications for principals and teachers.* Portland, OR: Northwestern Regional Educational Laboratory. Accessed at https://educationnorthwest.org/sites/default/files/trust.pdf on March 1, 2021.

Brookhart, S. M., & Moss, C. M. (2014). Learning targets on parade. *Educational Leadership, 72*(2), 28–33.

Brown, B. (2012). *Daring greatly: How the courage to be vulnerable transforms the way we live, love, parent, and lead.* New York: Gotham Books.

Buffum, A., Mattos, M., & Malone, J. (2018). *Taking action: A handbook for RTI at Work.* Bloomington, IN: Solution Tree Press.

Buffum, A., Mattos, M., & Weber, C. (2009). *Pyramid response to intervention: RTI, professional learning communities, and how to respond when kids don't learn.* Bloomington, IN: Solution Tree Press.

Buffum, A., Mattos, M., & Weber, C. (2012). *Simplifying response to intervention: Four essential guiding principles.* Bloomington, IN: Solution Tree Press.

Bustos, J. (2015, May 8). *Pre-Assessment in the classroom* [Video file]. Accessed at https://youtube.com/watch?v=xJSppChW9n8 on January 25, 2021.

Bryk, A. S., & Schneider, B. (2002). *Trust in schools: A core resource for improvement.* New York: Russell Sage Foundation.

Byrd, I. (n.d.). *Six traits of quality pre-assessments.* Accessed at www.byrdseed.com/six-traits-of-quality-pre-assessments on January 26, 2021.

Carroll, T. (2009). The next generation of learning teams. *Phi Delta Kappan, 91*(2), 8–13.

Clayton, H. (2017). Learning targets. *Making the standards come alive! VI*(1). Alexandria, VA: Just ASK. Accessed at https://justaskpublications.s3.amazonaws.com/Learning_Targets_5.pdf on March 10, 2021.

Coleman, M. R. (2010, October 19). *RTI for gifted students* [Interview transcript]. Accessed at www .rtinetwork.org/mpdf_print.php?htc=YToxOntzOjEzOiJyZXBvcnRfaWRjaGF0IjtzOjI6IjI0Ijt9 on March 17, 2021.

Conzemius, A. E., & O'Neill, J. (2014). *The handbook for SMART school teams: Revitalizing best practices for collaboration* (2nd ed.). Bloomington, IN: Solution Tree Press.

Covey, S. M. R. (2006). *The speed of trust: The one thing that changes everything.* New York: Free Press.

Crockett, H. (2013). *How I CAN statements can work for you.* Accessed at https://theartofed.com/2013/02 /21/how-i-can-statements-can-work-for-you on September 14, 2020.

Crow, T. (2012). Leadership through learning: When people are enlightened, they want to take action. *Journal of Staff Development, 33*(6), 16–22.

Daniels, H., & Steineke, N. (2011). *Texts and lessons for content-area reading.* Portsmouth, NH: Heinemann.

Dimich, N. (2015). *Design in five: Essential phases to create engaging assessment practice.* Bloomington, IN: Solution Tree Press.

Domina, T., Lewis, R., Agarwal, P., & Hanselman, P. (2015). Professional sense-makers: Instructional specialists in contemporary schooling. *Educational Researcher, 44*(6), 359–364.

DuFour, R. (2004). What is a professional learning community? *Educational Leadership, 61*(8), 6–11. Accessed at www.ascd.org/publications/educational-leadership/may04/vol61/num08/What-Is-a -Professional-Learning-Community%C2%A2.aspx on March 9, 2021.

DuFour, R. (2018). *Passion and persistence: How to develop a Professional Learning Community at Work* [DVD] (Revised ed.). Bloomington, IN: Solution Tree Press.

DuFour, R., DuFour, R., & Eaker, R. (2008). *Revisiting Professional Learning Communities at Work: New insights for improving schools.* Bloomington, IN: Solution Tree Press.

DuFour, R., DuFour, R., Eaker, R., & Karhanek, G. (2004). *Whatever it takes: How professional learning communities respond when kids don't learn.* Bloomington, IN: Solution Tree Press.

DuFour, R., DuFour, R., Eaker, R., & Karhanek, G. (2010). *Raising the bar and closing the gap: Whatever it takes.* Bloomington, IN: Solution Tree Press.

DuFour, R., DuFour, R., Eaker, R., & Many, T. (2006). *Learning by doing: A handbook for Professional Learning Communities at Work* (1st ed.). Bloomington, IN: Solution Tree Press.

DuFour, R., DuFour, R., Eaker, R., & Many, T. (2010). *Learning by doing: A handbook for Professional Learning Communities at Work* (2nd ed.). Bloomington, IN: Solution Tree Press.

DuFour, R., DuFour, R., Eaker, R., Many, T. W., & Mattos, M. (2016). *Learning by doing: A handbook for Professional Learning Communities at Work* (3rd ed.). Bloomington, IN: Solution Tree Press.

DuFour, R., Eaker, R., & DuFour, R. (2007). *The power of Professional Learning Communities at Work: Bringing the big ideas to life* [DVD]. Bloomington, IN: Solution Tree Press.

DuFour, R., & Fullan, M. (2013). *Cultures built to last: Systemic PLCs at Work.* Bloomington, IN: Solution Tree Press.

DuFour, R., & Marzano, R. J. (2011). *Leaders of learning. How district, school, and classroom leaders improve student achievement.* Bloomington, IN: Solution Tree Press.

DuFour, R., & Reeves, D. (2016). The futility of PLC lite. *Phi Delta Kappan, 97*(6), 69–71.

Dunne, D. W. (2012, August 15). *Teachers learn from looking together at student work.* Accessed at https://education-world.com/a_curr/curr246.shtml on March 17, 2021.

Dyer, K. (2016, January 19). *Three ways to put assessment data to work in the classroom* [Blog post]. Accessed at https://nwea.org/blog/2016/three-ways-to-put-assessment-data-to-work-in-the-classroom on August 29, 2020.

Eaker, R., & Dillard, H. (2017, Fall). Why collaborate? Because it enhancers student learning! *AllThingsPLC Magazine,* 46–47.

Eaker, R., & Keating, J. (2009, July 22). *Team leaders in a professional learning community* [Blog post]. Accessed at www.allthingsplc.info/blog/view/54/team-leaders-in-a-professional-learning-community on January 26, 2021.

Easton, L. B. (2009). *Protocols for professional learning.* Alexandria, VA: Association for Supervision and Curriculum Development.

Forman, M. L. (2005, July 15). *The use of assessment to improve instruction: The Data Wise Project helps schools turn student assessment data into a tool to enhance organizational performance* [Blog post]. Accessed at https://gse.harvard.edu/news/uk/05/07/use-assessment-improve-instruction on March 16, 2021.

Fulton, K., & Britton, T. (2011). *STEM teachers in professional learning communities: From good teachers to great teaching.* Washington, DC: National Commission on Teaching and America's Future.

Gareis, C. R., & Grant, L. W. (2008). *Teacher-made assessments: How to connect curriculum, instruction, and student learning.* Larchmont, NY: Eye on Education.

Gierl, M. J., Bulut, O., Guo, Q., & Zhang, X. (2017). Developing, analyzing, and using distractors for multiple-choice tests in education: A comprehensive review. *Review of Educational Research, 87*(6), 1082–1116.

The Glossary of Education Reform. (2014). *Selected response.* Accessed at www.edglossary.org on January 9, 2020.

Glaude, C. (2011). *Protocols for professional learning conversations: Cultivating the art and discipline.* Bloomington, IN: Solution Tree Press.

Gooden, J., Petrie, G., Lindauer, P., & Richardson, M. (1998). Principals' needs for small-group process skills. *NASSP Bulletin, 82*(596), 102–107.

Gordon, T., & Burch, N. (1977). *T. E. T. teacher effectiveness training, instructors' guide.* New York: David McKay.

Gordon, T., & Burch, N. (1974). *Teacher effectiveness training: The program proven to help teachers bring out the best in students of all ages.* New York: Three Rivers Press.

Gregory, G. H., & Kuzmich, L. (2007). *Teacher teams that get results: Sixty-one strategies for sustaining and renewing professional learning communities.* Thousand Oaks, CA: Corwin Press.

Griffiths, D. M. (2006, March). *Are you drowning in a sea of information? Managing information: A practical guide.* Accessed at www.managing-information.org.uk on January 26, 2021.

Grinder, M. (1997). *The science of nonverbal communication.* Battleground, WA: Author.

Guskey, T. R. (2003). How classroom assessments improve learning. *Educational Leadership, 60*(5), 6–11.

Guskey, T. R. (2010). Formative assessment: The contribution of Benjamin S. Bloom. In H. L. Andrade & G. J. Cizek (Eds.), *Handbook of formative assessment* (pp. 106–124). New York: Routledge.

Hattie, J. (2009). *Visible learning: A synthesis of over 800 meta-analyses relating to achievement.* New York: Routledge.

Hattie, J. (2015, June). *What works best in education: The politics of collaborative expertise.* London: Pearson. Accessed at www.pearson.com/content/dam/corporate/global/pearson-dot-com/files/hattie/150526_ExpertiseWEB_V1.pdf on September 30, 2015.

Hulme, P. (2014, July 28). Bridging the knowing-doing gap: know-who, know-what, know-why, know-how and know-when. Accessed at https://doi.org/10.1111/1365-2664.12321 on April 19, 2021.

Joyce, B., & Showers, B. (2002). *Student achievement through staff development* (3rd ed.). Alexandria, VA: Association for Supervision and Curriculum Development.

Kao, D. (2014, July). *Perception vs observation* [Blog post]. Accessed at www.diplateevo.com/perception-vs-observation on March 14, 2020.

Killion, J. (2008). Are you coaching heavy or light? *Teachers Teaching Teachers, 3*(8), 1–4.

Killion, J. (2010). Reprising coaching heavy and light. *Learning Forward, 6*(4), 8–9.

Killion, J., & Harrison, C. (2017). *Taking the lead: New roles for teachers and school-based coaches* (2nd ed.). Oxford, OH: Learning Forward.

Killion, J., Harrison, C., Bryan, C., & Clifton, H. (2012). *Coaching matters.* Oxford, OH: Learning Forward.

King, K. V., Gardner, D. A., Zucker, S., & Jorgensen, M. A. (2004, July). *The distractor rationale taxonomy: Enhancing multiple-choice items in reading and mathematics.* San Antonio, TX: Pearson.

Knight, J., van Nieuwerburgh, C., Campbell, J., & Thomas, S. (2019). Seven ways principals can improve professional conversations. *Principle Leadership, 19.* Accessed at www.nassp.org/2019/01/01/role-call-january-2019 on February 3, 2020.

Kozlowski, W. (2020, August 6). *Accidental teams* [Blog post]. Accessed at https://waltkozlowski.wordpress.com/2020/08/06/accidental-teams on March 1, 2021.

Kraft, M. A., & Blazar, D. (2018). Taking teacher coaching to scale. *Education Next, 18*(4), 68–74. Accessed at https://educationnext.org/taking-teacher-coaching-to-scale-can-personalized-training-become-standard-practice on March 2, 2021.

Kruse, S., Louis, K. S., & Bryk, A. (1994). Building professional learning in schools. Accessed at http://dieppestaff.pbworks.com/w/file/fetch/66176267/Professional%20Learning%20communities.pdf on March 9, 2021.

Larner, M. (2007). *Tools for leaders: Indispensable graphic organizers, protocols, and planning guidelines for working and learning together.* New York: Scholastic.

Lencioni, P. (2006). *Silos, politics, and turf wars: A leadership fable about destroying the barriers that turn colleagues into competitors.* San Francisco: Jossey-Bass.

Lipton, L., & Wellman, B. M. (1999). *Pathways to understanding: Patterns and practices in the learning-focused classroom* (3rd ed.). Guilford, VT: Pathways.

Lipton, L., & Wellman, B. M. (2011). *Groups at work: Strategies and structures for professional learning.* Charlotte, VT: MiraVia.

Lipton, L., & Wellman, B. (2012). *Got data? Now what? Creating and leading cultures of inquiry.* Bloomington, IN: Solution Tree Press.

Little, J. W. (2006, December). *Professional community and professional development in the learning-centered school.* Washington, DC: National Education Association. Accessed at https://citeseerx .ist.psu.edu/viewdoc/download?doi=10.1.1.159.5197&rep=rep1&type=pdf on February 8, 2020.

Louis, K. S., Kruse, S. D., & Bryk, A. S. (1995). Professionalism and community: What is it and why is it important in urban schools? In K. S. Louis & D. Kruse (Eds.), *Professionalism and community: Perspectives on reforming urban schools* (pp. 3–22). Thousand Oaks, CA: Corwin Press.

Lubniewski, K. L., Cosgrove, D. F., & Robinson, T. Y. (Eds.). (2019). *Supervision modules to support educators in collaborative teaching: Helping to support and maintain consistent practice in the field.* Charlotte, NC: Information Age.

Many, T. W. (2016, Summer). Is it R.E.A.L. or not? *PLC Magazine,* 34–35.

Many, T. W. (2019). Coaching collaborative teams: Drill deeper to achieve advanced levels of PLC practice. *TESPA News, 76*(2). Accessed at https://tepsa.org/resource/coaching-collaborative-teams -drill-deeper-to-achieve-advanced-levels-of-plc-practice on March 1, 2021.

Many, T. W., Maffoni, M. J., Sparks, S. K., & Thomas, T. F. (2018). *Amplify your impact: Coaching collaborative teams in PLCs at Work.* Bloomington, IN: Solution Tree Press.

Many, T. W., Maffoni, M. J., Sparks, S. K., & Thomas, T. F. (2020). *How schools thrive: Building a coaching culture for collaborative teams in PLCs at Work.* Bloomington, IN: Solution Tree Press.

Marshall, K. (2006). *Interim assessments: Keys to successful implementation.* New York: New Leaders. Accessed at https://marshallmemo.com/articles/Interim%20Assmt%20Report%20Apr.%2012,%2006.pdf on March 1, 2021.

Marshall, K. (2008). Interim assessments: A user's guide. *Phi Delta Kappan, 90*(1), 64–68. Accessed at https://marshallmemo.com/articles/IA%20User%20Guide.pdf on March 16, 2021.

Marzano, R. J. (2003). *What works in schools: Translating research into action.* Alexandria, VA: Association for Supervision and Curriculum Development.

Marzano, R. J. (2007). *The art and science of teaching.* Alexandria, VA: Association for Supervision and Curriculum Development.

Marzano, R. J. (2010). When students track their progress. *Educational Leadership, 67*(4), 86–87.

Marzano, R. J., & Simms, J. A. (2013). *Coaching classroom instruction.* Bloomington, IN: Marzano Resources.

Marzano, R. J., Yanoski, D. C., Hoegh, J. K., & Simms, J. A. (2013). *Using Common Core standards to enhance classroom instruction and assessment.* Bloomington, IN: Marzano Resources.

Marzano, R. J., Warrick, P. B., Rains, C. L., & DuFour, R. (2018). *Leading a high reliability school.* Bloomington, IN: Marzano Resources.

Mattos, M., DuFour, R., DuFour, R., Eaker, R., & Many, T. W. (2016). *Concise answers to frequently asked questions about Professional Learning Communities at Work.* Bloomington, IN: Solution Tree Press.

McCauley, C. D., & Van Velsor, E. (Eds.). (2003). *The Center for Creative Leadership handbook of leadership development* (2nd ed.). San Francisco: Jossey-Bass.

McDonald, J. P., Mohr, N., Dichter, D., & McDonald, E. C. (2007). *The power of protocols: An educator's guide to better practice* (2nd ed.). New York: Teachers College Press.

McLaughlin, M. W., & Talbert, J. E. (2006). *Building school-based teacher learning communities: Professional strategies to improve student achievement.* New York: Teachers College Press.

McTighe, J., & Silver, H. F. (2020). *Teaching for deeper learning: Tools to engage students in meaning making.* Alexandria, VA: Association for Supervision and Curriculum Development.

Mizell, H. (2010). *Why professional development matters.* Oxford, OH: Learning Forward. Accessed at https://learningforward.org/wp-content/uploads/2017/08/professional-development-matters.pdf on March 4, 2021.

Moss, C. M., & Brookhart, S. M. (2012). *Learning targets: Helping students aim for understanding in today's lesson.* Alexandria, VA: Association for Supervision and Curriculum Development.

Moss, C. M., Brookhart, S. M., & Long, B. A. (2011). Knowing your learning target. *Educational Leadership, 68*(6), 66–69.

Muir, T. (2019). *The collaborative classroom: Teaching students how to work together now and for the rest of their lives.* San Diego, CA: Burgess.

National Governors Association Center for Best Practices & Council of Chief State School Officers. (2010). *Common Core State Standards for English language arts and literacy in history/social studies, science, and technical subjects.* Washington, DC: Authors. Accessed at www.corestandards.org/assets /CCSSI_ELA%20Standards.pdf on March 11, 2021.

National Turning Points Center. (2001). *Turning Points: Transforming middle schools—Looking collaboratively at student and teacher work.* Boston: Author. Accessed at https://cce.org/uploads/files /Looking-at-Student-and-Teacher-Work.pdf on March 16, 2021.

Neufeld, B., & Roper, D. (2003). *Coaching: A strategy for developing instructional capacity—Promises and practicalities.* Washington, DC: Aspen Institute Program on Education. Accessed at ww.annenberginstitute.org/sites/default/files/product/268/files/Coaching.pdf on July 12, 2017.

Parker, W. D. (2018). *Collaborating for results: Interview with Dr. Judi Barber* [Audio podcast]. Accessed at https://williamdparker.com/2018/01/24/pmp099-collaborating-for-results-interview-with-dr -judi-barber on March 2, 2021.

Pfeffer, J., & Sutton, R. I. (2001). *The knowing-doing gap: How smart companies turn knowledge into action.* Boston: Harvard Business School Press.

Pierce, J., & Jackson, D. (2017). *Ten steps to make RTI work in schools.* Accessed at https://air.org/resource /ten-steps-make-rti-work-schools on January 26, 2021.

Popham, W. J. (2000). *Modern educational measurement: Practical guidelines for educational leaders* (3rd ed.). Boston: Pearson.

Popham, W. J. (2008). *Transformative assessment.* Alexandria, VA: Association for Supervision and Curriculum Development.

Psencik, K. (2011). *The coach's craft: Powerful practices to support school leaders.* Oxford, OH: Learning Forward.

Raywid, M. A. (1993). Finding time for collaboration. *Educational Leadership, 51*(1), 30–34.

Redding, S. (2006). *The mega system: Deciding. Learning. Connecting—A handbook for continuous improvement within a community of the school.* Lincoln, IL: Academic Development Institute. Accessed at www.adi.org/mega on January 26, 2021.

Reeves, D. (2002). *Making standards work: How to implement standard-based assessments in the classroom, school, and district* (3rd ed.). Englewood, CO: Advanced Learning Press.

Reeves, D. (Ed.). (2007). *Ahead of the curve: The power of assessment to transform teaching and learning.* Bloomington IN: Solution Tree Press.

Riggins, C., & Knowles, D. (2020). Caught in the trap of PLC lite: Essential steps needed for implementation of a true professional learning community. *Education, 141*(1), 46–54.

Roberts, M. (2020). *Shifting from me to we: How to jump-start collaboration in a PLC at Work.* Bloomington, IN: Solution Tree Press.

Rouda, R. (2018, March 28). *A framework for effective data use in schools* [Blog post]. Accessed at https://Learningforaction.com/lfa-blogpost/data-matters-framework on August 25, 2020.

Sanderson, B. E. (2005). *Talk it out! The educator's guide to successful difficult conversations.* Larchmont, NY: Eye On Education.

Saphier, J. (2005). *John Adams' promise: How to have good schools for all our children, not just for some.* Acton, MA: Research for Better Teaching.

Schmader, W. (n.d.). *It's time to give Noel Burch some credit* [Blog post]. Accessed at https://exceptionalleaderslab.com/its-time-to-give-noel-burch-some-credit on January 26, 2021.

Schmoker, M. (2001). *The results fieldbook: Practical strategies from dramatically improved schools.* Alexandria, VA: Association for Supervision and Curriculum Development.

Schmoker, M. (2004). Learning communities at the crossroads: A response to Joyce and Cook. *Phi Delta Kappan, 86*(1), 84–89.

School Reform Initiative (SRI). (2014). *A community of learners, version 3.* Denver, CO: Author.

Smith, W. R. (2015). *How to launch PLCs in your district.* Bloomington, IN: Solution Tree Press.

Sonbert, M. C. (2020). *Skyrocket your teacher coaching: How every school leader can become a coaching superstar.* San Diego, CA: Burgess.

Sparks, D. (2004). Broader purpose calls for higher understanding: An interview with Andy Hargreaves. *Journal of Staff Development, 25*(2), 46–50.

Sparks, S. D. (2015). Study: RTI practice falls short of promise. *Education Week.* Accessed at www.edweek.org/ew/articles/2015/11/11/study-rti-practice-falls-short-of-promise.html on January 26, 2021.

Sparks, S. K. (2008). Creating intentional collaboration. In *The collaborative teacher: Working together as a professional learning community* (pp. 31–55). Bloomington, IN: Solution Tree Press.

Sparks, S. K., & Many, T. W. (2015). *How to cultivate collaboration in a PLC.* Bloomington, IN: Solution Tree Press.

Stephenson, S. (2009). *Leading with trust: How to build strong school teams.* Bloomington, IN: Solution Tree Press.

Stiggins, R. J. (2002). Assessment crisis: The absence of assessment *for* learning. *Phi Delta Kappan*, *83*(10), 758–765.

Stiggins, R. J. (2007). Five assessment myths and their consequences. *Education Week*, *27*(8), 28–29.

Stiggins, R. J., Arter, J. A., Chappuis, J., & Chappuis, S. (2004). *Classroom assessment* for *student learning: Doing it right—Using it well*. Portland, OR: Assessment Training Institute.

Stiggins, R., & DuFour, R. (2009). Maximizing the power of formative assessments. *Phi Delta Kappan*, *90*(9), 640–644.

Supovitz, J. A., & Christman, J. B. (2003). Developing communities of instructional practice: Lessons from Cincinnati and Philadelphia. *CPRE Policy Brief*. Accessed at https://repository.upenn.edu /cpre_policybriefs/28 on March 2, 2021.

Sweeney, D. (2011). *Student-centered coaching: A guide for K–8 coaches and principals*. Thousand Oaks, CA: Corwin Press.

Sweeny, D., & Harris, L. S. (2017). *Student-centered coaching: The moves*. Thousand Oaks, CA: Corwin Press.

Thomas, T. (2015, November 23). *Pathways for coaching collaborative teams*. Presented at East Detroit Public Schools, Eastpointe, MI.

Thomas, T. (2019). *The implications of coaches' participation in professional learning community collaborative team meetings* (Doctoral Dissertation, University of Michigan-Flint, Flint, Michigan, United States). Accessed at htps://deepblue on January 26, 2021.

Tomlinson, C. A. (2007/2008). Learning to love assessment. *Educational Leadership*, *65*(4), 8–13.

Trach, S. A. (2014). Inspired instructional coaching: Stimulate teaching by structuring meaningful observations and feedback that will improve instruction schoolwide. *Principal*, *94*(2), 13–16. Accessed at https://naesp.org/sites/default/files/Trach_ND14.pdf on March 2, 2021.

Tschannen-Moran, M. (2004). *Trust matters: Leadership for successful schools*. San Francisco: Jossey-Bass.

Venables, D. R. (2014). *How teachers can turn data into action*. Alexandria, VA: Association for Supervision and Curriculum Development.

Waltman, J. (n.d.a). *I can statements* [Video file]. Accessed at https://sophia.org/tutorials/i-can-statements -2 on September 25, 2020.

Waltman, J. (n.d.b). *Why should students track their own progress?* [Video file]. Accessed at https://sophia .org/tutorials/why-should-students-track-their-own-progress-2 on March 9, 2021.

Watts, G. D., & Castle, S. (1993). The time dilemma in school restructuring. *Phi Delta Kappan*, *75*(4), 306–310.

Wellman, B., & Lipton, L. (2004). *Data-driven dialogue: A facilitator's guide to collaborative inquiry*. Charlotte, VT: MiraVia.

Wiliam, D. (2018). *Embedded formative assessment* (2nd ed.). Bloomington, IN: Solution Tree Press.

Willis, O. (2016, October 11). *Three steps to organize student data—and find joy* [Blog post]. Accessed at www.edsurge.com/news/2016–10–11-3-steps-to-organize-student-data on July 3, 2020.

Wong, H. K., & Wong, R. T. (2018). *The first days of school: How to be an effective teacher* (5th ed.). Mountain View, CA: Author.

INDEX

Amplify Your Impact
Thomas W. Many, Michael J. Maffoni, Susan K. Sparks, and Tesha Ferriby Thomas
Amplify Your Impact presents K–12 educators with a framework for improving collaboration in their PLCs. The authors share best practices and processes teams can rely on to ensure they are doing the right work in a cycle of continuous improvement. Discover concrete action steps your school can take to adopt proven collaborative coaching methods, fortify teacher teams, and ultimately improve student learning in classrooms.
BKF794

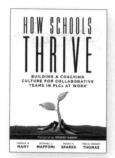

How Schools Thrive
Thomas W. Many, Michael J. Maffoni, Susan K. Sparks, and Tesha Ferriby Thomas
Strengthen your PLC by building a highly effective coaching culture for collaborative teams. This companion to *Amplify Your Impact* drills deeper into the more complex aspects of PLC at Work®. Coaches and leaders will acquire new insights and strategies for improving their team's professional practice around the essential elements of the PLC process, including continuous improvement, collective inquiry, action orientation, and a focus on results.
BKF855

Learning by Doing, Third Edition
Richard DuFour, Rebecca DuFour, Robert Eaker, Thomas W. Many, and Mike Mattos
Discover how to close the knowing-doing gap and transform your school or district into a high-performing PLC. The powerful third edition of this comprehensive action guide updates and expands on new and significant PLC topics. Explore fresh strategies, tools, and tips for hiring and retaining new staff, creating team-developed common formative assessments, implementing systematic interventions, and more.
BKF746

Make It Happen
Kim Bailey and Chris Jakicic
Ensure every educator is engaged in the right work with a collective focus on improved student learning. Aligned to the Professional Learning Communities (PLC) at Work model, this resource includes processes, protocols, templates, tips, and strategies designed to support the multidimensional work of instructional coaches and PLC training. Each chapter includes action steps and reflection activities, as well as suggestions for navigating some of the most common issues instructional coaches face.
BKF840

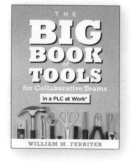

The Big Book of Tools for Collaborative Teams in a PLC at Work
William M. Ferriter
Build your team's capacity to become agents of positive change. Organized around the four critical questions of a PLC at Work, this comprehensive book of field-tested, easy-to-use tools provides an explicit structure for collaborative teams. Rely on these resources and best practices to help you establish team norms, navigate common challenges, develop collective teacher efficacy, and more.
BKF898

Solution Tree | Press

a division of
Solution Tree

Visit SolutionTree.com or call 800.733.6786 to order.